Ladies on the Loose

Ladies on the Loose

WOMEN TRAVELLERS OF THE 18TH and 19TH CENTURIES

EDITED, WITH AN INTRODUCTION BY
Leo Hamalian

DODD, MEAD & COMPANY
NEW YORK

Copyright © 1981 by Leo Hamalian
All rights reserved
No part of this book may be reproduced in any form
without permission in writing from the publisher
Printed in the United States of America

1 2 3 4 5 6 7 8 9 10

Library of Congress Cataloging in Publication Data
Main entry under title:
Ladies on the loose.
  Bibliography: p.
  1. Voyages and travels.
  2. Travelers, Women—Biography.
  I. Hamalian, Leo.
G465.L32   910′.8

81-7846
AACR2
ISBN 0-396-08009-X

Contents

Introduction ix

PART I
Europe

1 The Glories of Naples 3
　HESTER LYNCH PIOZZI

2 Journey Through Sweden 15
　MARY WOLLSTONECRAFT

3 Roman Fever 27
　MARGARET FULLER

4 Hassles in Spain 48
　KATE FIELD

5 Saunas and Swimming 57
　MRS. ALEC TWEEDIE

PART II
The Middle East

6	The Turkish Embassy LADY MARY WORTLEY MONTAGU	73
7	Life in the Lebanon LADY HESTER STANHOPE	92
8	The Secrets of the Hareem HARRIET MARTINEAU	99
9	Pilgrimage to the Holy Land FREDERIKA BREMER	115
10	Hyena and Locust for Dinner LADY ANN BLUNT	134

PART III
The Far East

11	Travelling Through China IDA PFEIFFER	149
12	Among the Aino ISABELLA BIRD	169
13	On a Mission to the Lepers KATE MARSDEN	185

14	The Customs of Burma MRS. ERNEST HART	198
15	Bicycling Through India FANNY BULLOCK WORKMAN	210

PART IV
Africa

16	Gondoroko ALEXINE TINNE	225
17	Journey into the Jungle MARY KINGSLEY	229

Bibliography	251
Other Accounts of Interest	253

Introduction

Writing about the theme of travel in women's literature of the nineteenth century, Ellen Moers in *Literary Women* (1976) isolates two dominant motifs: indoor travel and outdoor travel. The "indoor" she associates with the Gothic novel: "In the long dark twisting haunted passageways of the Gothic castle, there is travel with danger, travel with exertion—a challenge to the heroine's enterprise, resolution, ingenuity, and physical strength." By the "outdoor" she means the genre of the romance: "The heroine flies through the air independently of the laws of gravity, time, perspective."

Whether indoors or out, these journeys were confined to the imagination. They were, as Ms. Moers notes, flights of the female fancy, unrelated to the actualities of travel. Those marvelous places that Ann Radcliffe and other women authors of her time described were derived from paintings, from theater backdrops, and most often from travel books written by men. It was not until the nineteenth century that there developed another genre of literature: the travel book based upon the actual rather than the imaginary experiences of women. In retrospect, it is possible to recognize that these women travellers left behind an imposing array of documents, letters, and diaries, many of them more fascinating than their fictional predecessors by unperipatetic authors.

Why was this explosion of female energy so delayed at a time when both travel and travel books (by men) had become familiar and even popular forms of entertainment? The answer emerges when we recall that during the seventeenth and eighteenth centuries, it was chiefly men and men only who went "abroad." Some went to study, some to fight, some on special embassies, and others on missions to gather confidential diplomatic intelligence. These were not pursuits regarded as suitable for ladies. Later, a different and more coherent pattern began to take shape (a period of residence in Paris or Rome, a tour of southern France or Italy during the winter and following spring, then summer in Switzerland or the north), but even fixing the timetable and itinerary apparently did little to open opportunities for women who wished to travel. Indeed notable rebels like Byron and Shelley moved entire entourages abroad, including their women, and often officers serving in the military forces allowed their wives and daughters to accompany them on foreign duty, but even this was, so to speak, a drop in the bucket.

For most women, immobilized as they were by the iron hoops of convention, the term "abroad" had a dreamlike, talismanic quality. It conjured up a vision composed of a whole cluster of myths, half-myths, and truths—of sunlight, of liberty, of innocence, of sexual freedom, of the fantastic and the healing, of the unknown and the mysterious—all those concepts that stood in direct confrontation to domesticity. When women did buy tickets to sail on ships to India or to ride the Orient Express to Baghdad, their real destination, more often than not, was a restorative idea rather than a place on a map.

Though this restorative idea sometimes led them to endure a long, uncomfortable, and frequently dangerous journey to remote and savage places where few of their countrymen had penetrated before them, there was no intent, according to Dorothy Middleton in *Victorian Lady Travellers*, to imitate or develop the male fashion for exploration, which was such a feature of the time. On the whole, discovery was not the aim of most women travellers, nor did their wanderings inspire other expeditions of ever greater size or ambition. And apparently these ladies on the move were not seeking camp camaraderie or team spirit—all those motives were left to the likes of Mungo Park, David Livingstone, Sir Richard Burton, John Speke, and Henry Stanley, whose names had become honored if not household words.

What, *specifically*, were women seeking "abroad"? From the various travel accounts, one can make some reasonable assumptions. For women of that era, travel seems to have been the individual gesture of the housebound, male-dominated, very proper lady. Desperate for an emotional outlet, she often found it, late in life, through travel. Aboard a boat, astride a donkey, perched atop a camel or an elephant, paddling an outrigger, she could enjoy a freedom of action and thought unthinkable at home. For those women who aspired to become more than domestic drudges or commodities on the marriage market, travel offered the kind of adventure imaginable to them heretofore only in the Gothic or romantic novels of the day—encounters with the exotic, with the exciting, the renewing, the inherently self-fulfilling. The woman within could emerge, at least temporarily. Above all, travel promised a segment of life, a span of time, over which a woman had maximum control. Through the medium of travel, women could approach what the French sociologist Emile Durkheim calls "the sacred experience."

But the motive for going abroad was more than a quest for the extraordinary. Travel satisfied that well-known Victorian passion for improvement—of oneself and of others. This passion, once regarded as the property of men only, was shared by the "new" woman. Writes Dorothy Middleton, "Fortified by a kind of innocent valour, convinced of the civilizing mission of woman, clothed in long skirts and armed with an umbrella or sunshade according to the climate, the nineteenth-century woman travellers covered thousands of miles—writing, painting, observing, botanizing, missionarizing, collecting, and latterly, photographing." Touring or residing in foreign lands, women learned history, geography, languages, and politics. They also learned about "strange" customs. Many vivid images were imprinted upon the memory that would have been poorer without them—of the oppressed peasant in Japan, of the habitués of the *hareem*, of the miserable lives of the Siberian lepers, of the treasures of Italian culture, of the bathing habits of the Finns, of unusual defenses against diseases. All these impressions they were able to contribute upon their return, to the enlargement of their own country's culture. Very simply said, they brought back a powerful commodity—knowledge. By educating themselves, these women travellers educated the public.

History put these women in a unique position, and they responded in a unique way: They created a small but impressive library of first-person narratives that combined genuine learning with the spirit of individualism. The following generation of women travellers—the daughters and the granddaughters of these pioneers—were impelled by essentially the same impetus, the desire for independence and for enlightenment. These were the twin forces which crystallized in the ongoing movement for equal rights. Thus, the once-lowly travel book, rather unexpectedly, became an important instrument for the emancipation of women.

There are questions that the would-be reader of an anthology must ask of the compiler. First, what principle determined the choice of selections? I used one criterion for these selections, and I hope it will not prove to be disappointing to more serious questioners—that of readability. I simply chose passages that struck me as most interesting and assumed that they would seem the same to my readers.

The reader is justified in raising another question: "Why?" Sometimes the reason for the choice was sheer literary merit; sometimes the dramatic character of the episodes; sometimes the revelation of human character; and sometimes the skilled evocation of place. The writing of these women travellers is so rich in variety that no one kind of sample would have done them justice. There is here, I think, material for all tastes and for all types of readers, from those who remain fascinated by the mysterious drums and sorceries of unknown Africa to those whose perceptions are trained to distill the subtlest flavors of irony, comedy, or pathos from these forthright records. For those who enjoy a good story, a tour described day by day makes a natural plot. Adventures with wild animals, which constitute the bulk of travel accounts written by men, are absent among these accounts, except for one; and there, the legitimate self-dramatization of the travel writer is never made distasteful. What emerges from these accounts and perhaps unifies them is evidence that women were the first masters of the genre of travel writing.

Ladies on the Loose

PART I
Europe

1

HESTER LYNCH PIOZZI

The Glories of Naples

FROM
*Observations Made in the Course of a
Journey Through France, Italy, and Germany*
(1789)

The maiden name of the lady well known to the literary world of the eighteenth century as Mrs. Thrale and subsequently as Mrs. Piozzi was Hester Lynch Salusbury. Born in 1740 at Bodvel in Caernarvonshire, the only daughter of an impoverished but ambitious squire, she was sent to London to live with relatives and was tutored there in languages. We are told by Mrs. Ann Elwood, the author of Overland Journey to India, *that "her richly-stored mind, lively wit, and pleasing manners rendered her a most delightful friend and companion, whilst her fine flow of spirits, which continued to the last, made her a general favorite in society."*

Thus, it is no surprise that both the affluent and the distinguished sought the company of this "cultivated and intelligent woman, who had read widely and with relish," according to one critic. She married Henry Thrale, a wealthy brewer and member of Parliament, and in time, presided over a large brood of children in her home at Streatham. She was able to entertain lavishly and was soon accepted on equal terms by Oliver Goldsmith, Sir Joshua Reynolds, Mrs. Siddons, and Fanny Burney. In 1764, she met Dr. Samuel Johnson and became his closest confidante and patroness. Johnson not only lived with the Thrales intermittently, but also accompanied them on visits to Brighton, Wales, and France.

When her husband fell ill of apoplexy, Mrs. Thrale assumed the management of the brewery, and after his death, sold it to Barclay's. In

3

1784, *despite opposition from her family and friends (especially Dr. Johnson), she married Gabriel Piozzi, an Italian musician with whom she had fallen in love some four years earlier.*

The Piozzis went to Italy to live, and for the next three years Mrs. Piozzi was free to write and to travel as never before. She finished Anecdotes of the Late Samuel Johnson *(1786) and prepared her* Letters to and from the Late Samuel Johnson *(1788), both primary sources of information for Johnson scholars. An inveterate journal keeper, she carried two notebooks with her on her travels, eventually to be known as "Italian Journey 1784" and "German Journey 1786." These notebooks, along with entries that she continued to make in* Thraliana, *the journal she had been keeping since 1776, were the raw materials for* Observations and Reflections Made in the Course of a Journey Through France, Italy, and Germany *(1789), which she completed in two months during the summer of 1788. Though the places she describes have been overrun by tourists, they were relatively unfamiliar to the English world when she visited them, and clearly she had the gift of fresh and subtle observation overlaid with the ability to imbue her narrative with the spirit of her volatile and vivacious personality. It was this distinctly female and unconventional book that inspired Ann Radcliffe, who had never been outside England, to write about "marvelous Italy" in* The Mysteries of Udolpho.

In this selection, as well as in all those that follow, the author's spelling and punctuation have been preserved.

On the tenth day of this month we arrived early at Naples, for I think it was about two o'clock in the morning; and sure the providence of God preserved us, for never was such weather seen by me since I came into the world; thunder, lightning, storm at sea, rain and wind, contending for mastery, and combining to extinguish the torches bought to light us the last stage: Vesuvius, vomiting fire, and pouring torrents of red hot lava down its sides, was the only object visible; and *that* we saw plainly in the afternoon thirty miles off, where I asked a Franciscan friar, If it was the famous volcano? "Yes," replied he, "that's our mountain, which throws up money for us, by calling foreigners to see the extraordinary effects of so surprising a phænomenon." The weather was quiet then, and we had no notion of passing such a horrible night; but an hour after dark, a storm came on, which was really dreadful to endure; or even look upon: the blue lightning, whose colour shewed the nature of the original minerals from which she drew her existence, shone round us in a broad expanse from time to time, and sudden darkness followed in an instant: no object then but the fiery river could be seen, till another flash discovered the waves tossing and breaking, at a height I never saw before.

Nothing sure was ever more sublime or awful than our entrance into Naples at the dead hour we arrived, when not a whisper was to be heard in the streets, and not a glimpse of light was left to guide us, except the small lamp hung now and then at a high window before a favourite image of the Virgin.

My poor maid had by this time nearly lost her wits with terror, and the French valet, crushed with fatigue, and covered with rain and sea-spray, had just life enough left to exclaim—"*Ah, Madame! il me semble que nous sommes venus icy exprès pour voir la fin du monde.*"[1]

The Ville de Londres inn was full, and could not accommodate our family; but calling up the people of the Crocelle, we obtained a noble apartment, the windows of which look full upon the celebrated bay which washes the wall at our door. Caprea lies opposite the drawing-room or gallery, which is magnificent; and my bed-chamber commands a complete view of the mountain, which I value more, and which called me the first night twenty times away from sleep and supper, though never so in want of both as at that moment surely.

Such were my first impressions of this wonderful metropolis, of which I had been always reading summer descriptions, and had regarded somehow as an Hesperian garden, an earthly paradise, where delicacy and softness subdued every danger, and general sweetness captivated every sense;—nor have I any reason yet to say it will not still prove so, for though wet, and weary, and hungry, we wanted no fire, and found only inconvenience from that they lighted on our arrival. It was the fashion at Florence to struggle for a Terreno, but here we are all perched up one hundred and forty two steps from the level of the land or

[1] Lord, Madam! it seems to me that we came here on purpose sure to see the end of the world.

sea; large balconies, apparently well secured, give me every enjoyment of a prospect, which no repetition can render tedious: and here we have agreed to stay till Spring, which, I trust, will come out in this country as soon as the new year calls it.

Our eagerness to see sights has been repressed at Naples only by finding every thing a sight; one need not stir out to look for wonders sure, while this amazing mountain continues to exhibit such various scenes of sublimity and beauty at exactly the distance one would chuse to observe it from; a distance which almost admits examination, and certainly excludes immediate fear. When in the silent night, however, one listens to its groaning; while hollow sighs, as of gigantic sorrow, are often heard distinctly in my apartment; nothing can surpass one's sensations of amazement, except the consciousness that custom will abate their keenness: I have not, however, yet learned to lie quiet, when columns of flame, high as the mountain's self, shoot from its crater into the clear atmosphere with a loud and violent noise; nor shall I ever forget the scene it presented one day to my astonished eyes, while a thick cloud, charged heavily with electric matter, passing over, met the fiery explosion by mere chance, and went off in such a manner as effectually baffles all verbal description.

Upon reflection it appears to me, that the men most famous at London and Paris for performing tricks with fire have been always Italians in my time, and commonly Neapolitans; no wonder, I should think, Naples would produce prodigious connoisseurs in this way; we have almost perpetual lightning of various colours, according to the soil from whence the vapours are exhaled; sometimes of a pale straw or lemon colour, often white like artificial flame produced by camphor, but oftenest blue, bright as the rays emitted through the coloured liquors set in the window of a chemist's shop in London—and with such thunder!!—"For God's sake, Sir," said I to some of them, "is there no danger of the ships in the harbour here catching fire? why, we should all fly up in the air directly, if once these flashes should communicate to the room where any of the vessels keep their powder."—"Gunpowder, Madam!" replies the man, amazed: "why if St. Peter and St. Paul came here with gunpowder on board, we should soon drive them out again: don't you know," added he, "that every ship discharges her contents at such a place (naming it), and never comes into our port with a grain on board?"

The palaces and churches have no share in one's admiration at Naples, who scorns to depend on man, however mighty, however skilful, for *her* ornaments; while Heaven has bestowed on her and her *contorni* all that can excite astonishment, all that can impress awe. We have spent three or four days upon Pozzuoli and its environs; its cavern scooped originally by nature's hand, assisted by the armies of Cocceius Nerva—ever tremendous, ever gloomy grotto!—which leads to the road that shews you Ischia, an old volcano, now an island apparently rent asunder by an earthquake, the division too plain to beg assistance from philosophy: this is commonly called the *Grotto di Posilippo* though; you pass through it to go to every place; not without flambeaux, if you would go safely, and avoid the necessity the poor are under, who, driving their carts through the subterranean passage, cry as they meet each other, to avoid jostling, *alla montagna*, or *alla marina, keep to the rock side*, or *keep to the sea side*. It is at the right hand, awhile before you enter this cavern, that climbing up among a heap of bushes, you find a hollow place, and there go down again—it is the tomb of Virgil; and, for other antiquities, I recollect nothing shewed me when at Rome that gave me as complete an idea how things were really carried on in former days, as does the temple of *Shor Apis* at Pozzuoli, where the area is exactly all it ever was; the ring remains where the victim was fastened to; the priests apartments, lavatories, &c. the drains for carrying the beast's blood away, all yet remains as perfect as it is possible. The end of Caligula's bridge too, but that they say is not his bridge, but a mole built by some succeeding emperor—a madder or a wickeder it could not be—though here Nero bathed, and here he buried his mother Agrippina. Here are the centum camerae, the prisons employed by that prince for the cruellest of purposes; and here are his country palaces reserved for the most odious ones: here effeminacy learned to subsist without delicacy or shame, hence honour was excluded by rapacity, and conscience stupefied by constant inebriation: here brainsick folly put nature and common sense upon the rack—Caligula in madness courted the moon to his embraces— and Sylla, satiated with blood, retired, and gave a premature banquet to those worms he had so often fed with the flesh of innocence: here dwelt depravity in various shapes, and here Pandora's chambers left scarcely a *Hope* at the bottom that better times should come:—who can write prose however in such places!

But it is time to tell of Herculaneum, Pompeia, and Portici; of a theatre, the scene of gaiety and pleasure, overwhelmed by torrents of liquid fire! the inhabitants of a whole town surprised by immediate and unavoidable destruction! Where that very town indeed was built with the lava produced by former eruptions, one would think it scarce possible that such calamities could be totally unexpected;—but no matter, life must go on, though we all know death is coming;—so the bread was baking in their ovens, the meat was smoking on their dishes, some of their wine already decanted for use, the rest in large jars *(amphora)*, now petrified with their contents inside, and fixed to the walls of the cellars in which they stand.—How dreadful are the thoughts which such a sight suggests! how *very* horrible the certainty, that such a scene may be all acted over again to-morrow; and that we, who to-day are spectators, may become spectacles to travellers of a succeeding century, who mistaking our bones for those of the Neapolitans, may carry some of them to their native country back again perhaps; as it came into my head that a French gentleman was doing, when I saw him put a human bone into his pocket this morning, and told him I hoped he had got the jaw of a Gaulish officer, instead of a Roman soldier, for future reflections to energize upon. Of all single objects offered here to one's contemplation, none are more striking than a woman's foot, the *print* of her foot I mean, taken apparently in the very act of running from the river of melted minerals that surrounded her, and which now serves as an intaglio to commemorate the misery it caused. Another melancholy proof of what needs no confirmation, is the impression of a sick female, known to be so from the *stole* she wore, a drapery peculiar to the sex; her bed, converted into a substance like plaster of Paris, still retains the form and covering of her who perished quietly upon it, without ever making even an effort to escape.

That one of these towns is crushed, or rather buried, under loads of heavy lava, and is therefore difficult to disentangle, all have heard; that Pompeia is only lightly covered with pumice-stones and ashes, is new to nobody; it is in the power, as a

Venetian gentleman said angrily, of an English hen and chickens to scratch it open in a week, though these lazy Neapolitans will leave it not half dislodged, before a new eruption swallows all again.

Our visit to Portici was more than equally provoking in the same way; to see deposited there all the antiques which are so curious in themselves, so *very* valuable when considered as specimens of ancient art, and of the mode of living practiced in ancient Rome, kept at a place where I do sincerely believe they will be again overwhelmed and confounded among the king of Naples's furniture, to the great torture of future antiquarians, and to the disgrace of present insensibility.

The *triclinia* and *stibadia* used at supper by these old Romans prove the verses which our critics have been working at so long, to have been at least well explained by them, and do infinite honour to those who, without the advantage of seeing how the utensils were constructed, knew perfectly well their way of carrying on life, from their acquaintance with a language long since *dead,* and I am sure *buried* under a heap of rubbish heavier and more difficult to remove than all the lava heaped on Herculaneum; but it is a source of perpetual wonder, and let me add perpetual pleasure too, to know that Cicero, and Virgil, and Horace, if alive, would find their writings as well understood, ay and as perfectly tasted, by the scholars of Paris and London, as they had ever been by their own old literary acquaintance.

20th January 1786—Here are the most excellent, the most incomparable fish I ever eat; red mullets, large as our maycril, and of singularly high flavour; besides the calamaro, or ink-fish, a dainty worthy of imperial luxury; almond and even apple trees in blossom, to delight those who can be paid for coarse manners and confined notions by the beauties of a brilliant climate. Here are all the hedges in blow as you drive towards Pozzuoli, and a snow of white May-flowers clustering round Virgil's tomb. So strong was the sun's heat this morning, even before eleven o'clock, that I carried an umbrella to defend me from his rays, as we sauntered about the walks, which are spacious and elegant, laid out much in the style of St. James's Park, but with the sea on one side of you, the broad street, called Chiaja, on the other. What trees are planted there however, either do not grow up so as to afford shade, or else they cut them, and trim them about to make them in pretty shapes forsooth, as we did in England half a century ago.

Be this as it will, the vaunted view from the castle of St. Elmo, though much more deeply *interesting,* is in consequence of this defect less *naturally* pleasing than the prospect from Lomellino's villa near Genoa, or Lord Clifford's park, called King's Weston, in Somersetshire; those two places being, in point of mere situation, possessed of beauties hitherto unrivalled by anything I have seen. Nor does the steady regularity of this Mediterranean sea make me inclined to prefer it to our more capricious or rather active channel. Sea views have at best too little variety, and when the flux and reflux of the tide are taken away from one, there remains only rough and smooth: whereas the hope which its ebb and flow keep constantly renovating, serves to animate, and a little change the course of one's ideas, just as its swelling and sinking is of use, to purify in some degree, and keep the whole from stagnation.

I made inquiry after the old story of Nicola Pesce, told by Kircher, and sweetly brought back to all our memories by Goldsmith, who, as Dr. Johnson said of him, touched nothing that he did not likewise adorn; but I could gain no addition to what we have already heard. That there was such a man is certain, who, though become nearly amphibious by living constantly in the water, only coming sometimes on shore for sleep and refreshment, suffered avarice to be his ruin, leaping voluntarily into the Gulph of Charybdis to fetch out a gold cup thrown in thither to tempt him—what could a gold cup have done one would wonder for Nicola Pesce?—yet knowing the dangers of the place, he braved them all it seems for this bright reward; and was supposed to be devoured by one of the polypus fish, who, sticking close to the rocks, extend their arms for prey. When I expressed my indignation that he should so perish; "He forgot perhaps," said one present, "to recommend himself to Santo Gennaro."

The castle on this hill, called the Castel St. Elmo, would be much my comfort did I fix at Naples; for here are eight thousand soldiers constantly kept, to secure the city from sudden insurrection; his majesty most wisely trusting their command only to Spanish or German officers, or some few gentlemen from the northern states of Italy, that no personal tenderness for any in the town below may intervene, if occasion for sudden severity should arise. We went to-day and saw their garrison, comfortably and even elegantly kept; and I was wicked enough to rejoice that the soldiers were never, but with the very utmost difficulty, permitted to go among the townsmen for a moment.

To-morrow we mount the Volcano, whose present peaceful disposition has tempted us to inspect it more nearly. Though it appears little less than presumption thus to profane with eyes of examination the favourite alembic of nature, while the great work of projection is carrying on; guarded as all its secret caverns are too with every contradiction; snow and flame! solid bodies heated into liquefaction, and rolling gently down one of its sides; while fluids congeal and harden into ice on the other; nothing can exceed the curiosity of its appearance, now the lava is less rapid, and stiffens as it flows; stiffens too in ridges very surprisingly, and gains an odd aspect, not unlike the pasteboard waves representing sea at a theatre, but black, because this year's eruption has been mingled with coal. The connoisseurs here know the different degrees, dates, and shades of lava to a perfection that amazes one; and Sir William Hamilton's courage, learning, and perfect skill in these matters, is more people's theme here than the Volcano itself. Bartolomeo, the Cyclop of Vesuvius as he is called, studies its effects and operations too with much attention and philosophical exactness, relating the adventures he has had with our minister on the mountain to every Englishman that goes up, with great success. The way one climbs is by tying a broad sash with long ends round this Bartolomeo, letting him walk before one, and holding it fast. As far as the Hermitage there is no great difficulty, and to that place some chuse to ride an ass, but I thought walking safer; and there you are sure of welcome and refreshment from the poor good old man, who sets up a little cross wherever the fire has stopt near his cell; shews you the place with a sort of polite solemnity that impresses, spreads his scanty provisions before you kindly, and tells the past and present state of the eruption accurately, inviting you to partake of

> His rushy couch, his frugal fare,
> His blessing and repose.
>
> GOLDSMITH

This Hermit is a Frenchman. *J'ai dansé dans mon lit tant de fois,*[2] said he: the expression was not sublime when speaking of an earthquake, to be sure; I looked among his books, however, and found Bruyère. "Would not the Duc de Rochefoucault have done better?" said I. "Did I never see you before, Madam?" said he; "yes, sure I have, and dressed you too, when I was a hairdresser in London, and lived with Mons. Martinant, and I dressed pretty Miss Wynne too in the same street. *Vit-elle encore? Vit-elle encore?*[3] Ah I am old now," continued he; "I remember when black pins first came up." This was charming, and in such an unexpected way, I could hardly prevail upon myself ever to leave the spot; but Mrs. Greatheed having been quite to the crater's edge with her only son, a baby of four years old; shame rather than inclination urged me forward; I asked the little boy what he had seen; I saw the chimney, replied he, and it was on fire, but I liked the elephant better.

That the situation of the crater changed in this last eruption is of little consequence; it will change and change again I suppose. The wonder is, that nobody gets killed by venturing so near, while red-hot stones are flying about them so. The Bishop of Derry did very near get his arm broke; and the Italians are always recounting the exploits of these rash Britons who look into the crater, and carry their wives and children up to the top; while we are, with equal justice, amazed at the courageous Neapolitans, who build little snug villages and dwell with as much confidence at the foot of Vesuvius, as our people do in Paddington or Hornsey. When I enquired of an inhabitant of these houses how she managed, and whether she was not frighted when the Volcano raged, lest it should carry away her pretty little habitation: "Let it go," said she, "we don't mind now if it goes to-morrow, so as we can make it answer by raising our vines, oranges, &c. against it for three years, our fortune is made before the fourth arrives; and then if the red river comes we can always run away, *scappar via,* ourselves, and hang the property. We only desire three years use of the mountain as a hot wall or forcing-house, and then we are above the world, thanks be to God and St. Januarius," who always comes in for a large share of

---

[2] I have danced in my bed so often this year.
[3] Is she yet alive? Is she yet alive?

their veneration; and this morning having heard that the Neapolitans still present each other with a cake upon New-year's day, I began to hug my favourite hypothesis closer, recollecting the old ceremony of the wheaten cake seasoned with salt, and called *Janualis* in the Heathen days. All this however must still end in mere conjecture; for though the weather here favours one's idea of Janus, who loosened the furrow and liquefied the frost, to which the melting of our martyr's blood might, without much straining of the matter, be made to allude; yet it must be recollected after all, that the miracle is not performed in this month but that of May, and that St. Januarius did certainly exist and give his life as testimony to the truth of our religion, in the third century. Can one wonder, however, if corruptions and mistakes should have crept in since? And would it not have been equal to a miracle had no tares sprung up in the field of religion, when our Saviour himself informs us that there is an enemy ever watching his opportunity to plant them?

These dear people too at Rome and Naples do live so in the very hulk of ship-wrecked or rather foundered Paganism, have their habitation so at the very bottom of the cask, can it fail to retain the scent when the lees are scarce yet dried up, clean or evaporated? That an odd jumble of past and present days, past and present ideas of dignity, events, and even manner of portioning out their time, still confuse their heads, may be observed in every conversation with them; and when a few weeks ago we revisited, in company of some newly-arrived English friends, the old baths of Baiæ, Locrine lake, &c.[,] Tobias, who rowed us over, bid us observe the Appian way under the water, where indeed it appears quite clearly, even to the tracks of wheels on its old pavement made of very large stones; and seeing me perhaps particularly attentive, "Yes, Madam," said he, "I do assure you, that *Don* Horace and *Don* Virgil, of whom we hear such a deal, used to come from Rome to their country-seats here in a day; over this very road, which is now overflowed as you see it, by repeated earthquakes, but which was then so good and so unbroken, that if they rose early in the morning they could easily gallop hither against the *Ave Maria.*"

It was very observable in our second visit paid to the Stufe San Germano, that they had increased prodigiously in heat since Mount Vesuvius had ceased throwing out fire, though at least fourteen miles from it, and a vast portion of the sea between them; it vexed me to have no thermometer again, but by what one's immediate feelings could inform us, there were many degrees of difference. I could not now bear my hand on any part of them for a moment. The same luckless dog was again produced, and again restored to life, like the lady in Dryden's Fables, who is condemned to be hunted, killed, recovered, and set on foot again for the amusement of her tormentors; a story borrowed from the Italian.

Solfaterra burned my fingers as I plucked an incrustation off, which allured me by the beauty of its colours, and roared with more violence than when I was there before. The horrible volcano is by no means extinguished yet, but seems pregnant with wonders, principally combustible, and likely to break with one at every step, all the earth round it being hollow as a drum, and I should think of no great thickness neither; so plainly does one hear the sighings underneath which some of the country people imagine to be tortured spirits howling with agony.

2

MARY WOLLSTONECRAFT
Journey Through Sweden

FROM
Letters Written During a Short Residence in Sweden, Norway, and Denmark (1796)

Author of A Vindication of the Rights of Women, *the first great feminist document, Mary Wollstonecraft was born in 1759 in the Spitalsfield district of London. Her family moved to Yorkshire, where for two years her father tried unsuccessfully to become a gentleman farmer.*

As a young woman, she made a living by keeping a school with her sister at Newington, and when it failed, as a governess for Lord Kingsborough in County Cork, Ireland. For a time she also lived by her pen as a translator and reader for the publishing firm of Johnson. In 1792, the success of her book on the rights of women made her famous and revered (though, as late as 1947, two psychologists could write: "That Mary Wollstonecraft was an extreme neurotic of a compulsive type there can be no doubt. Out of her illness arose the ideology of feminism . . .")[1] She decided to visit France, then in the throes of a revolution that in principle she supported. She had already declared her growing radicalism in A Vindication of the Rights of Men, *which attacked Edmund Burke for his conservative defense of the monarchy, the church, and the aristocracy, and now she wanted to witness the struggle against these institutions firsthand.*

Late in 1792, she sailed for the Continent, and soon settled into a circle of American, English, and French radicals in Paris. There she fell in love with Gilbert Imlay, an American author, explorer, and entrepreneur. When the fighting intensified, she moved to the suburb of Neuilly, and in relative safety worked on her history of the French Revolution.

---

[1] See Ferdinand Lundberg and Marynia Farnham, *Modern Women: The Lost Sex* (Harper and Bros., 1947).

Although she and Imlay were registered as man and wife in the American Embassy in Paris, they never married. This was only to obtain protection for Mary, because to be British (and a woman) in Paris then was to be in danger. The following year she was pregnant, and when Imlay left Paris on business, she nursed the infant alone in the cold and dreary city.

In April of 1795, she returned to London with her daughter and a nursemaid and learned that Imlay was ready to abandon her. To divert her attention, Imlay hit upon the scheme of sending her to the Scandinavian countries as his business envoy. The chronicle of that summer of 1795, in the form of letters to Imlay, was published the following year.

Back in England, she discovered that Imlay had taken a strolling actress as his mistress. She soaked her skirts (to increase their weight) and threw herself off Putney Bridge. Rescued by Thames boatmen, she painfully and gradually conquered her passion for Imlay and began to rebuild her shattered life. She married William Godwin, the "little man with the big head," and soon her zest for living revived. Unfortunately, she died right after giving birth to her second daughter, Mary, who was to become the wife of Percy Bysshe Shelley and the author of **Frankenstein.** *Some scholars link Wollstonecraft's name with* **The Emigrants,** *published posthumously in 1797.*

The series of twenty-five epistles that make up **Letters Written During a Short Residence in Sweden, Norway, and Denmark** *is, in the words of Carol H. Poston, the editor of the text, "possibly the perfect fusion of the personal and intellectual selves of Mary Wollstonecraft." The modern reader should find appealing her contemporary attitudes toward prison reform, capital punishment, child care, and the plight of Scandinavian women. Furthermore, there is her spirit of adventure. Though accompanied by her year-old daughter Fanny and a nursemaid, she frequently found time to take side trips on her own, brief solo encounters with the Swedish countryside that permitted her more intimate feelings to come into play, as in the following letter (Number Five).*

Had I determined to travel in Sweden merely for pleasure, I should probably have chosen the road to Stockholm, though convinced, by repeated observation, that the manners of a people are best discriminated in the country. The inhabitants of the capital are all of the same genus; for the varieties in the species we must, therefore, search where the habitations of men are so separated as to allow the difference of climate to have its natural effect. And with this difference we are, perhaps, most forcibly struck at the first view, just as we form an estimate of the leading traits of a character at the first glance, of which intimacy afterwards makes us almost lose sight.

As my affairs called me to Stromstad (the frontier town of Sweden) in my way to Norway, I was to pass over, I heard, the most uncultivated part of the country. Still I believe that the grand features of Sweden are the same every where, and it is only the grand features that admit of description. There is an individuality in every prospect, which remains in the memory as forcibly depicted as the particular features that have arrested our attention; yet we cannot find words to discriminate that individuality so as to enable a stranger to say, this is the face, that the view. We may amuse by setting the imagination to work; but we cannot store the memory with a fact.

As I wish to give you a general idea of this country, I shall continue in my desultory manner to make such observations and reflections as the circumstances draw forth, without losing time, by endeavouring to arrange them.

Travelling in Sweden is very cheap, and even commodious, if you make but the proper arrangements. Here, as in other parts of the continent, it is necessary to have your own carriage, and to have a servant who can speak the language, if you are unacquainted with it. Sometimes a servant who can drive would be found very useful, which was our case, for I travelled in company with two gentlemen, one of whom had a German servant who drove very well. This was all the party; for not intending to make a long stay, I left my little girl behind me.

As the roads are not much frequented, to avoid waiting three or four hours for horses, we sent, as is the constant custom, an *avant courier* the night before, to order them at every post, and we constantly found them ready. Our first set I jokingly termed *requisition* horses; but afterwards we had almost always little spirited animals that went on at a round pace.

The roads, making allowance for the ups and downs, are uncommonly good and pleasant. The expence, including the postillions and other incidental things, does not amount to more than a shilling the Swedish mile.[2]

---

[2] A Swedish mile is nearly six English miles. [Author's note].

The inns are tolerable; but not liking the rye bread, I found it necessary to furnish myself with some wheaten before I set out. The beds too were particularly disagreeable to me. It seemed to me that I was sinking into a grave when I entered them; for, immersed in down placed in a sort of box, I expected to be suffocated before morning. The sleeping between two down beds, they do so even in summer, must be very unwholesome during any season; and I cannot conceive how the people can bear it, especially as the summers are very warm. But warmth they seem not to feel; and, I should think, were afraid of the air, by always keeping their windows shut. In the winter, I am persuaded, I could not exist in rooms thus closed up, with stoves heated in their manner, for they only put wood into them twice a day; and, when the stove is thoroughly heated, they shut the flue, not admitting any air to renew its elasticity, even when the rooms are crowded with company. These stoves are made of earthenware, and often in a form that ornaments an apartment, which is never the case with the heavy iron ones I have seen elsewhere. Stoves may be economical; but I like a fire, a wood one, in preference; and I am convinced that the current of air which it attracts renders this the best mode of warming rooms.

We arrived early the second evening at a little village called Quistram, where we had determined to pass the night; having been informed that we should not afterwards find a tolerable inn until we reached Stromstad.

Advancing towards Quistram, as the sun was beginning to decline, I was particularly impressed by the beauty of the situation. The road was on the declivity of a rocky mountain, slightly covered with a mossy herbage and vagrant firs. At the bottom, a river, straggling amongst the recesses of stone, was hastening forward to the ocean and its grey rocks, of which we had a prospect on the left, whilst on the right it stole peacefully forward into the meadows, losing itself in a thickly wooded rising ground. As we drew near, the loveliest banks of wild flowers variegated the prospect, and promised to exhale odours to add to the sweetness of the air, the purity of which you could almost see, alas! not smell, for the putrifying herrings, which they use as manure, after the oil has been extracted, spread over the patches of earth, claimed by cultivation, destroyed every other.

It was intolerable, and entered with us into the inn, which was in other respects a charming retreat.

Whilst supper was preparing I crossed the bridge, and strolled by the river, listening to its murmurs. Approaching the bank, the beauty of which had attracted my attention in the carriage, I recognized many of my old acquaintance growing with great luxuriancy.

Seated on it, I could not avoid noting an obvious remark. Sweden appeared to me the country in the world most proper to form the botanist and natural historian: every object seemed to remind me of the creation of things, of the first efforts of sportive nature. When a country arrives at a certain state of perfection, it looks as if it were made so; and curiosity is not excited. Besides, in social life too many objects occur for any to be distinctly observed by the generality of mankind; yet a contemplative man, or poet, in the country, I do not mean the country adjacent to cities, feels and sees what would escape vulgar eyes, and draws suitable inferences. This train of reflections might have led me further, in every sense of the word; but I could not escape from the detestable evaporation of the herrings, which poisoned all my pleasure.

After making a tolerable supper, for it is not easy to get fresh provisions on the road, I retired, to be lulled to sleep by the murmuring of a stream, of which I with great difficulty obtained sufficient to perform my daily ablutions.

The last battle between the Danes and Swedes, which gave new life to their ancient enmity, was fought at this place 1788; only seventeen or eighteen were killed; for the great superiority of the Danes and Norwegians obliged the Swedes to submit; but sickness, and a scarcity of provisions, proved very fatal to their opponents, on their return.

It would be very easy to search for the particulars of this engagement in the publications of the day; but as this manner of filling my pages does not come within my plan, I probably should not have remarked that the battle was fought here, were it not to relate an anecdote which I had from good authority.

I noticed, when I first mentioned this place to you, that we descended a steep before we came to the inn; an immense ridge of rocks stretching out on one side. The inn was sheltered under them; and about a hundred yards from it was a bridge that crossed the river, whose murmurs I have celebrated; it was not fordable. The Swedish general received orders to stop at the bridge, and dispute the passage; a most advantageous post for an army so much inferior in force: but the influence of beauty is not confined to courts. The mistress of the inn was handsome: when I saw her there were still some remains of beauty; and, to preserve her house, the general gave up the only tenable station. He was afterwards broke for contempt of orders.

Approaching the frontiers, consequently the sea, nature resumed an aspect ruder and ruder, or rather seemed the bones of the world waiting to be clothed with every thing necessary to give life and beauty. Still it was sublime.

The clouds caught their hue of the rocks that menaced them. The sun appeared afraid to shine, the birds ceased to sing, and the flowers to bloom; but the eagle fixed his nest high amongst the rocks, and the vulture hovered over this abode of desolation. The farm houses, in which only poverty resided, were formed of logs scarcely keeping off the cold and drifting snow; out of them the inhabitants seldom peeped, and the sports or prattling of children was neither seen nor heard. The current of life seemed congealed at the source: all were not frozen; for it was summer, you remember; but every thing appeared so dull, that I waited to see ice, in order to reconcile me to the absence of gaiety.

The day before, my attention had frequently been attracted by the wild beauties of the country we passed through.

The rocks which tossed their fantastic heads so high were often covered with pines and firs, varied in the most picturesque manner. Little woods filled up the recesses, when forests did not darken the scene; and vallies and glens, cleared of the trees, displayed a dazzling verdure which contrasted with the gloom of the shading pines. The eye stole into many a covert where tranquility seemed to have taken up her abode, and the number of little lakes that continually presented themselves added to the peaceful composure of the scenery. The little cultivation which appeared did not break the enchantment, nor did castles rear their turrets aloft to crush the cottages, and prove that man is more savage than the natives of the woods. I heard of the bears, but never saw them stalk forth, which I was sorry for; I wished to have seen one in its wild state. In the winter, I am told, they sometimes catch a stray cow, which is a heavy loss to the owner.

The farms are small. Indeed most of the houses we saw on the road indicated poverty, or rather that the people could just live. Towards the frontiers they grew worse and worse in their appearance, as if not willing to put sterility itself out of countenance. No gardens smiled round the habitations, not a potatoe or cabbage to eat with the fish drying on a stick near the door. A little grain here and there appeared, the long stalks of which you might almost reckon. The day was gloomy when we passed over this rejected spot, the wind bleak, and winter seemed to be contending with nature, faintly struggling to change the season. Surely, thought I, if the sun ever shines here, it cannot warm these stones; moss only cleaves to them, partaking of their hardness; and nothing like vegetable life appears to cheer with hope the heart.

So far from thinking that the primitive inhabitants of the world lived in a southern climate, where Paradise spontaneously arose, I am led to infer, from various circumstances, that the first dwelling of man happened to be a spot like this which led him to adore a sun so seldom seen; for this worship, which probably preceded that of demons or demi-gods, certainly never began in a southern climate, where the continual presence of the sun prevented its being considered as a god; or rather the want of it never being felt, this glorious luminary would carelessly have diffused its blessings without being hailed as a benefactor. Man must therefore have been placed in the north, to tempt him to run after the sun, in order that the different parts of the earth might be peopled. Nor do I wonder that hordes of barbarians always poured out of these regions to seek for milder climes, when nothing like cultivation attached them to the soil; especially when we take into the view that the adventuring spirit, common to man, is naturally stronger and more general during the infancy of society. The conduct of the followers of Mahomet, and the crusaders, will sufficiently corroborate my assertion.

Approaching nearer to Stromstad, the appearance of the town proved to be quite in character with the country we had just passed through. I hesitated to use the word country, yet could not find another; still it would sound absurd to talk of fields of rocks.

The town was built on, and under them. Three or four

weather-beaten trees were shrinking from the wind; and the grass grew so sparingly, that I could not avoid thinking Dr. Johnson's hyperbolical assertion "that the man merited well of his country who made a few blades of grass grow where they never grew before," might here have been uttered with strict propriety. The steeple likewise towered aloft; for what is a church, even amongst the Lutherans, without a steeple? But to prevent mischief in such an exposed situation, it is wisely placed on a rock at some distance, not to endanger the roof of the church.

Rambling about, I saw the door open, and entered, when to my great surprise I found the clergyman reading prayers, with only the clerk attending. I instantly thought of Swift's "Dearly beloved Roger";[3] but on enquiry I learnt that some one had died that morning, and in Sweden it is customary to pray for the dead.

The sun, who I suspected never dared to shine, began now to convince me that he came forth only to torment; for though the wind was still cutting, the rocks became intolerably warm under my feet; whilst the herring effluvia, which I before found so very offensive, once more assailed me. I hastened back to the house of a merchant, the little sovereign of the place, because he was by far the richest, though not the mayor.

Here we were most hospitably received, and introduced to a very fine and numerous family. I have before mentioned to you the lillies of the north, I might have added, water lillies, for the complexion of many, even of the young women seem to be bleached on the bosom of snow. But in this youthful circle the roses bloomed with all their wonted freshness, and I wondered from whence the fire was stolen which sparkled in their fine blue eyes.

Here we slept; and I rose early in the morning to prepare for my little voyage to Norway. I had determined to go by water, and was to leave my companions behind; but not getting a boat

---

[3]Lord Orrery, in his *Remarks* (1751), one of the earliest biographies of Jonathan Swift, tells that when Swift was in charge of a small church in Laracor, near Dublin, he faced, the first day, a church empty save for the presence of his faithful clerk Roger, whom he addressed, saying, "Dearly beloved Roger, the Scripture moveth you and me" (cited in Henry Craik, *The Life of Jonathan Swift* [London, 1894], 1:119).

immediately, and the wind being high and unfavourable, I was told that it was not safe to go to sea during such boisterous weather; I was therefore obliged to wait for the morrow, and had the present day on my hands; which I feared would be irksome, because the family, who possessed about a dozen French words amongst them, and not an English phrase, were anxious to amuse me, and would not let me remain alone in my room. The town we had already walked round and round; and if we advanced farther on the coast, it was still to view the same unvaried immensity of water, surrounded by barrenness.

The gentlemen wishing to peep into Norway, proposed going to Fredericshall, the first town, the distance was only three Swedish miles. There, and back again, was but a day's journey, and would not, I thought, interfere with my voyage. I agreed, and invited the eldest and prettiest of the girls to accompany us. I invited her, because I liked to see a beautiful face animated by pleasure, and to have an opportunity of regarding the country, whilst the gentlemen were amusing themselves with her.

I did not know, for I had not thought of it, that we were to scale some of the most mountainous cliffs of Sweden, in our way to the ferry which separates the two countries.

Entering amongst the cliffs, we were sheltered from the wind; warm sun-beams began to play, streams to flow, and groves of pines diversified the rocks. Sometimes they became suddenly bare and sublime. Once, in particular, after mounting the most terrific precipice, we had to pass through a tremendous defile, where the closing chasm seemed to threaten us with instant destruction, when turning quickly, verdant meadows and a beautiful lake relieved and charmed my eyes.

I have never travelled through Switzerland; but one of my companions assured me, that I should not there find any thing superior, if equal to the wild grandeur of these views.

As we had not taken this excursion into our plan, the horses had not been previously ordered, which obliged us to wait two hours at the first post. The day was wearing away. The road was so bad, that walking up the precipices consumed the time insensibly. But as we desired horses at each post ready at a certain hour, we reckoned on returning more speedily.

We stopt to dine at a tolerable farm. They brought us out ham, butter, cheese, and milk; and the charge was so moderate, that I scattered a little money amongst the children who were peeping at us, in order to pay them for their trouble.

Arrived at the ferry, we were still detained; for the people who attend at the ferries have a stupid kind of sluggishness in their manner, which is very provoking when you are in haste. At present I did not feel it; for scrambling up the cliffs, my eye followed the river as it rolled between the grand rocky banks; and to complete the scenery, they were covered with firs and pines, through which the wind rustled, as if it were lulling itself to sleep with the declining sun.

Behold us now in Norway; and I could not avoid feeling surprise at observing the difference in the manners of the inhabitants of the two sides of the river; for every thing shews that the Norwegians are more industrious and more opulent. The Swedes, for neighbours are seldom the best friends, accuse the Norwegians of knavery, and they retaliate by bringing a charge of hypocrisy against the Swedes. Local circumstances probably render both unjust, speaking from their feelings, rather than reason: and is this astonishing when we consider that most writers of travels have done the same, whose works have served as materials for the compilers of universal histories. All are eager to give a national character; which is rarely just, because they do not discriminate the natural from the acquired difference. The natural, I believe, on due consideration, will be found to consist merely in the degree of vivacity or thoughtfulness, pleasure, or pain, inspired by the climate, whilst the varieties which the forms of government, including religion, produce, are much more numerous and unstable.

A people have been characterized as stupid by nature; what a paradox! because they did not consider that slaves, having no object to stimulate industry, have not their faculties sharpened by the only thing that can exercise them, self-interest. Others have been brought forward as brutes, having no aptitude for the arts and sciences, only because the progress of improvement had not reached that stage which produces them.

Those writers who have considered the history of man, or of the human mind, on a more enlarged scale, have fallen into similar errors, not reflecting that the passions are weak where the necessaries of life are too hardly or too easily obtained.

Travellers who require that every nation should resemble

their native country, had better stay at home. It is, for example, absurd to blame a people for not having that degree of personal cleanliness and elegance of manners which only refinement of taste produces, and will produce every where in proportion as society attains a general polish. The most essential service, I presume, that authors could render to society, would be to promote inquiry and discussion, instead of making those dogmatical assertions which only appear calculated to gird the human mind round with imaginary circles, like the paper globe which represents the one he inhabits.

This spirit of inquiry is the characteristic of the present century, from which the succeeding will, I am persuaded, receive a great accumulation of knowledge; and doubtless its diffusion will in a great measure destroy the factitious national characters which have been supposed permanent, though only rendered so by the permanency of ignorance.

Arriving at Fredericshall, at the siege of which Charles XII lost his life, we had only time to take a transient view of it, whilst they were preparing us some refreshment.

Poor Charles! I thought of him with respect. I have always felt the same for Alexander; with whom he has been classed as a madman, by several writers, who have reasoned superficially, confounding the morals of the day with the few grand principles on which unchangeable morality rests. Making no allowance for the ignorance and prejudices of the period, they do not perceive how much they themselves are indebted to general improvement for the acquirements, and even the virtues, which they would not have had the force of mind to attain, by their individual exertions in a less advanced state of society.

The evening was fine, as is usual at this season; and the refreshing odour of the pine woods became more perceptible; for it was nine o'clock when we left Fredericshall. At the ferry we were detained by a dispute relative to our Swedish passport, which we did not think of getting countersigned in Norway. Midnight was coming on; yet it might with such propriety have been termed the noon of night, that had Young ever travelled towards the north, I should not have wondered at his becoming enamoured of the moon. But it is not the queen of night alone who reigns here in all her splendor, though the sun, loitering just below the horizon, decks her with a golden tinge from his car, illuminating the cliffs that hide him; the heavens also, of a clear softened blue, throw her forward, and the evening star appears a lesser moon to the naked eye. The huge shadows of the rocks, fringed with firs, concentrating the views, without darkening them, excited that tender melancholy which, sublimating the imagination, exalts, rather than depresses the mind.

My companions fell asleep:—fortunately they did not snore; and I contemplated, fearless of idle questions, a night such as I had never before seen or felt to charm the senses, and calm the heart. The very air was balmy, as it freshened into morn, producing the most voluptuous sensations. A vague pleasurable sentiment absorbed me, as I opened my bosom to the embraces of nature; and my soul rose to its author, with the chirping of the solitary birds, which began to feel, rather than see, advancing day. I had leisure to mark its progress. The grey morn, streaked with silvery rays, ushered in the orient beams,—how beautifully varying into purple!—yet, I was sorry to lose the soft watery clouds which preceded them, exciting a kind of expectation that made me almost afraid to breathe, lest I should break the charm. I saw the sun—and sighed.

One of my companions, now awake, perceiving that the postillion had mistaken the road, began to swear at him, and roused the other two, who reluctantly shook off sleep.

We had immediately to measure back our steps, and did not reach Stromstad before five in the morning.

The wind had changed in the night, and my boat was ready.

A dish of coffee, and fresh linen, recruited my spirits; and I directly set out again for Norway; purposing to land much higher up the coast.

Wrapping my great coat round me, I lay down on some sails at the bottom of the boat, its motion rocking me to rest, till a discourteous wave interrupted my slumbers, and obliged me to rise and feel a solitariness which was not so soothing as that of the past night.

Adieu!

3

MARGARET FULLER
"Roman Fever"

FROM
Memoirs, Volume II (1852)

A host of European women, especially from England, travelled in America and wrote about their travels during the eighteenth and nineteenth centuries. By contrast, few American women who went abroad during the same period apparently thought it was worth recording their impressions of the Old World. The notable exceptions are Harriet Beecher Stowe, the author of Uncle Tom's Cabin, *and Margaret Fuller, a prominent writer and feminist of that period.*

Margaret Fuller was born in Cambridgeport, Massachusetts, in 1810. Her father, a stern and arrogant lawyer, submitted her to a grueling education that damaged her health but made her an intellectual prodigy. The grown-up Margaret lamented the loss of her childhood: "I wish that I had read no books at all till later—that I had lived with toys, and played in the open air." At Harvard University, she was remembered as a homely girl, dumpy, long-necked, and nearsighted, who was more interested in current writers in Europe, such as Carlyle and Coleridge, than in her studies.

In 1835, she was introduced by Harriet Martineau to Ralph Waldo Emerson, whose favor she eventually gained. When her father died the next year, he became a father figure for her, and during the next decade, she became one of the leading lights of the Transcendentalist movement.

After a term of teaching in Providence, she returned to Boston and edited the prestigious The Dial *for two years. She also held Saturday "conversations" in her home and wrote critical articles for the* New York Tribune. *In 1846, in the company of two wealthy friends, she headed for Italy, the "proper home" of her heart. Travelling through Europe, she* mingled with the prominent authors of the day and met Giovanni Angelo, Marquis Ossoli, ten years her junior, and became his lover. When she became pregnant, she went to Rieti to have her child. (Later they were apparently married.)

Ossoli was a patriot and her friend Giuseppe Mazzini was the leader of Italy's struggle for independence. When that short-lived Roman Republic was proclaimed in February of 1848, Margaret Fuller wrote: "Art is not important to me now. . . . I see the future dawning." The Catholic states of Europe sent troops to besiege Rome and to restore the pope to his temporal power as head of the Roman government. During the city's resistance, Margaret supervised a Roman hospital. But after two months, French troops reimposed papal rule on Rome, and Margaret sobbed, "Here in Rome I shall no longer wish to live. O Rome, my country."

For a period the Ossolis lived in Florence (and made friends with Robert and Elizabeth Browning) before finally deciding to leave for America. In 1850, they set sail, but disaster struck. Their vessel was shipwrecked off Fire Island and all the passengers drowned. The body of their infant son Angelo was washed ashore, the only body to be recovered.

This paradoxical New Englander published a number of books, among them Summer on the Lakes *(1844)* and Women in the Nineteenth Century *(1846),* the first American plea for women's rights. As the first American woman journalist abroad, she covered (for Greeley's New York Tribune) a revolution in Italy that foreshadowed much of European history to come. Directly or by implication, she argued vigorously for the right of a woman to do as she pleased with her person, especially to travel, to love, and to live alone as she did, without censure or shame. For her troubles James Russell Lowell attacked her in A Fable for Critics *and Nathaniel Hawthorne modeled his Zenobia in* The Blithedale Romance *after her. Today she is read only by a small circle of intellectuals—a pity, as the following selection from Volume Two of her* Memoirs *(1852) should indicate.*

TO HER MOTHER

Lago di Garda, Aug. 1, 1847—Do not let what I have written disturb you as to my health. I have rested now, and am as well as usual. This advantage I derive from being alone, that, if I feel the need of it, I can stop.

I left Venice four days ago; have seen well Vicenza, Verona,

Mantua, and am reposing, for two nights and a day, in this tranquil room which overlooks the beautiful Lake of Garda. The air is sweet and pure, and I hear no noise except the waves breaking on the shore.

I think of you a great deal, especially when there are flowers. Florence was all flowers. I have many magnolias and jasmines. I always wish you could see them. The other day, on the island of San Lazaro, at the Armenian Convent, where Lord Byron used to go, I thought of you, seeing the garden full of immense oleanders in full bloom. One sees them everywhere at Venice.

TO R. W. E.

Milan, Aug. 10, 1847—Since writing you from Florence, I have passed the mountains; two full, rich days at Bologna; one at Ravenna; more than a fortnight at Venice, intoxicated with the place, and with Venetian art, only to be really felt and known in its birth-place. I have passed some hours at Vicenza, seeing mainly the Palladian structures; a day at Verona,—a week had been better; seen Mantua, with great delight; several days in Lago di Garda,—truly happy days there; then, to Brescia, where I saw the Titians, the exquisite Raphael, the Scavi, and the Brescian Hills. I could charm you by pictures, had I time.

To-day, for the first time, I have seen Manzoni.[1] Manzoni has spiritual efficacy in his looks; his eyes glow still with delicate tenderness, as when he first saw Lucia, or felt them fill at the image of Father Cristoforo. His manners are very engaging, frank, expansive; every word betokens the habitual elevation of his thoughts; and (what you care for so much) he says distinct, good things; but you must not expect me to note them down. He lives in the house of his fathers, in the simplest manner. He has taken the liberty to marry a new wife for his own pleasure and companionship, and the people around him do not like it, because she does not, to their fancy, make a good pendant to him. But I liked her very well, and saw why he married her. They asked me to return often, if I pleased, and I mean to go once or twice, for Manzoni seems to like to talk with me.

[1] Alessandro Manzoni, the poet and novelist, author of *I promessi sposi*.

Rome, Oct. 1847—Leaving Milan, I went on the Lago Maggiore, and afterward into Switzerland. Of this tour I shall not speak here; it was a little romance by itself.

Returning from Switzerland, I passed a fortnight on the Lake of Como, and afterward visited Lugano. There is no exaggeration in the enthusiastic feeling with which artists and poets have viewed these Italian lakes. The *"Titan"* of Richter, the *"Wanderjahre"* of Goethe, the Elena of Taylor, the pictures of Turner, had not prepared me for the visions of beauty that daily entranced the eyes and heart in those regions. To our country, Nature has been most bounteous, but we have nothing in the same class that can compare with these lakes, as seen under the Italian heaven. As to those persons who have pretended to discover that the effects of light and atmosphere were no finer than they found in our own lake scenery, I can only say that they must be exceedingly obtuse in organization,—a defect not uncommon among Americans.

Nature seems to have labored to express her full heart in as many ways as possible, when she made these lakes, moulded and planted their shores. Lago Maggiore is grandiose, resplendent in its beauty; the view of the Alps gives a sort of lyric exaltation to the scene. Lago di Garda is so soft and fair on one side,—the ruins of ancient palaces rise softly with the beauties of that shore; but at the other end, amid the Tyrol, it is so sublime, so calm, so concentrated in its meaning! Como cannot be better described in generals than in the words of Taylor: "Softly sublime, profusely fair."

Lugano is more savage, more free in its beauty. I was on it in a high gale; there was little danger, just enough to exhilarate; its waters wild, and clouds blowing across its peaks. I like the boatmen on these lakes; they have strong and prompt character; of simple features, they are more honest and manly than Italian men are found in the thoroughfares; their talk is not so witty as that of the Venetian gondoliers, but picturesque, and what the French call *incisive*. Very touching were some of their histories, as they told them to me, while pausing sometimes on the lake. Grossi gives a true picture of such a man in his family relations; the story may be found in "Marco Visconti."

On this lake, I met Lady Franklin, wife of the celebrated navigator. She has been in the United States, and showed equal penetration and candor in remarks on what she had seen there. She gave me interesting particulars as to the state of things in Van Diemen's Land, where she passed seven years, when her husband was in authority there.

TO C. S.

Lake of Como, Aug. 22, 1847—Rome was much poisoned to me. But, after a time, its genius triumphed, and I became absorbed in its proper life. Again I suffered from parting, and have since resolved to return, and pass at least a part of the winter there. People may write and prate as they please of Rome, they cannot convey thus a portion of its spirit. The whole heart must be yielded up to it. It is something really transcendent, both spirit and body. Those last glorious nights, in which I wandered about amid the old walls and columns, or sat by the fountains in the Piazza del Popolo, or by the river, were worth an age of pain,— only one hates pain in Italy.

Tuscany I did not like as well. It is a great place to study the history of character and art. Indeed, there I did really begin to study, as well as gaze and feel. But I did not like it. Florence is more in its spirit like Boston, than like an Italian city. I knew a good many Italians, but they were busy and intellectual, not like those I had known before. But Florence is full of really good, great pictures. There first I saw some of the great masters. Andrea del Sarto, in particular, one sees only there, and he is worth much. His wife, whom he always paints, and for whom he was so infatuated, has some bad qualities, and in what is good a certain wild nature or *diablerie*.

Bologna is truly an Italian city, one in which I should like to live; full of hidden things, and its wonders of art are very grand. The Caracci and their friends had vast force; not much depth, but enough force to occupy one a good while,—and Domenichino, when good at all, is very great.

Venice was a dream of enchantment; *there* was no disappointment. Art and life are one. There is one glow of joy, one deep shade of passionate melancholy; Giorgione, as a man, I care more for now than any of the artists, though he had no ideas.

In the first week, floating about in a gondola, I seemed to find myself again.

I was not always alone in Venice, but have come through the fertile plains of Lombardy, seen the lakes Garda and Maggiore, and a part of Switzerland, alone, except for occasional episodes of companionship, sometimes romantic enough.

In Milan I stayed a while, and knew some radicals, young, and interested in ideas. Here, on the lake, I have fallen into contact with some of the higher society,—duchesses, marquises, and the like. My friend here is Madame Arconati, Marchioness Visconti. I have formed connection with a fair and brilliant Polish lady, born Princess Radzivill. It is rather pleasant to come a little on the traces of these famous histories; also, both these ladies take pleasure in telling me of spheres so unlike mine, and do it well.

The life here on the lake is precisely what we once imagined as being so pleasant. These people have charming villas and gardens on the lake, adorned with fine works of art. They go to see one another in boats. You can be all the time in a boat, if you like; if you want more excitement, or wild flowers, you climb the mountains. I have been here for some time, and shall stay a week longer. I have found soft repose here.

TO R. W. E.

Rome, Oct. 28, 1847—I am happily settled for the winter, quite by myself, in a neat, tranquil apartment in the Corso, where I see all the motions of Rome,—in a house of loving Italians, who treat me well, and do not interrupt me, except for service. I live alone, eat alone, walk alone, and enjoy unspeakably the stillness, after all the rush and excitement of the past year.

I shall make no acquaintance from whom I do not hope a good deal, as my time will be like pure gold to me this winter; and, just for happiness, Rome itself is sufficient.

To-day is the last of the October feasts of the Trasteverini. I have been, this afternoon, to see them dancing. This morning I was out, with half Rome, to see the Civic Guard maneuvering in that great field near the tomb of Cecilia Metella, which is full of ruins. The effect was noble, as the band played the Bolognese march, and six thousand Romans passed in battle array amid these fragments of the great time.

TO R. F. F.

Rome, Oct. 29, 1847—I am trying to economize,—anxious to keep the Roman expenses for six months within the limits of four hundred dollars. Rome is not as cheap a place as Florence, but then I would not give a pin to live in Florence.

We have just had glorious times with the October feasts, when all the Roman people were out. I am now truly happy here, quiet and familiar; no longer a staring, sight-seeing stranger, riding about finely dressed in a coach to see muses and sibyls. I see these forms now in the natural manner, and am contented.

Keep free from false ties; they are the curse of life. I find myself so happy here, alone and free.

TO ———

Rome, morning of the 17th Nov., 1847—It seems great folly to send the enclosed letter. I have written it in my nightly fever. All day I dissipate my thoughts on outward beauty. I have many thoughts, happiest moments, but as yet I do not have even this part in a congenial way. I go about in a coach with several people; but English and Americans are not at home here. Since I have experienced the different atmosphere of the European mind, and been allied with it, nay, mingled in the bonds of love, I suffer more than ever from that which is peculiarly American or English. I should like to cease from hearing the language for a time. Perhaps I should return to it; but at present I am in a state of unnatural divorce from what I was most allied to.

There is a Polish countess here, who likes me much. She has been very handsome, still is, in the style of the full-blown rose. She is a widow, very rich, one of the emancipated women, naturally vivacious, and with talent. This woman *envies me;* she says, "How happy you are; so free, so serene, so attractive, so self-possessed!" I say not a word, but I do not look on myself as particularly enviable. A little money would have made me much more so; a little money would have enabled me to come here long ago, and find those that belong to me, or at least try my experiments; then my health would never have sunk, nor the best years of my life been wasted in useless friction. Had I money now,—could I only remain, take a faithful servant, and live alone, and still see those I love when it is best, that would suit me. It seems to me, very soon I shall be calmed, and begin to enjoy.

TO HER MOTHER

Rome, Dec. 16, 1847—My life at Rome is thus far all I hoped. I have not been so well since I was a child, nor so happy ever, as during the last six weeks. I wrote you about my home; it continues good, perfectly clean, food wholesome, service exact. For all this I pay, but not immoderately. I think the sum total of my expenses here, for six months, will not exceed four hundred and fifty dollars.

My *marchesa,* of whom I rent my rooms, is the greatest liar I ever knew, and the most interested, heartless creature. But she thinks it for her interest to please me, as she sees I have a good many persons who value me; and I have been able, without offending her, to make it understood that I do not wish her society. Thus I remain undisturbed.

Every Monday evening, I receive my acquaintance. I give no refreshment, but only light the saloon, and decorate it with fresh flowers, of which I have plenty still. How I wish *you* could see them!

Among the frequent guests are known to you Mr. and Mrs. Cranch, Mr. and Mrs. Story. Mr. S. has finally given up law, for the artist's life. His plans are not matured, but he passes the winter at Rome.

On other evenings, I do not receive company, unless by appointment. I spend them chiefly in writing or study. I have now around me the books I need to know Italy and Rome. I study with delight, now that I can verify everything. The days are invariably fine, and each day I am out from eleven till five, exploring some new object of interest, often at a great distance.

AMERICANS IN ITALY

The Americans took their share in this occasion, and Greenough,—one of the few Americans who, living in Italy, takes the pains to know whether it is alive or dead, who penetrates beyond the cheats of tradesmen, and the cunning of a mob corrupted by centuries of slavery, to know the real mind, the vital blood of Italy,—took a leading part. I am sorry to say that a large portion of my countrymen here take the same slothful and prejudiced view as the English, and, after many years' sojourn, betray entire ignorance of Italian literature and Italian life beyond what is attainable in a month's passage through the thoroughfares.

In reference to what I have said of many Americans in Italy, I will only add that they talk about the corrupt and degenerate state of Italy as they do about that of our slaves at home. They come ready trained to that mode of reasoning which affirms, that, because men are degraded by bad institutions, they are not fit for better.

I will only add some words upon the happy augury I draw from the wise docility of the people. With what readiness they listened to wise counsel and the hopes of the Pope that they would give no advantage to his enemies at a time when they were so fevered by the knowledge that conspiracy was at work in their midst! That was a time of trial. On all these occasions of popular excitement their conduct is like music, in such order, and with such union of the melody of feeling with discretion where to stop; but what is wonderful is that they acted in the same manner on that difficult occasion. The influence of the Pope here is without bounds; he can always calm the crowd at once. But in Tuscany, where they have no such one idol, they listened in the same way on a very trying occasion. The first announcement of the regulation for the Tuscan National Guard terribly disappointed the people. They felt that the Grand Duke, after suffering them to demonstrate such trust and joy on this feast of the 12th, did not really trust, on his side; that he meant to limit them all he could; they felt baffled, cheated; hence young men in anger tore down at once the symbols of satisfaction and respect; but the leading men went among the people, begged them to be calm, and wait till a deputation had seen the Grand Duke. The people listened at once to men who, they were sure, had at heart their best good—waited; the Grand Duke became convinced, and all ended without disturbance. If the people continue to act thus, their hopes cannot be baffled.

The American in Europe would fain encourage the hearts of these long-oppressed nations, now daring to hope for a new era, by reciting triumphant testimony from the experience of his own country. But we must stammer and blush when we speak of many things. I take pride here, that I may really say the liberty of the press works well, and that checks and balances naturally evolve from it, which suffice to its government. I may say, that the minds of our people are alert, and that talent has a free chance to rise. It is much. But dare I say, that political ambition is not as darkly sullied as in other countries? Dare I say, that men of most influence in political life are those who represent most virtue, or even intellectual power? Can I say, our social laws are generally better, or show a nobler insight into the wants of man and woman? I do indeed say what I believe, that voluntary association for improvement in these particulars will be the grand means for my nation to grow, and give a nobler harmony to the coming age. Then there is this cancer of slavery, and this wicked war that has grown out of it. How dare I speak of these things here? I listen to the same argument against the emancipation of Italy, that are used against the emancipation of our blacks; the same arguments in favor of the spoliation of Poland, as for the conquest of Mexico.

TO R. W. E.

Rome, March 14, 1848—Mickiewicz is with me here, and will remain some time; it was he I wanted to see, more than any other person, in going back to Paris, and I have him much better here. France itself I should like to see, but remain undecided, on account of my health, which has suffered so much, this winter, that I must make it the first object in moving for the summer. One physician thinks it will of itself revive, when once the rains have passed, which have now lasted from 16th December to this day. At present, I am not able to leave the fire, or exert myself at all.

In all the descriptions of the Roman Carnival, the fact has been omitted of daily rain. I felt, indeed, ashamed to perceive it, when no one else seemed to, whilst the open windows caused me convulsive cough and headache. The carriages, with their cargoes of happy women dressed in their ball dresses and costumes, drove up and down, even in the pouring rain. The two handsome *contadine,* who serve me, took off their woolen gowns, and sat five hours at a time, in the street, in white cambric dresses, and straw hats turned up with roses. I never saw anything like the merry good-humor of these people. I should always be ashamed to complain of anything here. But I had always looked forward to the Roman Carnival as a time when I could play too; and it even surpassed my expectations, with its exuberant gayety and innocent frolic, but I was unable to take much part. The others threw flowers all day, and went to masked balls all night; but I went out only once, in a carriage, and was more exhausted with the storm of flowers and sweet looks than I could be by a storm of hail. I went to the German Artists' ball, where were some pretty costumes, and beautiful music; and to the Italian masked ball, where interest lies in intrigue.

I have scarcely gone to the galleries, damp and cold as tombs; or to the mouldy old splendor of churches, where, by the way, they are just wailing over the theft of St. Andrew's head, for the sake of the jewels. It is quite a new era for this population to plunder the churches; but they are suffering terribly, and Pio's municipality does, as yet, nothing.

TO W. H. C.

Rome, March 29, 1848—I have been engrossed, stunned almost, by the public events that have succeeded one another with such rapidity and grandeur. It is a time such as I always dreamed of, and for long secretly hoped to see. I rejoice to be in Europe at this time and shall return possessed of a great history. Perhaps I shall be called to act. At present, I know not where to go, what to do. War is everywhere. I cannot leave Rome, and the men of Rome are marching out every day into Lombardy. The citadel of Milan is in the hands of my friends, Guerriere, &c., but there may be need to spill much blood yet in Italy. France and Germany are not in such a state that I can go there now. A glorious flame burns higher and higher in the heart of the nations.

The rain was constant through the Roman winter, falling in torrents from 16th December to 19th March. Now the Italian heavens wear again their deep blue, the sun is glorious, the melancholy lustres are stealing again over the Campagna, and hundreds of larks sing unwearied above its ruins. Nature seems in sympathy with the great events that are transpiring. How much has happened since I wrote!—the resistance of Sicily, and the revolution of Naples; now the fall of Louis Philippe; and Metternich is crushed in Austria. I saw the Austrian arms dragged through the streets here, and burned in the Piazza del Popolo. The Italians embraced one another, and cried, *miracolo, Providenza!* the Tribune Ciceronachio fed the flame with fagots; Adam Mickiewicz, the great poet of Poland, long exiled from his country, looked on; while Polish women brought little pieces that had been scattered in the street, and threw into the flames. When the double-headed eagle was pulled down from the lofty portal of the Palazzo di Venezia, the people placed there, in its stead, one of white and gold, inscribed with the name, ALTA ITALIA; and instantly the news followed, that Milan, Venice, Modena, and Parma, were driving out their tyrants. These news were received in Rome with indescribable rapture. Men danced, and women wept with joy along the street. The youths rushed to enrol themselves in regiments to go to the frontier. In the Colosseum, their names were received.

Rome, April 1, 1848—Yesterday, on returning from Ostia, I find the official news, that the Viceroy Ranieri has capitulated at Verona; that Italy is free, independent, and one. I trust this will prove no April foolery. It seems too good, too speedy a realization of hope.

Rome, April 30, 1848—It is a time such as I always dreamed of; and that fire burns in the hearts of men around me which can keep me warm. Have I something to do here? or am I only to cheer on the warriors, and after write the history of their deeds? The first is all I have done yet, but many have blessed me for my sympathy, and blest me by the action it impelled.

My private fortunes are dark and tangled; my strength to govern them (perhaps that I am enervated by this climate) much diminished. I have thrown myself on God, and perhaps he will make my temporal state very tragical. I am more of a child than ever, and hate suffering more than ever, but suppose I shall live with it, if it must come.

I did not get your letter, about having the rosary blessed for ———, before I left Rome, and now, I suppose, she would not wish it, as none can now attach any value to the blessing of Pius IX. Those who loved him can no longer defend him. It has become obvious, that those first acts of his in the papacy were merely the result of a kindly, good-natured temperament; that he had not thought to understand their bearing, nor force to abide by it. He seems quite destitute of moral courage. He is not resolute either on the wrong or right side. First, he abandoned the liberal party; then, yielding to the will of the people, and uniting, in appearance, with a liberal ministry, he let the cardinals betray it, and defeat the hopes of Italy. He cried peace, peace! but had not a word of blame for the sanguinary acts of the King of Naples, a word of sympathy for the victims of Lombardy. Seizing the moment of dejection in the nation, he put in this retrograde ministry; sanctioned their acts, daily more impudent; let them neutralize the constitution he himself had given; and when the people slew his minister, and assaulted him in his own palace, he yielded anew; he dared not die, or even run the slight risk,—for only by accident could he have perished. His person as a Pope is still respected, though his character as a man is despised. All the people compare him with Pius VII, saying to the French, "Slay me if you will; I *cannot* yield," and feel the difference.

I was on Monte Cavallo yesterday. The common people were staring at the broken windows and burnt door of the palace where they have so often gone to receive a blessing, the children playing, *"Sedia Papale. Morte ai Cardinali, e morte al Papa!"*

The men of straw are going down in Italy everywhere; the real men rising into power. Montanelli, Guerazzi, Mazzini, are real men; their influence is of character. Had we only been born a little later! Mazzini has returned from his seventeen years' exile, "to see what he foresaw." He has a mind far in advance of his times, and yet Mazzini sees not all.

Rome, May 7, 1848—Good and loving hearts will be unprepared, and for a time must suffer much from the final dereliction of Pius IX, to the cause of freedom. After the revolution opened in Lombardy, the troops of the line were sent thither; the volunteers rushed to accompany them, the priests preached the war as a crusade, the Pope blessed the banners. The report that the Austrians had taken and hung as a brigand one of the Roman Civic Guard,—a well-known artist engaged in the war of Lombardy,—roused the people; and they went to the Pope, to demand that he should declare war against the Austrians. The Pope summoned a consistory, and then declared in his speech that he had only intended local reforms; that he regretted the misuse that had been made of his name; and wound up by lamenting the war as offensive to the spirit of religion. A nation, in which the words *traitor* and *imbecile* were heard, received this astounding speech. The Pope was besieged with deputations, and, after two days' struggle, was obliged to place the power in the hands of persons most opposed to him, and nominally acquiesce in their proceedings.

TO MADAME ARCONATI

Rome, May 27, 1848—This is my last day at Rome. I have been passing several days at Subiaco and Tivoli, and return again to the country to-morrow. These scenes of natural beauty have filled my heart, and increased, if possible, my desire that the people who have this rich inheritance may no longer be deprived of its benefits by bad institutions.

The people of Subiaco are poor, though very industrious, and cultivating every inch of ground, with even English care and neatness;—so ignorant and uncultivated, while so finely and strongly made by Nature. May God grant now, to this people, what they need!

An illumination took place last night, in honor of the "Illustrious Gioberti." He is received here with great triumph, his carriage followed with shouts of *"Viva Gioberti, morte ai Jesuiti!"* which must be pain to the many Jesuits, who, it is said, still linger here in disguise. His triumphs are shared by Mamiani and Orioli, self-trumpeted celebrities, self-constituted rulers of the

Roman states,—men of straw, to my mind, whom the fire already kindled will burn into a handful of ashes.

I sit in my obscure corner, and watch the progress of events. It is the position that pleases me best, and, I believe, the most favorable one. Everything confirms me in my radicalism; and, without any desire to hasten matters, indeed with surprise to see them rush so like a torrent, I seem to see them all tending to realize my own hopes.

My health and spirits now much restored, I am beginning to set down some of my impressions. I am going into the mountains, hoping there to find pure, strengthening air, and tranquillity for so many days as to allow me to do something.

TO R. F. F.

Rieti, July 1, 1848—Italy is as beautiful as even I hoped, and I should wish to stay here several years, if I had a moderate fixed income. One wants but little money here, and can have with it many of the noblest enjoyments. I should have been very glad if fate would allow me a few years of congenial life, at the end of not a few of struggle and suffering. But I do not hope it; my fate will be the same to the close,—beautiful gifts shown, and then withdrawn, or offered on conditions that make acceptance impossible.

TO MADAME ARCONATI

Corpus Domini, June 22, 1848—I write such a great number of letters, having not less than a hundred correspondents, that it seems, every day, as if I had just written to each. There is no one, surely, this side of the salt sea, with whom I wish more to keep up the interchange of thought than with you.

I am no bigoted Republican, yet I think that form of government will eventually pervade the civilized world. Italy may not be ripe for it yet, but I doubt if she finds peace earlier; and this hasty annexation of Lombardy to the crown of Sardinia seems, to me, as well as I can judge, an act unworthy and unwise. Base, indeed, the monarch, if it was needed, and weak no less than base; for he was already too far engaged in the Italian cause to retire with honor or wisdom.

I am here, in a lonely mountain home, writing the narrative of my European experience. To this I devote great part of the day. Three or four hours I pass in the open air, on donkey or on foot. When I have exhausted this spot, perhaps I shall try another. Apply as I may, it will take three months, at least, to finish my book. It grows upon me.

TO R. W. E.

Rieti, July 11, 1848—Once I had resolution to face my difficulties myself, and try to give only what was pleasant to others; but now that my courage has fairly given way, and the fatigue of life is beyond my strength, I do not prize myself, or expect others to prize me.

Some years ago, I thought you very unjust, because you did not lend full faith to my spiritual experiences; but I see you were quite right. I thought I had tasted of the true elixir, and that the want of daily bread, or the pangs of imprisonment, would never make me a complaining beggar. A widow, I expected still to have the cruse full for others. Those were glorious hours, and angels certainly visited me; but there must have been too much earth,— too much taint of weakness and folly, so that baptism did not suffice. I know now of those same things, but at present they are words, not living spells.

I hear, at this moment, the clock of the Church del Purgatorio telling noon in this mountain solitude. Snow yet lingers on these mountain-tops, after forty days of hottest sunshine, last night broken by a few clouds, prefatory to a thunder storm this morning. It has been so hot here, that even the peasant in the field says, *"Non porro piu resistere,"* and slumbers in the shade, rather than the sun. I love to see their patriarchal ways of guarding the sheep and tilling the fields. They are a simple race. Remote from the corruptions of foreign travel, they do not ask for money, but smile upon and bless me as I pass,—for the Italians love me; they say I am so *"simpatica."* I never see any English or Americans, and now think wholly in Italian; only the surgeon who bled me, the other day, was proud to speak a little French, which he had learned at Tunis! The ignorance of this people is amusing. I am to them a divine visitant,—an instructive Ceres,—telling them wonderful tales of foreign customs, and even legends of the lives of their own saints. They are people whom I could love and live with. Bread and grapes among them would suffice me.

TO HER MOTHER

Rome, Nov. 16, 1848—I am again in Rome, situated for the first time entirely to my mind. I have but one room, but large; and everything about the bed so gracefully and adroitly disposed that it makes a beautiful parlor, and of course I pay much less. I have the sun all day, and an excellent chimney. It is very high and has pure air, and the most beautiful view all around imaginable. Add, that I am with the dearest, delightful old couple one can imagine, quick, prompt, and kind, sensible and contented. Having no children, they like to regard me and the Prussian sculptor, my neighbor, as such; yet are too delicate and too busy ever to intrude. In the attic, dwells a priest, who insists on making my fire when Antonia is away. To be sure, he pays himself for his trouble, by asking a great many questions. The stories below are occupied by a frightful Russian princess with moustaches, and a footman who ties her bonnet for her; and a fat English lady, with a fine carriage, who gives all her money to the church, and has made for the house a terrace of flowers that would delight you. Antonia has her flowers in a humble balcony, her birds, and an immense black cat; always addressed by both husband and wife as "Amoretto," (little love!)

The house looks out on the Piazza Barberini, and I see both that palace and the Pope's. The scene to-day has been one of terrible interest. The poor, weak Pope has fallen more and more under the dominion of the cardinals, till at last all truth was hidden from his eyes. He had suffered the minister, Rossi, to go on, tightening the reins, and, because the people preserved a sullen silence, he thought they would bear it. Yesterday, the Chamber of Deputies, illegally prorogued, was opened anew.

Rossi, after two or three most unpopular measures, had the imprudence to call the troops of the line to defend him, instead of the National Guard. On the 14th, the Pope had invested him with the privileges of a Roman citizen: (he had renounced his country when an exile, and returned to it as ambassador of Louis Philippe.) This position he enjoyed but one day. Yesterday, as he descended from his carriage, to enter the Chamber, the crowd howled and hissed; then pushed him, and, as he turned his head in consequence, a sure hand stabbed him in the back. He said no word, but died almost instantly in the arms of a cardinal. The act was undoubtedly the result of the combination of many, from the dexterity with which it was accomplished, and the silence which ensued. Those who had not abetted beforehand seemed entirely to approve when done. The troops of the line, on whom he had relied, remained at their posts, and looked coolly on. In the evening, they walked the streets with the people, singing, "Happy the hand which rids the world of a tyrant!" Had Rossi lived to enter the Chamber, he would have seen the most terrible and imposing mark of denunciation known in the history of nations,—the whole house, without a single exception, seated on the benches of opposition. The news of his death was received by the deputies with the same cold silence as by the people. For me, I never thought to have heard of a violent death with satisfaction, but this act affected me as one of terrible justice.

To-day, all the troops and the people united and went to the Quirinal to demand a change of measures. They found the Swiss Guard drawn out, and the Pope dared not show himself. They attempted to force the door of his palace, to enter his presence, and the guard fired. I saw a man borne by wounded. The drum beat to call out the National Guard. The carriage of Prince Barberini has returned with its frightened inmates and liveried retinue, and they have suddenly barred up the court-yard gate. Antonia, seeing it, observes, "Thank Heaven, we are poor, we have nothing to fear!" This is the echo of a sentiment which will soon be universal in Europe.

Never feel any apprehensions for my safety from such causes. There are those who will protect me, if necessary, and, besides, I am on the conquering side. These events have, to me, the deepest interest. These days are what I always longed for,—were I only free from private care! But, when the best and noblest want bread to give to the cause of liberty, I can just not demand *that* of them; their blood they would give me.

You cannot conceive the enchantment of this place. So much I suffered here last January and February, I thought myself a little weaned; but, returning, my heart swelled even to tears with the cry of the poet: "O, Rome, *my* country, city of the soul!" Those have not lived who have not seen Rome. Warned, however, by the last winter, I dared not rent my lodgings for the year. I hope I am acclimated. I have been through what is called the grape-cure, much more charming, certainly, than the water-cure. At present I am very well; but, alas! because I have gone to bed early, and done very little. I do not know if I can maintain any labor. As to my life, I think that it is not the will of Heaven it should terminate very soon. I have had another strange escape. I had taken passage in the diligence to come to Rome; two rivers were to be passed,—the Turano and the Tiber,—but passed by good bridges, and a road excellent when not broken unexpectedly by torrents from the mountains. The diligence sets out between three and four in the morning, long before light. The director sent me word that the Marchioness Crispoldi had taken for herself and family a coach extraordinary, which would start two hours later, and that I could have a place in that, if I liked; so I accepted. The weather had been beautiful, but, on the eve of the day fixed for my departure, the wind rose, and the rain fell in torrents. I observed that the river which passed my window was much swollen, and rushed with great violence. In the night, I heard its voice still stronger, and felt glad I had not to set out in the dark. I rose with twilight, and was expecting my carriage, and wondering at its delay, when I heard, that the great diligence, several miles below, had been seized by a torrent; the horses were up to their necks in water, before any one dreamed of the danger. The postilion called on all the saints, and threw himself into the water. The door of the diligence could not be opened, and the passengers forced themselves, one after another, into the cold water,—dark too. Had I been there I had fared ill; a pair of strong men were ill after it, though all escaped with life.

For several days, there was no going to Rome; but, at last, we set forth in two great diligences, with all the horses of the route. For many miles, the mountains and ravines were covered with snow; I seemed to have returned to my own country and climate. Few miles passed, before the conductor injured his leg under the wheel, and I had the pain of seeing him suffer all the way, while "Blood of Jesus," "Souls of Purgatory," was the mildest beginning of an answer to the jeers of the postilions upon his paleness. We stopped at a miserable osteria, in whose cellar we found a magnificent remain of Cyclopean architecture,—as indeed in Italy one is paid at every step, for discomfort or danger, by some precious subject of thought. We proceeded very slowly, and reached just at night a solitary little inn, which marks the site of the ancient home of the Sabine virgins, snatched away to become the mothers of Rome. We were there saluted with the news that the Tiber, also, had overflowed its banks, and it was very doubtful if we could pass. But what else to do? There were no accommodations in the house for thirty people, or even for three, and to sleep in the carriages, in that wet air of the marshes, was a more certain danger than to attempt the passage. So we set forth; the moon, almost at the full, smiling sadly on the ancient grandeurs, then half draped in mist, then drawing over her face a thin white veil. As we approached the Tiber, the towers and domes of Rome could be seen, like a cloud lying low on the horizon. The road and the meadows, alike under water, lay between us and it, one sheet of silver. The horses entered; they behaved nobly; we proceeded, every moment uncertain if the water would not become deep; but the scene was beautiful, and I enjoyed it highly. I have never yet felt afraid when really in the presence of danger, though sometimes in its apprehension.

At last we entered the gate; the diligence stopping to be examined, I walked to the gate of Villa Ludovisi, and saw its rich shrubberies of myrtle, and its statues so pale and eloquent in the moonlight.

Is it not cruel that I cannot earn six hundred dollars a year, living here? I could live on that well, now I know Italy. Where I have been, this summer, a great basket of grapes sells for one cent!—delicious salad, enough for three or four persons, one cent,—a pair of chickens, fifteen cents. Foreigners cannot live so, but I could, now that I speak the language fluently, and know the price of everything. Everybody loves, and wants to serve me, and I cannot earn this pitiful sum to learn and do what I want.

Of course, I wish to see America again; but in my own time, when I am ready; and not to weep over hopes destroyed and projects unfulfilled.

Many Americans have shown me great and thoughtful kindness, and none more so than W.S——— and his wife. They are now in Florence, but may return. I do not know whether I shall stay here or not; shall be guided much by the state of my health.

All is quieted in Rome. Late at night the Pope had to yield, but not till the door of his palace was half burnt, and his confessor killed. This man, Parma, provoked his fate by firing on the people from a window. It seems the Pope never gave order to fire; his guard acted from a sudden impulse of their own. The new ministry chosen are little inclined to accept. It is almost impossible for any one to act, unless the Pope is stripped of his temporal power, and the hour for that is not yet quite ripe; though they talk more and more of proclaiming the Republic, and even of calling my friend Mazzini.

If I came home at this moment, I should feel as if forced to leave my own house, my own people, and the hour which I had always longed for. If I do come in this way, all I can promise is to plague other people as little as possible. My own plans and desires will be postponed to another world.

Do not feel anxious about me. Some higher power leads me through strange, dark, thorny paths, broken at times by glades opening down into prospects of sunny beauty, into which I am not permitted to enter. If God disposes for us, it is not for nothing. This I can say, my heart is in some respects better, it is kinder and more humble. Also, my mental acquisitions have certainly been great, however inadequate to my desires.

4

KATE FIELD
Hassles in Spain

FROM
Ten Days in Spain (1875)

Kate Field deserves to be remembered perhaps not so much for what she wrote or where she ventured, but more for what she represented—the accomplishments of an intelligent and independent woman during the late Victorian era in America.

Born Mary Katherine Keemle Field in 1838, she was the only daughter of an actress and newspaper publisher in St. Louis. When her father died, she became at the age of eighteen the ward of a wealthy uncle, Milton L. Sanford. He provided her with a genteel education and took her to Italy, where she became a favorite of Anthony Trollope and other members of the writers' colony in Florence. However, when she supported the Union cause in the Civil War, her uncle, a Southern sympathizer, decided not to make her his heir.

To support herself, she tried a variety of jobs, among them writing for newspapers and acting in the theater. She also wrote commercial publicity, advertising copy, and amusing accounts of travelling in Europe. In 1890, she was able to found her own newspaper, Kate Field's Washington, *which gave her a platform for her views. She died in 1896 in Hawaii, where she had gone to regain her health after the newspaper had failed.*

Her writings reveal a range of interests. She published many articles in Atlantic Monthly, *one of them a memorial tribute to Mrs. Elizabeth Browning (this article brought the English poet to the attention of Emily Dickinson, for whom Mrs. Browning became a spiritual mentor).* Pen Photographs of Charles Dickens' Readings *(1868) captured the aura of the great novelist on his lecture tour of America and helped Miss*

Field to shape her own successful lecture on Dickens while she was working the lyceum circuit.

A keen sense of humor and a flair for social satire inform her two best books, Hap-Hazard *(1873) and* Ten Days in Spain *(1875), from which the following selection is taken. The first is a collection of letters from the New York* Tribune *concerning a lady lecturer who makes fun of both the British monarchy and American tourists. The second, combining some typical middle-class American prejudices with an amiable wit, is largely an account of the difficulties faced by a woman travelling in a country undergoing political upheaval (in this case, the Carlist Wars).*

Not a militant feminist, she used her newspaper chiefly to express her special commitments, such as those to cremation, prohibition of Mormon polygamy, international copyright laws, civil service reform, the arts, and drawing-room comedies, several of which were performed. She was the first woman in America to found and run her own weekly newspaper and among the first to travel alone in Spain.

Spain acquaints one with strange bedfellows. There is an untiring industry about them worthy of a better cause. Would that the Republic's Minister of Finance and its commanding generals possessed the activity of its fleas! Why will Nature be such a spendthrift? Were she to economize on fleas, there might be sufficient energy in the Peninsula to start the trains punctually and occasionally turn promises into deeds. Why there should be so many Spanish fleas weird William Blake would quickly tell us. When completing his curious drawing of the Ghost of a Flea, the lively ghost informed Blake that all fleas were inhabited by the souls of such men as were by nature bloodthirsty to excess, and were therefore providentially confined to the size and form of insects. With this strange light thrown upon Spain's largest population, it is most wasteful management that fails to utilize fleas for war purposes. Placed at the head of the army, they would soon drive the Carlists howling into the Bay of Biscay.

Santander is not a big town, otherwise we might be wandering about to this hour. When cigarettes are to be smoked with tender appreciation, distances become great; but we found the sanitary bureau and harangued the mighty potentate thereof. I was an American whose stay in Spain was limited to a few days. Could I have my trunk?

"No."

"Why not?"

"Because there is cholera in Paris?"

"But I've not come from Paris, nor have any other passengers."

"It matters little. We are held responsible for the introduction of cholera into Spain, and every province exercises its own discretion in this matter."

The potentate heeded neither argument nor sarcasm. He smoked a cigarette, and seemed perfectly resigned to my fate. I wrestled with the Spanish intellect. I tried to make him realize that the eyes of Europe and America would be everlastingly fixed upon him if he forced me to go to Madrid with one gown. At this final threat the potentate relented. "You cannot have your trunk," he said. "That would cost me my office, but I will give you such a paper as will enable you to take out its entire contents." And the potentate gave me a written order addressed to the quarantine officers. To the last he did not seem to appreciate the absurdity of persecuting my innocent trunk.

Thanking the potentate, we went in search of banker and American Consul, as it seemed to me that such a ridiculous law might be overruled by powerful influence. The Spanish banker received me with stately dignity, looked at my letter of credit, heard my pathetic story, and said he could do nothing. Law was law. This, from a native of the country that makes more laws and fulfils fewer than any nation in the world, impressed me. We bade each other farewell with profound bows, and soon I stood in the small office of the American Consulate. Of course the Consul was a Spaniard who could not speak English; but I am assured that he is efficient, and that his assistant understands our language. Half a dozen men were smoking, all of whom stopped puffing as the thrilling tale was told. They examined the order, and then the Consul said: "Madam, I don't know how you have obtained this document, but you are given extraordinary privileges. No human being can obtain more. Take your clothes, and I will send the trunk back to Bayonne." There was no power behind the Consul. The telegraph-wire to Madrid was cut, and I gave up the contest.

What next was to be done? To go in search of the *Four Friends*. And where was it? In the neighborhood of quarantine? And where was quarantine? Across the harbor, five miles away. It was half past ten o'clock, and the Madrid train started at two. How long would it take to go and return? About two hours, if nothing happened. As something always happens when one is in a hurry, I begged the Blinker[1] to secure the lightest boat and strongest rowers. He smiled, went to the quay, returned, and escorted me to a heavy tub commanded by an old man and manned by a small boy. I said nothing. Of what use? The Blinker would have assured me that the boat was the best in the harbor. "Now, my good friends, hurry. I've no time to lose," I exclaimed. Whereupon man and boy sat down to indulge in a dialogue as to whether they should or should not carry a sail. Deciding affirmatively, the boy went in search of one, and in the course of twenty minutes the unwieldy thing was in place. "Now we are off," I thought. No, we were not. Then began the most important work of the day,—making cigarettes. The entire Spanish nation begins and ends in smoke. With the first puff we were under way so far as concerned the sailing; but, as the wind was very light, I suggested rowing. Would the noble, independent Spaniards row? No; they preferred smoking and conversation. Why should they wear themselves out? The sea glittered like molten silver, the air was soft, the sky beautiful. Why exert the muscles? To talk about being in haste seemed to them an evidence of insanity.

When we arrived finally at quarantine the *Four Friends* was spluttering and shrieking, backing and filling, trying to effect a landing. Heeding our pantomime, she stopped, and by a repetition of the gymnastics practised on a more formidable occasion, I went aboard.

The quarantine officer looked at the order, said it was queer, but that there was nothing to prevent my emptying the trunk inside out. This I knew, and in five minutes we jumped into our boat with the biggest, absurdest-looking bundle I ever saw in the possession of any one not an emigrant. It was half past twelve o'clock. Both current and wind were against us, and I began to despair. Would the good men row? Well, yes, they would. They did not want me to be left by the train. And they dipped their oars into the water with something akin to vigor. It was not what

---

[1] A fellow American whom Kate Field met in Spain.

I call rowing, but I had begun to grow reasonable, and not to expect Yankee energy from Spanish lazzaroni. Slowly we approached the town, the wind helping us on the last tack.

With a beggar running in advance, carrying my ridiculous bundle on his head, for which I felt an apology was due to the gaping multitude, we strode into the hotel. Where was the station? Near by. Where was a carriage? None to be had. Everybody walked. Should I be in time for the train? My friend the *maître d'hôtel* did not know. I could but try. The Blinker disappeared. I cried aloud for more beggars. They swarmed. To my room I rushed, collected more bundles, consigned them to my small army, paid the hotel bill, and then looked about for the Blinker. The *maître d'hôtel* rushed up stairs after my enterprising courier.

"Where is your carpet bag?" I asked.

"O, are you really going?" he exclaimed, retiring, and returning with his luggage. "Good by," he said blandly to the *maître d'hôtel*. "We'll be back directly."

Was not this insulting? Was it not enough to make an American perform a war-dance? In single file we hurried to the station.

Such a crowd! It seemed as though half of the world had assembled on the platform to bid an everlasting farewell to the other half huddled together in the train. I felt somewhat like a victim, as going to Madrid was not the safe journey it had been. An accident had occurred not many days before, the sum total of which was seventeen killed and several wounded. Some maintained it to have been the result of a Carlist conspiracy; others blamed the road. Nobody knew, and I trusted to about all one can trust,—luck. Every place was occupied but a coupé, into which I climbed,—for that is what entering a European railway-carriage means,—the beggars and the Blinker barricading me with bundles. I have always had a contempt for women who traveled with bundles. Bundles are but one remove from bandboxes. And here was I with the contents of a trunk in my arms! Of course everybody's eyes were fastened on that blue-and-white checkered bundle,—done up in a morning wrapper,—and of course I could not rise to explain.

I wanted to put my head out of the window and assure people I was not a receiver of stolen goods.

We departed at twenty minutes past two! Hereafter I shall

never despair of catching a Spanish train, for, although it may have started, I shall be sure to catch up with it by walking over the track, because it stands still much more than it goes ahead. Why trains should stop at any way-station seems curious, nobody appearing to enter or leave them. Whenever the train for Madrid did stop, however, I concluded it was for the night. I believe the cause of detention is due to tobacco,—heaven's last, best gift to man. At every station engineer, fireman, all, make cigarettes, and do not start until the last puff has been drawn. Time was made for slaves. Are Spaniards slaves? They are the cause of slavery in others.

Converting my checkered bundle into a pillow, I congratulated myself on having a coupé wherein to be moderately comfortable. I had had nothing to eat for two days except a few grapes; but it is astonishing how one can live without eating after becoming accustomed to it. Was I allowed to remain in peace? Certainly not. While we were fondly lingering at a station not many miles from Santander, a young man opened the door and politely asked me if I had a coupé ticket.

"No; I saw the coupé empty. No official could or would give me any information about it, and I got in."

"There are others who wish the coupé."

"Possession is nine points of the law."

"Certainly, madam, but there are three gentlemen who wish to occupy the other seats, and unless you take the compartment they have a right to them."

"Are they Spaniards?"

"Yes, madam."

"Do they smoke?"

"Certainly, madam."

"It is impossible. I can't endure smoke all night. There is no compartment for women. I must take the coupé."

"But, madam, you will ruin yourself. The coupé will cost you a great deal of money."

"How much?"

The polite young man sat down and did sums for ten minutes, at the end of which time he presented a bill that staggered my intellect and frightened my purse. In all my experience I had never known such extortion.

"What does this mean?"

"It means that the government taxes railroads to such a degree as to put up fares. I thought you did not know Spain. It really will not pay you to take this coupé. At——a carriage with compartment for *Dames Seules* will be put on, and then I advise you to change. Until then you can have the coupé to yourself."

Such interest in my pocket touched me. How did that unknown young man divine my financial status? Why did he not take me for an "American Princess"? Was it being without a trunk, travelling with a steerage bundle, that revealed my abject squalor? Yes, a woman is known by her trunks. I did not inform my economical friend that I owned a courier. I was so glad to be rid of the Blinker that I would not have called for his assistance had my bundle been borne off by brigands. Upon arriving at ———, true to his word, the polite young man appeared with porters, escorted me and my bundles to a woman's compartment, and bade me a good night.

On general principles I object to the compartment for *Dames Seules:* first, because *Dames Seules* usually carry as many bundles as I did on this exceptional occasion, and stow them away in the places where legs ought to go; second, because they travel with babies that cry or small children that eat candy or cake and then wipe their dear, dirty little fingers on your new travelling-gown; third, because they have as much as they can do to take care of themselves, and never volunteer to help you in or out of the carriage, or fetch you a glass of water, or say civil things to you. I always avoid *Dames Seules,* but in Spain I was grateful for them. On entering, I beheld three ladies and two children. They were exceedingly courteous, gave me two seats and fastened their black eyes on my bundle. To vindicate my right to respectability, I told them the story of the quarantine. They listened gravely, never dreamed of smiling, and merely remarked that I was very brave to come to Spain at such a time. "But," they added, "American women are not like European. They travel about like men. It must be very fatiguing, and to come to Spain! After seeing Paris, what is there in Madrid, especially now?"

"You are not republicans?"

"O no; nor any one else," replied the most voluble of the señoras.

"Are you in favor of Don Carlos?"

"Not at all. It is a great trial to be torn to pieces by civil war, but we are obliged to endure it. The best Spaniards are Alphonsists. The Queen we do not want. She has disgraced us; but her son is our legitimate sovereign. Unfortunately, he is very young. We fear a regency, and so accept the present government."

"Then you regard the republic as a *pis-aller*."

"Precisely."

"Dinner! dinner! twenty minutes for dinner!" and off everybody rushed to the dining-room of a restaurant. It was the only occasion on which I saw Spaniards in a hurry, although Gautier declares that they are the greatest walkers and most agile runners. They would have done credit to a Western steamboat, as described by Dickens thirty years ago. I had succeeded so well without eating, that to dine seemed like throwing away money. However, early prejudices still clung to me, and I sat down beside a nice-looking Spanish woman, who immediately began to talk broken English. It really is provoking not to be able to pass for somebody else occasionally, but the Anglo-Saxon is so branded with national characteristics as to render concealment impossible. This woman ate; I could not. There came soup with oil in it; then dry fish with oil on it, followed by pork and oil. I fell back on a bit of done-to-death beef and underdone potato. At least I made the effort, but had no knife.

"Bring me a knife," I said to a waiter laden with dishes.

"Certainly," said the waiter, and never returned.

"Bring madam a knife," said the Spanish woman to another waiter.

"Certainly," he replied, and never returned.

Both, probably, came back the next day. The one word in everybody's mouth is *mañana* (tomorrow). It appears to be the appropriate answer to any question, and has so taken possession of the Spanish mind that I don't believe Castelar himself would dare to do to-day what he could put off until to-morrow. It was not feasible to postpone my dinner, so I poised my beef on the point of a fork and gnawed it, to the amazement of some old Spaniards opposite, who picked their teeth in chorus, and glared. Said they, probably, when seated smoking in a hermetically concealed compartment, "What queer people are the English! They never use a knife. They stick their meat on a fork, and bite around it." I didn't like gnawing, and, after deferring to my stomach by indulging in several mouthfuls, I arose.

It is a long night that has no morrow. Long as it was, the end came before I died for want of fresh air. Thinking me asleep, my neighbors stole to the window and closed it, counted their beads, and said their prayers in unison. The sound was like the hum of bees. Then the ladies removed their bonnets, took off their hair, tied their remains up in silk handkerchiefs, and I watched them, nod, nod, nodding until daylight.

The view within did not excite, nor did that without. When Dickens wishes to describe desolation, he says, "Few children were to be seen, and no dogs." Had he visited Spain, he would have drawn a picture of naked, russet mountains, stretching north and south, east and west, staring out of an atmosphere so clear and thin as to render their bleak monotony all the more startling, without cultivation, without habitation, saving here and there the wretched ruin of a wretched stone sty, in which once may have wallowed mediæval beggars, giving no hope for either time or eternity. I became more and more oppressed by the absence of life. That a railroad track should be laid down in such a region, that a train should be slowly climbing an inclined plane, that occasional dreary stations, seemingly attached to no town, should punctuate our progress, seemed a ghastly joke; and when, early in the morning, we passed the Escorial, built high in the air, and starting out of the solitude like the great grim parody on humanity that it is, I saw in its gridiron the bier of past and present Spain. This is the country that once ruled the world, the country to which America owes its discovery!

Is anything as incredible as history?

5

MRS. ALEC TWEEDIE
Saunas and Swimming
FROM
Through Finland in Carts (1897)

Edith Harley ("Mrs. Alec Tweedie") was born in London in about 1866, the daughter of a prominent Harley Street physician, and was more or less rocked in her cradle by the likes of Paul Du Chaillu, the French-American explorer, and Dr. John Rae, the discoverer of the Franklin Expedition remains in the Arctic.

*She gave up her aspirations to become an actress (*Behind the Footlights, *1914, describes her early romance with the theater) in favor of marriage to Alexander Tweedie, also of a medical family. In 1887, the Tweedies set up house in Regent's Park and there entertained such notables as Marchese Marconi, the inventor of the telegraph; Johnston Forbes-Robertson, the great Shakespearean actor; and Henrik Ibsen (*My Table-Clothe, *1916, is a reminiscence about that time).*

*When the unexpected death of her husband left her a young widow with two sons (both of whom were to die in uniform) and no money, she cultivated her talents as a traveller and a writer, covering more than fifty thousand miles from the Sudan to Scandinavia and publishing, to the amusement of a generation of readers, a succession of lively and original travel books. At the same time, before failing eyesight caused her retirement a year before her death in 1940, she managed to work ardently for women's rights, for improved conditions in English hospitals, and for philanthropic causes elsewhere in the world. In 1912, the Italian government thanked her officially for helping the sufferers in the great earthquake that devastated Sicily, a place Mrs. Tweedie had visited and loved (*Sunny Sicily, *1904). The Royal Geographic Society acknowledged her accomplishments by electing her a Fellow.*

An early tour of geyser and volcano formations resulted in Girl's Ride to Iceland *(1899), and her visits to Mexico produced* Mexico as I Saw It *(1901) and* Porfirio Diaz *(1904). After she had journeyed around the United States several times, she wrote* America as I Saw It *(1913). Her impressions of Russia, Siberia, China, and Japan are contained in* An Adventurous Journey *(1926), in which she predicted that Japan would attack the United States in Hawaii and the Philippines and win the ensuing war. Her other books include* A Woman on Four Battle Fronts *(1919) and* George Harley: Life of a London Physician *(1899).*

Perhaps her most entertaining book of travel is Through Finland in Carts *(1897), an early effort that depicts life in a land most travellers, especially women, chose to avoid. For her readers, Mrs. Tweedie combined the qualities of boldness and bashfulness in exactly the right degree, and today her account of the bathing habits of the Finns is as readable as it was eighty-five years ago.*

No one can be many days in Finland without hearing murmurs of the bath-house.

A Finnish bath once taken by man or woman can never be forgotten!

A real native bath is one of the specialities of the country. Even in the old songs of the *Kalevala* they speak of the "cleansing and healing vapours of the heated bath-room."

Poets have described the bath in verse, artists have drawn it on canvas, and singers have warbled forth its charms; nevertheless, it is not every traveller who has penetrated the strange mystery. Most strange and most mysterious it is! But I anticipate.

Every house in the country, however humble that house may be, boasts its *bastu,* or bath-house, called in Finnish *Sauna.* As we passed along the country roads, noting the hay piled up on a sort of tent erection made of pine trunks, to dry in the sun before being stowed away into small wooden houses for protection during the winter or nearly drove over one of those strange long-haired pigs, the bristles on whose backs reminded one of a hog-maned polo pony, one saw these *bastus* continually. Among the cluster of little buildings that form the farm, the bath-house, indeed, stands forth alone, and is easily recognisable, one of its

Saunas and Swimming

walls, against which the stove stands, being usually black, even on the outside, from smoke.

Every Saturday, year in, year out, that stove is heated, and the whole family have a bath—not singly, or dear, no, but altogether, men, women, and children; farmer, wife, brothers, sisters, labourers, friends, and the dogs too, if they have a mind; so that once in each week the entire population of Finland is clean, although few of them know what daily ablutions, even of the most primitive kind, mean, while hot water is almost as difficult to procure in *Suomi,* as a great auk's egg in England!

Naturally any institution so purely national as the Finnish *bastu* was worth investigating—in fact, could not be omitted from our programme. Bathing with the peasants themselves, however, being impossible, we arranged to enjoy the extraordinary pleasure at a friend's house, where we could be washed by one of her own servants; for, be it understood, there is always one servant in every better-class establishment who understands the *bastu,* and can, and does wash the family.

When *she* is washed, we unfortunately omitted to inquire! In towns, such as Helsingfors, there are professional women-washers, who go from house to house to bathe and massage men and women alike. Theirs is a regular trade, and as the higher class of the profession receive about a shilling for "attending" each bath given at a private house, the employment is not one to be despised. Neither is it, as proved by the fact that there are over 300 public bathing-women in Finland.

On the eventful night of our initiation, supper was over, the house-party and guests were all assembled on the balcony, the women engaged in needlework, and the men smoking cigarettes, when Saima, the Finnish servant, arrived to announce that the English ladies' bath was ready. Taking a fond farewell of the family, we marched solemnly behind the flaxen-haired Saima, who had thoroughly entered into the spirit of the joke of giving an English lady a Finnish bath, neither the bather nor attendant being able to understand one word of what the other spoke. Down an avenue overshadowed by trees we proceeded, getting a peep of a perfectly glorious sunset which bathed one side of the lake in yellow hues, while the other was lighted by an enormous blood-red moon, for in those Northern climes many strange natural effects occur, we little wot of in England. It was a wonderful evening, and we paused to consider which was the more beautiful, the departing day or the coming night.

Saima would brook no delay however, so we had to hurry on. Immediately before us was the *bastu*—a wee wooden house like a small Swiss châlet, the outer room, where we undressed, containing a large oven. The inner room boasted only one small window, through which the departing day did not shine very brilliantly, luckily for our modesty. Its furniture was only a large-sized tin bath filled with cold water, opposite to which were seven very wide wooden steps like a staircase, the top step forming a kind of platform where there was just room to sit without one's head touching the tarred ceiling above. The steps and the platform were covered with straw—Finnish fashion—for the great occasion.

We wondered what next, but we had not much time for speculation, for Saima—who only took off her outer dress—grasped us by the hand, her face aglow with the intense heat, led us up the wooden staircase, and signed her will that we should sit on the straw-strewn platform afore honourably mentioned!

Oh, the heat! Many of us know Turkish baths; but then we take them gradually, whereas in the *bastu* one plunges into volcanic fires at once. Blinking in the dim light, we found that beside us was a brick-built stove, for which the fire, as we had noticed while disrobing, is in the outer chamber, and when the washingwoman threw a pail of water upon the surface of the great heated stones, placed for the purpose inside the stove, the steam ascended in volumes, and the temperature went up, until we exclaimed, in one of the few Swedish sentences we knew, *"Mycket hett"* (very hot), at which agonised remark Saima laughed uproariously, and, nodding and smiling, fetched another pail of water from the cold bath, and threw its contents on the brick furnace in order that more steaming fumes might ascend. Almost stifled we blinked, and gasped, and groaned by turns, we repeated again and again, *"Mycket hett,"* *"alltför hett"* (too hot), *"Tack så mycket"* (thank you), in tones of anguish. Much amused, Saima—who, be it understood, was a Swedish-speaking Finn—stood smiling cheerfully at our discomfiture; but, happily, at last she seemed to think we might have had enough, for, after waving our hands hopelessly to the accompaniment of *"Nej tack,*

Saunas and Swimming 61

nej tack" (no thank you), she apparently understood and desisted.

A moment later, through the steam, we saw her smiling face ascending the stairs, with a pail of hot water in one hand, and a lump of soft soap in the other, on which was a large bundle of white fibre, something like hemp. Dipping this in the pail, she soon made a lather with the soap, and, taking up limb after limb, scrubbed us hard and long—scrubbed until our skin tingled, and in the damp mysterious heat we began to wonder how much of our bodies would emerge from the ordeal. This scrubbing was a long process, and if the Finns wash one another as industriously as Saima washed us, no one in Finland should ever be dirty, although most of them must lose several skins a year. Pails of water were then thrown over us, over the straw, over everything, and we heard the soapy water gurgling away into the lake below, which was covered with yellow and white water-lilies. Lilies cannot object to soap, or they would never bloom in Finland as they do!

"*Mycket bra*" (very good), we called again and again, hoping our appreciation might perhaps make Saima desist, as our exclamations at the heat did not seem to alarm her. More water was thrown on to the steaming bricks, and Saima retired, returning immediately with a great bundle of birch leaves, tied up with a string, such as we had often seen her on former occasions sweeping the floors with. Dipping the branches of the birch into a pail of hot water she proceeded to beat us all over! She laughed, and we laughed; but the more we laughed the harder she thumped, till the sharp edges of the leaves left almost a sting, while the strong healthy Saima beat us harder and harder, dipping the leaves into hot water continually.

The peasantry in Finland are occasionally good enough to wash one another, and stories are told of a dozen of them sitting in rows on the wooden steps, each man vigorously beating his neighbour with birch boughs.

At harvest time, when the heat is very great, and the work very hard, laborers have a bath *every night*! Frequently, after our wonderful experience at Ilkeäsaari, we saw, while journeying farther into the country, shoals of human beings strolling off to enjoy their *bastu* or *Sauna*.

It was an awful experience! We were really beginning to feel the heat dreadful by this time, and were confident the blood must be galloping through our veins. Finally the good-tempered Finnish maid appeared to be of our mind, for she fetched a pail of cold water, and, pouring a good drop on our heads—which made us jump—she dipped her birch branches therein and switched them over us. Had we followed true Finnish fashion we should then have plunged straight into the lake outside,—or in winter taken a roll in the snow,—but, our bath being rather more aristocratic, we only descended the slippery steps and jumped into that bath of cold water previously mentioned, before—clad only in burning hot towels—returning to the outer room to dress.

We puffed and panted, and, quite exhausted, longed for a Turkish divan and quiet rest before, robed in fur coats and thick under-garments, we trotted home to bed.

Our bath was taken, the mystery unravelled; we had been washed according to native ideas and customs, and understood what the whole thing meant.

Whether it was the heat, or exhaustion, or the loss of one skin or many, we know not; but after a glass of *mjöd*, that most delicious and refreshing of Finnish drinks, we slept splendidly, and felt fit next morning for any amount of hard work, even for a journey to Russia through Finland, though we did not speak or understand the language of either country.

The Finnish peasant thinks nothing of being seen by his friends or his neighbours in a state of nature, *apropos* of which peculiarity a well-known general told us the following story—

He had been inspecting a district, and for his benefit parades, etc., were held. Some hours afterwards he went for a ride, and on returning to the village he passed a *Sauna,* where the folk were enjoying their primitive kind of Turkish bath. According to the usual custom one of the men came out to dress himself; but, having left his clothes in a little pile some 20 feet from the *Sauna* door, he had hardly looked out his things when he noticed that the general was upon him. Though not in the least confused by the fact of his nakedness, for which he made no apology, he nevertheless exclaimed in tones of horror, "The general! the general!" and began rummaging among the articles on the ground, till at last he pulled forth a wig, which, all in a hurry, he clapped on his head wrong side up, then standing proudly erect he saluted the general as he passed!

The poor fellow evidently considered his wig of much more importance than his shirt.

Another amusing story is told of an elegant Englishman who had heard so much of Finnish baths that he determined to try one; having arrived at some small town, he told the *Isvoschtschik* to go to the *bastu*. Away they drove, and finally drew up at a very nice house, where he paid the twopence halfpenny fare for his cab, rang the bell, and was admitted by a woman servant. He only knew half a dozen words in Swedish, but repeated *bastu* to the smiling lass, being surprised at the elegance of the furniture in the room into which he had been shown. The girl smiled again and left him. However, thinking it was all right, he proceeded to undress, and, having entirely disrobed, he stood ready to be escorted into the bath, and accordingly rang for the woman to come and wash and massage him. A few moments later the door opened, and a very beautiful young dame stood before him. She was no masseuse, but the wife of the pastor, into whose house he had come by mistake owing to his want of knowledge of the pronunciation of the language. Tableau!

We had many curious experiences when bathing in the lakes, and seemed to excite as much interest in the peasantry of Finland as a Chinaman with his pigtail would in a small country village in England. At Sordavala, for instance, there was a charming little bath-house belonging to our host, for which we got the key and prepared to enjoy ourselves. A bathing-dress was not to be bought for love or money. No one had ever heard of such a thing, but my sister's modesty forbade her appearing without one so near a town, and, now that we had left our kind hostess at Ilkeäsaari, she could no longer borrow one. Through the town of Sordavala, therefore, we marched from shop to shop until we lighted upon a sort of store where linen goods were procurable. Blue and white-striped galatea exactly suited the purpose, as it would be light for packing, and the colour could not run. We bought it, we paid for it, and home we marched. In less than an hour that gown was cut out by the aid of a pair of nail scissors, without any kind or sort of pattern whatever, and was sewn up ready for use. Out my sister went to bathe, triumphant;

but so rare was a bathing-dress that the onlookers thought the English lady had fallen into the water by mischance with all her clothes on.

My sister had hardly taken a plunge from the springboard into the water below, before every man, woman, and child in the neighbourhood began exclaiming one to the other, "The English lady has tumbled in," and, absolutely, before the bather's head could appear again from the depths of the water they had all run to the bank to have a look at the phenomenon. Of course their interest was heightened by the appearance of a proper dress and cap, for even the better-class Finlanders very rarely wear any covering on their bodies while bathing, and as the women never dive or swim under water a cap is not necessary to keep their hair dry. They evidently considered my sister and her attire something remarkably funny.

Again at Iisalmi, another place of some importance, when we went down to the bath-house we found it surrounded by dozens of boys of all ages and descriptions, who were enjoying themselves gamboling in the water.

A Finnish gentleman of the town, to whom we had an introduction, kindly came with us to unlock the door and see that everything was satisfactory, and he quickly explained to the boys they must go away into the next cove as strange ladies were about to bathe. Very reluctantly they went; and, wishing us good-bye and a pleasant dip, he went too.

We undressed, donned our aquatic attire, plunged into the water, to discover, in a few moments, a row of grinning spectators, varying in age from three years old to thirty, sitting up on the banks like monkeys in a cage, thoroughly enjoying the joke. They laughed and they chatted, they pointed, they waved their arms, and they evidently considered our performances very extraordinary.

These are only two instances out of many, for everywhere we went we caused interest and some amusement.

One of our party through Northern Finland was a magnificent swimmer. He had a cheery way of jumping into a boat, rowing himself far out into the lake, and then taking a header which excited the admiration of all beholders.

At Kuopio he did this as was his usual habit, while the old

women of the bath-house watched his performance from the shore. One minute went by, and he did not reappear; two minutes went by, and they still did not see his head. "He is drowned, he is drowned," they shrieked in despair, and great was the hubbub and dismay which ensued before he came up again smiling some distance from the spot where he had originally plunged from the boat. Besides being a strong swimmer, he was a remarkable diver, and if two minutes and a half be the length of time a human being can breathe under water, then we can safely say two minutes and a half was the length of time he always stayed, for in every town we halted he invariably caused consternation in the heart of some one, who thought the stranger in their midst had gone to a watery grave. He preferred the boat for the sake of his dive, but, as a rule, every one in Finland bathes in the bath-houses, where there are little rooms for undressing, in front of which a big stretch of the lake is walled in as a swimming bath. A penny is the usual charge, and an extra penny for the towel.

Although every Finlander bathes, as, indeed, they must do during their hot summers, every Finlander does not swim, and it is a remarkable thing that among the women, who go daily—sometimes twice a day—to the swimming bath, most of them will sit on the steps or haul themselves round by means of a rope, and never learn how to keep themselves afloat without artificial help.

Walking through the park at Kuopio one day with the Baroness Michaeloff, my attention was arrested by the extraordinary number of ant hills we passed.

"They are used for baths," she explained.

"For what?" I asked, thinking I could not have heard aright.

"For baths," she repeated; "formerly these *muurahainen* (ant-heap baths) were quite commonly employed as a cure for rheumatism and many other ailments; but now I fancy it is only the peasants who take them, or very old folk, perhaps."

"Can an ant bath be had here?"

"Certainly. But surely you don't think of taking one?"

"Indeed I do, though. I am trying all the baths of Finland, and an ant-heap bath must not be omitted, if it is possible to have such a thing."

The kindly lady laughed heartily as she said, "Mais, Madame, est-ce que possible que vous vouliez prendre un de ces bains?"

"Certainment, cela me fait plaisir," I replied, and accordingly we then and there marched off to the bath-house to see how my desire might best be accomplished.

The whole matter did not take long to arrange. Next day, at ten o'clock, the *muurahainen* bath was to be ready, and, in spite of all the chaff round the governor's dinner-table that night about my queer experiment, nothing daunted I presented myself at the appointed hour. The head *Fröken*, who luckily spoke German, explained that my bath was ready.

Into a dear little room I went, and lo, the hot water in the bath was brown! while, floating on the surface, I saw a small linen sack, shaped like a pillow-case, securely tied at the end. The cushion contained the ant-heap, on which boiling water had been poured, so that the animals were really dead, the colour of the water having come from their bodies.

Did I shiver at the thought? Well, a little, perhaps; nevertheless, I tumbled into the warm water, and was scrubbed Finnish fashion by the old bath-woman, with her scrubbing brush, her soft soap, her birch branches, and, afterwards, her massage, the *Fröken* sitting all the while on the sofa, chatting affably, and describing how the peasants omitted the sacks and simply threw the ant-heap *au naturel* into the bath.

The small room had two doors—one opening into the passage, and one into the douche-chamber, which also served for another bathroom. Presently the first of the doors opened, and a girl, without apology, entered and took away a sponge. Did this intrusion make me feel shy? Well, why! one gets over shyness after being washed like a baby once or twice; but she had hardly disappeared before the other door opened, giving admission to a second woman, who came in and deposited a towel; a moment later some one else appeared, and after a good stare departed; then came a fourth on some pretext or other, and I was beginning to think of the queer stories told of Japan, where the whole paper wall slides back, and the natives enjoy the spectacle of English folk bathing, when yet a fifth came into the room. This was too much, and I asked the *Fröken* why they had all forgotten so many things.

She laughed merrily.

"I'm afraid it's curiosity to see an English lady having an ant-heap bath, so please don't be angry," and she laughed again.

A spectacle, verily! But who could be angry with such innocent people? I had come to try a strange Finnish bath which interested me—why should they not come to see a queer Englishwoman if it amused them? Flinging shyness to the winds, therefore, I smiled and grinned at the next woman who entered as though I liked being on view, and she went away happily.

What was a *muurahainen* like? Candidly, it resembled any other ordinary warm bath, only the water was very black, and there was a strange aromatic odour about it; but there was nothing horrible in the experience, although I had a good douche—three kinds of good douches in fact—for the sake of peace of mind afterwards.

A douche is very delightful, especially on a hot day, and the bath-woman was particularly anxious that we should try the various kinds arranged from the floor, the ceiling, and the walls of the room.

"But," we explained to the lady, with a good deal of patting and gesticulation, "long hair cannot be wet every day, even in the summer time, and to have a shower-bath, as she did not possess a cap, was impossible."

She looked distressed, but she was not going to be beaten, and beckoning for us to wait, she departed, returning a few minutes afterwards with a small white china basin; this she put on her head upside down, to show us that it would serve the purpose of a cap, and holding the rim with both hands she moved it round and round, in a way which indicated that wherever the water of a shower-bath was falling most was the side to move the basin to.

It was an original idea this shower-bath trick, and it answered very well, but then baths in Finland are an art, and Finland without its bath-houses would not be Finland at all.

The reason that the *muurahainen* bath is efficacious for rheumatism and of strengthening property is due to the amount of formic acid the ants contain. Added to which, these industrious little animals live upon the pine needles, and therefore suck all the strength from the most juicy part of the turpentiny pine, and, as we all know, turpentine is much employed in all kinds of embrocation used for rheumatism, lumbago, sprains, etc.

The next strange bath we experienced was in a waterfall, and was yet more remarkable. Yes, in a real waterfall where a tremendous volume of water dashed down about 10 feet! It was at Kajana, a town lying on a stretch of the famous Uled rapids. The real fall is about 40 feet, over which not even the tar-boats—described in a later chapter—dare venture; consequently, two locks, each containing 20 feet of water, have been made for their use. No one could swim, even in the calmer waters above or below the locks, because of the cataracts, so a bath-house has been erected beside the fall, to which the water is brought, by means of a wooden trough, to a sort of small chamber, where it rushes in. That waterfall bath was a most alarming place. It was almost dark as we entered the little chamber through which the water passed.

How shall we describe it? It was a small room about 8 or 10 feet square, with a wooden floor and walls. The top of the wall facing us did not join the roof by about a foot, so as to enable the water to rush in, and the bottom of the wall behind us did not reach the floor by another foot, so as to allow the water to rush out. Some half-dozen stairs descended from the platform on which we stood to the floor below, but as the only light came in where the falling water was always dripping, the walls were soaking wet, and therefore quite black. It was dull and mystic to say the least of it. Once the full force of the water was turned on by the large wooden arm, it poured in with such tremendous force from about 10 feet above, that in a moment the floor below was a bubbling, seething, frothing pool, and as we descended the steps into this bath, now some 2 or 3 feet deep, the force of the stream was so great that we had actually to hold on by the rail of the stairs to keep our feet at all on the slippery floor below. It was a lovely sensation. A piece of bacon bubbling about in the fat of the frying-pan must experience something like the same movements as we did, bobbing up and down in this rapidly flowing stream. It almost bumped us over, it lifted us off our feet, and yet, as the water swirled round us, the feeling was delicious, and its very coldness was most enjoyable after the heat outside, and the dust we had travelled through.

As we grew courageous and accustomed to the darkness, we walked more under the fall itself, but the water, simply thumping on our back and shoulders, came with such force, that we felt exactly as if we were being well pummelled with a pair of boxing-gloves, or being violently massaged, a delicious tingling sensation being the result. It washed our hair and rinsed it in a way it had never been rinsed before; but the force of the water was so large that it was impossible to keep our whole head under the fall for more than a second at a time, as it almost stunned us. The volume was so great that it would have rendered us insensible very quickly. We women all emerged from the waterfall-bath like drowned rats; or, to put it more poetically, like mermaids, feeling splendidly refreshed, and wider awake than we had probably ever felt in our lives before. The magnitude and force of that waterfall-bath makes me gasp even now to remember. It requires a stout heart to stand underneath it; nevertheless, how delicious the experience to the travel-stained and weary traveller, who had been suffering from tropical sun, and driving for days along dusty roads in carts.

We had all taken the opportunity of washing our powdered hair, the accumulation of many days dust, back to its natural colour, and, as we all possessed locks which fell considerably below our waists, they would not dry in five minutes, therefore, each with a towel over her shoulders, we came up on to the little pier, hat in hand, and our hair hanging down our backs. It certainly was somewhat primitive to sit all in a row, with our backs to the sun, on the fashionable promenade or pier of the town. But the town was not very big, and the fashion was not very great, and we gradually screwed up our courage, and finally walked home through the streets in the same way, carrying our hats, with towels over our shoulders for cloaks. That was all very well, but when we reached the small hotel the dinner was already on the table, for we had dallied so long over our bath that our gentlemen were impatiently waiting for our advent, and persuaded us not to stop to dress our hair as they were starving, so down we sat, just as we were, to partake of the meal.

But one hardly ever does anything uncommon or a little out of the ordinances of society, in this world, without being sorry for it afterwards, and having put off struggling with knots, tangled plaits, and hair-pins, until after dinner, we were horrified when the door opened and three unknown men marched in to join our meal. There was no escape; we were caught like rats in cages. What on earth they thought of strange women sitting in towels, and with dishevelled locks, we dare not think! Imagine our confusion!

PART II
The Middle East

6

LADY MARY WORTLEY MONTAGU
The Turkish Embassy

FROM
The Selected Letters, 1716-1718

Lady Mary Wortley Montagu's deserved fame as one of the shining letter writers and feminists of the eighteenth century is almost eclipsed by her reputation as a fearless traveller and expatriate. Few women of her time have caught the modern imagination as she has.

Her astounding career was hardly predictable from her early circumstances. She was born in 1689 in London. Her mother, Evelyn Pierrepont, died when Mary was young, and her father, the Duke of Kingston, was (according to a member of the family) "far too fine a gentleman to be a tender or even considerate parent." Nonetheless, she received a good education at home, in part through a governess, in larger part through a well-furnished library. In 1712, against her father's wishes, she married Edward Wortley Montagu, a member of Parliament and a familiar of Addison. Before long, she was frequenting the court of George I with her husband and cultivating the friendship of wits and writers, especially Alexander Pope, who accepted her as an equal.

In 1716, she accompanied her husband to Turkey, where he was to serve as British ambassador. Her journey took her over the plains of Hungary, down the Danube, through the Balkans, and up to the Bosphorus. She stayed in Constantinople for two years, and on her return voyage to England, she braved the dangers of the Dardanelles and the Mediterranean, along the way making sure to stop at the ruins of Troy and Carthage. She went ashore in Italy to climb the Alps before crossing France to the English Channel.

In England, she participated in the significant social and intellectual life, and had a falling out with Pope, who portrayed her as Sappho in the

Dunciad. *From 1739, after an unhappy love affair, she lived abroad without her husband (with whom she seemed to remain on friendly terms) in various Italian cities, especially Venice, until in response to her daughter's urging, she returned to England in 1762. She died of cancer later that year.*

Her letters give us an excellent account of what she witnessed during her travels. Alert and perceptive, she had one great advantage over the male traveller of equal wit and intellect: As a woman, she could share in the social life forbidden to men in Turkey. In the words of Robert Halsband, "She visited the luxurious baths for women and called on sultans in their own palaces to observe an opulence that matched what she had read in Oriental tales." Free of insularity, she was open to useful ideas. She saw the security against smallpox attained in Turkey by inoculation and had it performed on her own two children, then introduced it to her countrymen despite the outcry against what one clergyman called "the impiety of seeking to take events out of the hands of Providence." The following excerpts from her grave, pert, sometimes gossipy, sometimes sober, letters reveal an epistolary art seldom equaled in the English language. And her range of interests is no less astonishing.

TO LADY ———

Adrianople, 1 April 1717—I am now got into a new world where everything I see appears to me a change of scene, and I write to your Ladyship with some content of mind, hoping at least that you will find the charm of novelty in my letters and no longer reproach me that I tell you nothing extraordinary. I won't trouble you with a relation of our tedious journey, but I must not omit what I saw remarkable at Sophia, one of the most beautiful towns in the Turkish Empire and famous for its hot baths that are resorted to both for diversion and health. I stopped here one day on purpose to see them. Designing to go incognito, I hired a Turkish coach. These *voitures* are not at all like ours, but much more convenient for the country, the heat being so great that glasses would be very troublesome. They are made a good deal in the manner of the Dutch coaches, having wooden lattices painted and gilded, the inside being painted with baskets and nosegays of flowers, intermixed commonly with little poetical mottoes. They are covered all over with scarlet cloth, lined with silk and very often richly embroidered and fringed. This covering entirely hides the persons in them, but may be thrown back at pleasure and the ladies peep through the lattices. They hold four people very conveniently, seated on cushions, but not raised.

In one of these covered wagons I went to the bagnio about ten o'clock. It was already full of women. It is built of stone in the shape of a dome with no windows but in the roof, which gives light enough. There were five of these domes joined together, the outmost being less than the rest and serving only as a hall where the porteress stood at the door. Ladies of quality generally give this woman the value of a crown or ten shillings, and I did not forget that ceremony. The next room is a very large one, paved with marble, and all round it raised two sofas of marble, one above another. There were four fountains of cold water in this room, falling first into marble basins and then running on the floor in little channels made for that purpose, which carried the streams into the next room, something less than this, with the same sort of marble sofas, but so hot with steams of sulphur proceeding from the baths joining to it, 'twas impossible to stay there with one's clothes on. The two other domes were the hot baths, one of which had cocks of cold water turning into it to temper it to what degree of warmth the bathers have a mind to.

I was in my travelling habit, which is a riding dress, and certainly appeared very extraordinary to them, yet there was not one of 'em that showed the least surprise or impertinent curiosity, but received me with all the obliging civility possible. I know no European court where the ladies would have behaved themselves in so polite a manner to a stranger. I believe in the whole there were two hundred women[1] and yet none of those disdainful smiles or satiric whispers that never fail in our assemblies when anybody appears that is not dressed exactly in fashion. They repeated over and over to me, 'Uzelle, pek uzelle', which is nothing but, 'Charming, very charming'. The first sofas were covered with cushions and rich carpets, on which sat the

---

[1] Ingres copied into a notebook several passages from this letter, beginning here, using a French translation of the 1805 edition. His famous painting *'Le Bain Turc'* (1862), now in the Louvre, shows the influence of Lady Mary's sensuous descriptions.

ladies, and on the second their slaves behind 'em, but without any distinction of rank by their dress, all being in the state of nature, that is, in plain English, stark naked, without any beauty or defect concealed, yet there was not the least wanton smile or immodest gesture amongst 'em. They walked and moved with the same majestic grace which Milton describes of our General Mother.[2] There were many amongst them as exactly proportioned as ever any goddess was drawn by the pencil of Guido or Titian, and most of their skins shiningly white, only adorned by their beautiful hair divided into many tresses hanging on their shoulders, braided either with pearl or riband, perfectly representing the figures of the Graces.

I was here convinced of the truth of a reflection that I had often made, that if 'twas the fashion to go naked the face would be hardly observed. I perceived that the ladies with the finest skins and most delicate shapes had the greatest share of my admiration, though their faces were sometimes less beautiful than those of their companions. To tell you the truth, I had wickedness enough to wish secretly that Mr. Jervas[3] could have been there invisible. I fancy it would have very much improved his art to see so many fine women naked in different postures, some in conversation, some working, others drinking coffee or sherbet, and many negligently lying on their cushions while their slaves (generally pretty girls of seventeen or eighteen) were employed in braiding their hair in several pretty manners. In short, 'tis the women's coffeehouse, where all the news of the town is told, scandal invented, etc. They generally take this diversion once a week, and stay there at least four or five hours without getting cold by immediate coming out of the hot bath into the cool room, which was very surprising to me. The lady that seemed the most considerable amongst them entreated me to sit by her and would fain have undressed me for the bath. I excused myself with some difficulty, they being all so earnest in persuading me. I was at last forced to open my skirt and show them my stays, which satisfied 'em very well, for I saw they believed I was so locked up in that machine that it was not in my own power to open it, which contrivance they attributed to my

---

[2] *Paradise Lost,* IV, 304-18.
[3] Charles Jervas, portrait painter and friend of the London wits.

husband. I was charmed with their civility and beauty and should have been very glad to pass more time with them, but Mr. Wortley resolving to pursue his journey the next morning early I was in haste to see the ruins of Justinian's church, which did not afford me so agreeable a prospect as I had left, being little more than a heap of stones.

Adieu, madam. I am sure I have now entertained you with an account of such a sight as you never saw in your life and what no book of travels could inform you of. 'Tis no less than death for a man to be found in one of these places.

TO LADY MAR

Adrianople, 1 April 1717—I wish to God (dear sister) that you was as regular in letting me have the pleasure of knowing what passes on your side of the globe as I am careful in endeavouring to amuse you by the account of all I see that I think you care to hear of. You content yourself with telling me over and over that the town is very dull. It may possibly be dull to you when everyday does not present you with something new, but for me that am in arrear at least two months' news, all that seems very stale with you would be fresh and sweet here; pray let me into more particulars. I will try to awaken your gratitude by giving you a full and true relation of the novelties of this place, none of which would surprise you more than a sight of my person as I am now in my Turkish habit, though I believe you would be of my opinion that 'tis admirably becoming. I intend to send you my picture; in the meantime accept of it here.

The first piece of my dress is a pair of drawers, very full, that reach to my shoes and conceal the legs more modestly than your petticoats. They are of a thin, rose-colour damask brocaded with silver flowers, my shoes of white kid leather embroidered with gold. Over this hangs my smock of a fine white silk gauze edged with embroidery. This smock has wide sleeves hanging half-way down the arm and is closed at the neck with a diamond button, but the shape and colour of the bosom very well to be distinguished through it. The *antery* is a waistcoat made close to the shape, of white and gold damask, with very long sleeves falling back and fringed with deep gold fringe, and should have diamond or pearl buttons. My caftan of the same stuff with my drawers is a robe exactly fitted to my shape and reaching to my feet, with very long strait falling sleeves. Over this is the girdle of about four fingers broad, which all that can afford have entirely of diamonds or other precious stones. Those that will not be at that expense have it of expensive embroidery on satin, but it must be fastened before with a clasp of diamonds. The *curdée* is a loose robe they throw off or put on according to the weather, being of a rich brocade (mine is green and gold) either lined with ermine or sables; the sleeves reach very little below the shoulders.

The head-dress is composed of a cap called *talpack,* which is in winter of fine velvet embroidered with pearls or diamonds and in summer of a light, shining silver stuff. This is fixed on one side of the head, hanging a little way down with a gold tassel and bound on either with a circle of diamonds (as I have seen several) or a rich embroidered handkerchief. On the other side of the head the hair is laid flat, and here the ladies are at liberty to show their fancies, some putting flowers, others a plume of heron's feathers, and, in short, what they please, but the most general fashion is a large bouquet of jewels made like natural flowers, that is, the buds of pearl, the roses of different coloured rubies, the jasmines of diamonds, jonquils of topazes, etc., so well set and enamelled 'tis hard to imagine anything of that kind so beautiful. The hair hangs at its full length behind, divided into tresses braided with pearl or riband, which is always in great quantity.

I never saw in my life so many fine heads of hair. I have counted one hundred and ten of these tresses of one lady's, all natural; but it must be owned that every beauty is more common here than with us. 'Tis surprising to see a young woman that is not very handsome. They have naturally the most beautiful complexions in the world and generally large black eyes. I can assure you with great truth that the Court of England (though I believe it the fairest in Christendom) cannot show so many beauties as are under our protection here. They generally shape their eyebrows, and the Greeks and Turks have a custom of putting round their eyes on the inside a black tincture that, at a distance or by candlelight, adds very much to the blackness of them. I fancy many of our ladies would be overjoyed to know this secret, but 'tis too visible by day. They dye their nails rose colour; I own I cannot enough accustom myself to this fashion to find any beauty in it.

As to their morality or good conduct, I can say like Harlequin, " 'Tis just as 'tis with you' "; and the Turkish ladies don't commit one sin the less for not being Christians. Now I am a little acquainted with their ways, I cannot forbear admiring either the exemplary discretion or extreme stupidity of all the writers that have given accounts of 'em. 'Tis very easy to see they have more liberty than we have, no woman of what rank soever being permitted to go in the streets without two muslins, one that covers her face all but her eyes and another that hides the whole dress of her head and hangs half-way down her back; and their shapes are wholly concealed by a thing they call a *ferigée*, which no woman of any sort appears without. This has strait sleeves that reach to their fingers' ends and it laps all round 'em, not unlike a riding hood. In winter 'tis of cloth, and in summer, plain stuff or silk. You may guess how effectually this disguises them, that there is no distinguishing the great lady from her slave, and 'tis impossible for the most jealous husband to know his wife when he meets her, and no man dare either touch or follow a woman in the street.

This perpetual masquerade gives them entire liberty of following their inclinations without danger of discovery. The most usual method of intrigue is to send an appointment to the lover to meet the lady at a Jew's shop, which are as notoriously convenient as our Indian houses, and yet even those that don't make that use of 'em do not scruple to go to buy penn'orths and tumble over rich goods, which are chiefly to be found amongst that sort of people. The great ladies seldom let their gallants know who they are, and 'tis so difficult to find it out that they can very seldom guess at her name they have corresponded with above half a year together.

You may easily imagine the number of faithful wives very small in a country where they have nothing to fear from their lovers' indiscretion, since we see so many that have the courage to expose themselves to that in this world and all the threatened punishment of the next, which is never preached to the Turkish damsels. Neither have they much to apprehend from the resentment of their husbands, those ladies that are rich having all their money in their own hands, which they take with 'em upon a divorce with an addition which he is obliged to give 'em. Upon the whole, I look upon the Turkish women as the only free people in the empire. The very Divan pays a respect to 'em, and the Grand Signior himself, when a pasha is executed, never violates the privileges of the harem (or women's apartment) which remains unsearched entire to the widow. They are queens of their slaves, which the husband has no permission so much as to look upon, except it be an old woman or two that his lady chooses. 'Tis true their law permits them four wives, but there is no instance of a man of quality that makes use of this liberty, or of a woman of rank that would suffer it. When a husband happens to be inconstant (as those things will happen) he keeps his mistress in a house apart and visits her as privately as he can, just as 'tis with you. Amongst all the great men here I only know the *tefterdar* (*i.e.* treasurer) that keeps a number of she slaves for his own use (that is, on his own side of the house, for a slave once given to serve a lady is entirely at her disposal), and he is spoke of as a libertine, or what we should call a rake, and his wife won't see him, though she continues to live in his house.

Thus you see, dear sister, the manners of mankind do not differ so widely as our voyage writers would make us believe. Perhaps it would be more entertaining to add a few surprising customs of my own invention, but nothing seems to me so agreeable as truth, and I believe nothing so acceptable to you. I conclude with repeating the great truth of my being, dear sister, etc.

TO SARAH CHISWELL

Adrianople, 1 April 1717—In my opinion, dear Sarah, I ought rather to quarrel with you for not answering my Nijmegen letter of August till December, than to excuse my not writing again till now. I am sure there is on my side a very good excuse for silence, having gone such tiresome land journeys, though I don't find the conclusion of 'em so bad as you seem to imagine. I am very easy here and not in the solitude you fancy me; the great quantity of Greek, French, English and Italians that are under our protection make their court to me from morning till night, and I'll assure you are many of 'em very fine ladies, for there is no possibility for a Christian to live easily under this government but by the protection of an ambassador, and the richer they are the greater their danger.

Those dreadful stories you have heard of the plague have very little foundation in truth. I own I have much ado to reconcile myself to the sound of a word which has always given me such terrible ideas, though I am convinced there is little more in it than a fever, as a proof of which we passed through two or three towns most violently infected. In the very next house where we lay, in one of 'em, two persons died of it. Luckily for me I was so well deceived that I knew nothing of the matter, and I was made believe that our second cook who fell ill there had only a great cold. However, we left our doctor to take care of him, and yesterday they both arrived here in good health and I am now let into the secret that he has had the plague. There are many that 'scape of it, neither is the air ever infected. I am persuaded it would be as easy to root it out here as out of Italy and France, but it does so little mischief, they are not very solicitous about it and are content to suffer this distemper instead of our variety, which they are utterly unacquainted with.

Apropos of distempers, I am going to tell you a thing that I am sure will make you wish yourself here. The smallpox, so fatal and so general amongst us, is here entirely harmless by the invention of engrafting (which is the term they give it). There is a set of old women who make it their business to perform the operation. Every autumn, in the month of September, when the great heat is abated, people send to one another to know if any of their family has a mind to have the smallpox. They make parties for this purpose, and when they are met (commonly fifteen or sixteen together) the old woman comes with a nutshell full of the matter of the best sort of smallpox and asks what veins you please to have opened. She immediately rips open that you offer to her with a large needle (which gives you no more pain than a common scratch) and puts into the vein as much venom as can lie upon the head of her needle, and after binds up the little wound with a hollow bit of shell, and in this manner opens four or five veins. The Grecians have commonly the superstition of opening one in the middle of the forehead, in each arm, and on the breast to mark the sign of the cross, but this has a very ill effect, all these wounds leaving little scars, and is not done by those that are not superstitious, who choose to have them in the legs or that part of the arm that is concealed. The children or young patients play together all the rest of the day and are in perfect health till the eighth. Then the fever begins to seize 'em and they keep their beds two days, very seldom three. They have very rarely above twenty or thirty in their faces, which never mark, and in eight days' time they are as well as before their illness. Where they are wounded there remains running sores during the distemper, which I don't doubt is a great relief to it. Every year thousands undergo this operation, and the French ambassador says pleasantly that they take the smallpox here by way of diversion as they take the waters in other countries. There is no example of anyone that has died in it, and you may believe I am very well satisfied of the safety of the experiment since I intend to try it on my dear little son.[4] I am patriot enough to take pains to bring this useful invention into fashion in England, and I should not fail to write to some of our doctors very particularly about it if I knew any one of 'em that I thought had virtue enough to destroy such a considerable branch of their revenue for the good of mankind, but that distemper is too beneficial to them not to expose to all their resentment the hardy wight that should undertake to put an end to it. Perhaps if I live to return I may, however, have courage to war with 'em. Upon this occasion, admire the heroism in the heart of your friend, etc.

TO THE ABBÉ CONTI[5]

Constantinople, 29 May 1717—I have had the advantage of very fine weather all my journey, and the summer being now in its beauty I enjoyed the pleasure of fine prospects; and the meadows being full of all sorts of garden flowers and sweet herbs, my berlin perfumed the air as it pressed 'em. The Grand

---

[4] She did so a year later.
[5] The Abbé Antonio Conti (1677-1749) was an Italian philosopher, savant, and poet. He had visited London in 1715.

Signior furnished us with thirty covered wagons for our baggage and five coaches of the country for my women. We found the road full of the great *spabis* and their equipages, coming out of Asia to the war. They always travel with tents, but I chose to lie in houses all the way. I will not trouble you with the names of the villages we passed in which there was nothing remarkable, but at Corlu we were lodged in a *conac,* or little seraglio, built for the use of the Grand Signior when he goes this road. I had the curiosity to view all the apartments destined for the ladies of his court. They were in the midst of a thick grove of trees, made fresh by fountains, but I was surprised to see the walls almost covered with little distiches of Turkish verse writ with pencils. I made my interpreter explain them to me and I found several of them very well turned, though I easily believed him that they lost much of their beauty in the translation. One runs literally thus in English:

We come into this world, we lodge, and we depart;
He never goes that's lodged within my heart.

The rest of our journey was through fine painted meadows by the side of the Sea of Marmara, the ancient Propontis. We lay the next night at Sclivria, anciently a noble town. It is now a very good seaport, and neatly built enough, and has a bridge of thirty-two arches. Here is a famous ancient Greek church. I had given one of my coaches to a Greek lady who desired the conveniency of travelling with me. She designed to pay her devotions and I was glad of the opportunity of going with her. I found it an ill built place, set out with the same sort of ornaments but less rich than the Roman Catholic churches. They showed me a saint's body, where I threw a piece of money, and a picture of the Virgin Mary drawn by the hand of St. Luke, very little to the credit of his painting, but, however, the finest Madonna of Italy is not more famous for her miracles. The Greeks have the most monstrous taste in their pictures, which for more finery are always drawn upon a gold ground. You may imagine what a good air this has, but they have no notion either of shade or proportion. They have a Bishop here, who officiated in his purple robe, and sent me a candle almost as big as myself for a present when I was at my lodging.

We lay the next night at a town called Büjük Cekmege or Great Bridge, and the night following at Küjük Cekmege, Little Bridge, in a very pleasant lodging, formerly a monastery of dervishes, having before it a large court encompassed with marble cloisters with a good fountain in the middle. The prospect from this place and the gardens round it are the most agreeable I have seen, and shows that monks of all religions know how to choose their retirements. 'Tis now belonging to a *bogia* or schoolmaster, who teaches boys here; and asking him to show me his own apartment I was surprised to see him point to a tall cypress tree in the garden, on the top of which was a place for a bed for himself, and a little lower, one for his wife and two children, who slept there every night. I was so much diverted with the fancy I resolved to examine his nest nearer, but after going up fifty steps I found I had still fifty to go and then I must climb from branch to branch with some hazard of my neck. I thought it the best way to come down again.

We arrived the next evening at Constantinople, but I can yet tell you very little of it, all my time having been taken up with receiving visits, which are at least a very good entertainment to the eyes, the young women being all beauties and their beauty highly improved by the good taste of their dress. Our palace is in Pera, which is no more a suburb of Constantinople than Westminster is a suburb to London. All the Ambassadors are lodged very near each other. One part of our house shows us the port, the city and the seraglio, and the distant hills of Asia, perhaps altogether the most beautiful prospect in the world. A certain French author says that Constantinople is twice as large as Paris.[6] Mr. Wortley is unwilling to own 'tis bigger than London, though I confess it appears to me to be so, but I don't believe 'tis so populous. The burying fields about it are certainly much larger than the whole city. 'Tis surprising what a vast deal of land is lost this way in Turkey. Sometimes I have seen burying places of several miles belonging to very inconsiderable villages which were formerly great towns and retain no other mark of their ancient grandeur. On no occasion they remove a stone that serves for a monument. Some of them are costly enough, being of very fine marble. They set up a pillar with a carved turban on

---

[6] Jean Dumont, *Nouveau Voyage du Levant* (1694).

the top of it to the memory of a man, and as the turbans by their different shapes show the quality or profession, 'tis in a manner putting up the arms of the deceased; besides, the pillar commonly bears a large inscription in gold letters. The ladies have a simple pillar without other ornament, except those that die unmarried, who have a rose on the top of it. The sepulchres of particular families are railed in and planted round with trees. Those of the Sultans and some great men have lamps constantly burning in them.

When I spoke of their religion I forgot to mention two particularities, one of which I had read of, but it seemed so odd to me I could not believe it. Yet 'tis certainly true that when a man has divorced his wife in the most solemn manner, he can take her again upon no other terms than permitting another man to pass a night with her, and there are some examples of those that have submitted to this law rather than not have back their beloved.[7] The other point of doctrine is very extraordinary: any woman that dies unmarried is looked upon to die in a state of reprobation. To confirm this belief, they reason that the end of the creation of woman is to increase and multiply, and she is only properly employed in the works of her calling when she is bringing [bearing] children or taking care of 'em, which are all the virtues that God expects from her; and indeed their way of life, which shuts them out of all public commerce, does not permit them any other. Our vulgar notion that they do not own women to have any souls is a mistake. 'Tis true they say they are not of so elevated a kind and therefore must not hope to be admitted into the paradise appointed for the men, who are to be entertained by celestial beauties; but there is a place of happiness destined for souls of the inferior order, where all good women are to be in eternal bliss. Many of 'em are very superstitious and will not remain widows ten days for fear of dying in the reprobate state of a useless creature.[8] But those that like their liberty and are not slaves to their religion content themselves with marrying when they are afraid of dying. This is a piece of

[7] Although this was true, other travellers remarked that the husband usually chose a friend whose tactful continence he could rely on.
[8] But according to Muslim doctrine matrimony does not affect the spiritual fate of women; and a widow is forbidden to remarry for a period of four months and ten days.

theology very different from that which teaches nothing to be more acceptable to God than a vow of perpetual virginity. Which divinity is most rational I leave you to determine.

I have already made some progress in a collection of Greek medals. Here are several professed antiquaries who are ready to serve anybody that desires them, but you can't imagine how they stare in my face when I inquire about 'em, as if nobody was permitted to seek after medals till they were grown a piece of antiquity themselves. I have got some very valuable of the Macedonian kings, particularly one of Perseus, so lively I fancy I can see all his ill qualities in his face.[9] I have a porphyry head finely cut of the true Greek sculpture, but who it represents is to be guessed at by the learned men when I return, for you are not to suppose these antiquaries (who are all Greeks) know anything. Their trade is only to sell. They have correspondents at Aleppo, Grand Cairo, in Arabia, and Palestine, who send them all they can find, and very often great heaps that are only fit to melt into pans and kettles. They get the best price they can for any of 'em, without knowing those that are valuable from those that are not. Those that pretend to skill generally find out the image of some saint in the medals of the Greek cities. One of them, showing me the figure of a Pallas with a victory in her hand on a reverse, assured me it was the Virgin holding a crucifix. The same man offered me the head of a Socrates on a sardonyx, and to enhance the value gave him the title of St. Augustine. I have bespoke a mummy, which I hope will come safe to my hands, notwithstanding the misfortune that befell a very fine one designed for the King of Sweden.[10] He gave a great price for it, and the Turks took it into their heads that he must certainly have some considerable project depending upon't. They fancied it the body of God knows who, and that the fate of their Empire mystically depended on the conservation of it. Some old prophecies were remembered upon this occasion, and the mummy committed prisoner to the Seven Towers, where it has remained under close confinement ever since. I dare not try my interest in so considerable a point as the release of it, but I hope mine will pass without

---

[9] Perseus, last king of the Macedonians, had his brother murdered.

[10] Charles XII, after being defeated in 1709, remained near Adrianople until 1714 as a 'guest' of the Turks.

examination.—I can tell you nothing more at present of this famous city. When I have looked a little about me you shall hear from me again. I am, sir, etc.

TO ALEXANDER POPE

Belgrade Village,[11] *17 June 1717*—I hope before this time you have received two or three of my letters. I had yours but yesterday, though dated the third of February, in which you suppose me to be dead and buried. I have already let you know that I am still alive, but to say truth I look upon my present circumstances to be exactly the same with those of departed spirits. The heats of Constantinople have driven me to this place which perfectly answers the description of the Elysian fields. I am in the middle of a wood consisting chiefly of fruit trees, watered by a vast number of fountains famous for the excellency of their water, and divided into many shady walks upon short grass, that seems to me artificial but I am assured is the pure work of nature, within view of the Black Sea, from whence we perpetually enjoy the refreshment of cool breezes that makes us insensible of the heat of the summer. The village is wholly inhabited by the richest amongst the Christians, who meet every night at a fountain forty paces from my house to sing and dance, the beauty and dress of the women exactly resembling the ideas of the ancient nymphs as they are given us by the representations of the poets and painters.[12] But what persuades me more fully of my decease is the situation of my own mind, the profound ignorance I am in of what passes amongst the living, which only comes to me by chance, and the great calmness with which I receive it. Yet I have still a hankering after my friends and acquaintance left in the world, according to the authority of that admirable author,

> That spirits departed are wondrous kind
> To friends and relations left behind,
> Which nobody can deny,

[11] Some ten miles from Constantinople.
[12] The author is speaking about the Armenian community long established near the Black Sea.

of which solemn truth I am a dead instance. I think Virgil is of the same opinion, that in human souls there will still be some remains of human passions.

Curae non ipsa in morte relinquunt;[13]

and 'tis very necessary to make a perfect Elysium that there should be a river Lethe, which I am not so happy to find. To say truth, I am sometimes very weary of this singing and dancing and sunshine, and wish for the smoke and impertinencies in which you toil, though I endeavour to persuade myself that I live in a more agreeable variety than you do, and that Monday setting of partridges, Tuesday reading English, Wednesday studying the Turkish language (in which, by the way, I am already very learned), Thursday classical authors, Friday spent in writing, Saturday at my needle, and Sunday admitting of visits and hearing music, is a better way of disposing the week than Monday at the Drawing Room,[14] Tuesday Lady Mohun's, Wednesday the opera, Thursday the play, Friday Mrs. Chetwynd's,[15] etc.: a perpetual round of hearing the same scandal and seeing the same follies acted over and over, which here affect me no more than they do other dead people. I can now hear of displeasing things with pity and without indignation. The reflection on the great gulf between you and me cools all news that comes hither. I can neither be sensibly touched with joy or grief when I consider that possibly the cause of either is removed before the letter comes to my hands; but (as I said before) this indolence does not extend to my few friendships. I am still warmly sensible of yours and Mr. Congreve's[16] and desire to live in your remembrances, though dead to all the world beside.

TO MISS ANNE THISTLETHWAYTE

Pera of Constantinople, 4 January 1718—I am infinitely obliged to you, dear Mrs. Thistlethwayte, for your entertaining letter.

[13] 'Even in death the pangs leave them not' *(Aeneid).*
[14] At St. James's Palace.
[15] Mary Chetwynd was the wife of an M.P. Her house was well known as a gossip centre.
[16] Lady Mary had known William Congreve, the dramatist, since her girlhood.

You are the only one of my correspondents that have judged right enough to think I would gladly be informed of the news amongst you. All the rest of 'em tell me (almost in the same words) that they suppose I know everything. Why they are pleased to suppose in this manner, I can guess no reason except they are persuaded that the breed of Mohammed's pigeon still subsists in this country and that I receive supernatural intelligence.[17] I wish I could return your goodness with some diverting accounts from hence, but I know not what part of the scenes here would gratify your curiosity or whether you have any curiosity at all for things so far distant. To say the truth, I am at this present writing not very much turned for the recollection of what is diverting, my head being wholly filled with the preparations necessary for the increase of my family, which I expect every day.[18] You may easily guess at my uneasy situation; but I am, however, in some degree comforted by the glory that accrues to me from it, and a reflection on the contempt I should otherwise fall under.

You won't know what to make of this speech, but in this country 'tis more despicable to be married and not fruitful than 'tis with us to be fruitful before marriage. They have a notion that whenever a woman leaves off bringing children, 'tis because she is too old for that business, whatever her face says to the contrary, and this opinion makes the ladies here so ready to make proofs of their youth (which is as necessary in order to be a received beauty as it is to show the proofs of nobility to be admitted Knight of Malta) that they do not content themselves with using the natural means, but fly to all sort of quackeries to avoid the scandal of being past child-bearing and often kill themselves by 'em. Without any exaggeration, all the women of my acquaintance that have been married ten year have twelve or thirteen children, and the old ones boast of having had five-and-twenty or thirty a piece and are respected according to the number they have produced. When they are with child, 'tis their common expression to say they hope God will be so merciful to 'em to send two this time, and when I have asked them some-

---

[17] A pigeon was said to have been taught by Mohammed to pick corn out of his ear, which the vulgar took to be the whispering of the Holy Ghost.
[18] A daughter, the future Countess of Bute, was born on 19 January and christened Mary.

times how they expected to provide for such a flock as they desire, they answer that the plague will certainly kill half of 'em; which, indeed, generally happens without much concern to the parents, who are satisfied with the vanity of having brought forth so plentifully. The French Ambassadress is forced to comply with this fashion as well as myself. She has not been here much above a year and has lain in once and is big again. What is most wonderful is the exemption they seem to enjoy from the curse entailed on the sex. They see all company the day of their delivery and at the fortnight's end return visits, set out in their jewels and new clothes.

I wish I may find the influence of the climate in this particular, but I fear I shall continue an English woman in that affair as well as I do in my dread of fire and plague, which are two things very little feared here, most families having had their houses burnt down once or twice, occasioned by their extraordinary way of warming themselves, which is neither by chimneys nor stoves, but a certain machine called a *tendour,* the height of two foot, in the form of a table, covered with a fine carpet or embroidery. This is made only of wood, and they put into it a small quantity of hot ashes and sit with their legs under the carpet. At this table they work, read, and very often sleep; and if they chance to dream, kick down the *tendour* and the hot ashes commonly sets the house on fire. There was five hundred houses burnt in this manner about a fortnight ago, and I have seen several of the owners since who seem not at all moved at so common a misfortune. They put their goods into a bark and see their houses burn with great philosophy, their persons being very seldom endangered, having no stairs to descend.

But having entertained you with things I don't like, 'tis but just I should tell you something that pleases me. The climate is delightful in the extremest degree. I am now sitting, this present fourth of January, with the windows open, enjoying the warm shine of the sun, while you are freezing over a sad sea-coal fire; and my chamber is set out with carnations, roses and jonquils, fresh from my garden. I am also charmed with many points of the Turkish law, to our shame be it spoken, better designed and better executed than ours, particularly the punishment of convicted liars (triumphant criminals in our country, God knows).

They are burnt in the forehead with a hot iron, being proved the authors of any notorious falsehood. How many white foreheads should we see disfigured? How many fine gentlemen would be forced to wear their wigs as low as their eyebrows were this law in practice with us? I should go on to tell you many other parts of justice, but I must send for my midwife.

7

LADY HESTER STANHOPE
Life in the Lebanon

FROM
The Memoirs (1845)

Lady Hester Stanhope was born in Kent in 1776, the daughter of Lord Charles Mahon, an eccentric inventor, and Lady Hester Pitt, whose father was the first Earl of Chatham, the famous "Elder Pitt."

Other than the fact that she kept house for her uncle, the "Younger Pitt," not much is known about the early life of Miss Stanhope, who would in time win notoriety as the first Western woman to explore the ancient Arab world. According to Virginia Woolf, "she had a conviction of the rights of the aristocracy, and ordered her life from an eminence which made her conduct almost sublime." "Principle," she once exclaimed, "what do you mean by principle? I am a Pitt." Uncle William is alleged to have said to her, "If you were a man, I would send you on the Continent with sixty thousand men, and give you carte blanche; and I am sure that not one of my plans would fail, and not one soldier would go with his shoes unblackened."

Driven by ambition but thwarted by the limitations placed on her sex, she retired to a cottage near Wales when her uncle died and left her fifteen hundred pounds (then a small fortune). There, curing the poor and keeping a diary occupied her until her thirty-second year. Then, convinced that English life was too tame for a person of her curiosity and command, she departed in 1810 for the Middle East. She was accompanied by her brother Henry and her personal physician, Charles Meryon, who would become her confidant and editor of her Memoirs. *In Athens, she met Lord Byron and disliked him (and he her). She then settled for about a year in Constantinople. When the British Embassy rejected her scheme to defeat Napoleon, she left in a huff for Egypt, surviving en route a shipwreck that cast her up on the island of Rhodes. Following a stay there, she emerged in Syria "astride her horse, in the trousers of a Turkish gentleman" (Woolf).*

She bought a convent at Dar Djoun on the slope of Mount Lebanon, and for the rest of her life, when she was not shaking her fist at England, she entertained Westerners who came her way (among them Alphonse de Lamartine, the French poet), gave advice to local chieftans, and wrote hundreds of indignant letters to her family and friends. But most important, in spite of civil wars among the Druze, rock-cracking heat, and primitive transport, she travelled throughout the still-mysterious world of the Arabs, unveiled and unafraid, and made her way alone across the Syrian desert to Palmyra (where she became known as the "Queen of Palmyra"). She made friends with the Bedouins in their tents and smoked a hookah, while continuing to live at Dar Djoun.

As her funds ran low, she rarely left her terraced garden overlooking the Mediterranean, and near the end, spent her time in bed "arguing, scolding, and ringing bells perpetually" (Woolf again). In 1839, word came down to Beirut from the crumbling house that Lady Hester Stanhope's heart had given out.

Her private correspondence was published in 1845 in three volumes, edited by Charles Meryon under the title The Memoirs of Lady Hester Stanhope, As Related Herself in Conversation With Her Physician, Comprising Her Opinions and Anecdotes of Some of the Most Remarkable Persons of Her Time. *Despite complaints from critics about her complete lack of literary style or coherence, these letters offer a fascinating glimpse into the personal life of a woman who was among the first to emancipate and educate herself through the experiences of travel and life abroad. The following excerpts are from letters that she wrote while travelling and living in the Middle East.*

[On February 10, 1810, Lady Hester sailed for the Mediterranean on board the frigate Jason. *At Gibraltar, her brother, Captain Charles Stanhope, left to join his regiment at Cadiz. At Athens, her party was joined by Lord Sligo and Lord Byron, who had just won fresh laurels by swimming the Hellespont. Here are Lady Stanhope's impressions of him:]*

I think Lord Byron was a strange character. His generosity was for a motive, his avarice was for a motive; one time he was mopish, and nobody was to speak to him; another, he was for being jocular with everybody. . . . At Athens I saw nothing in him but a well-bred man, like many others: for as for poetry, it is easy enough to write verses; and as for the thoughts, who knows where he got them? Many a one picks up some old book that nobody knows anything about, and gets his ideas out of it. He had a great deal of vice in his looks—his eyes set close together, and a contracted brow. O Lord! I am sure he was not a liberal man, whatever else he might be. The only good thing about his looks was this part [drawing her hands under her cheek, and down the front of her neck], and the curl on his forehead.

[In November, the Jason sprang a leak and had to be abandoned. The passengers were rescued and taken ashore at Rhodes. Here is Lady Hester's account of the disaster:]

I write one line by a ship which came in here for a few hours, just to tell you we are safe and well. Starving thirty hours on a bare rock, without even fresh water, being half naked and drenched with wet, having traversed an almost trackless country over dreadful rocks and mountains, laid me up at a village for a few days, but I have since crossed the island on an ass, going for six hours a day, which proves I am pretty well, now, at least. . . . My locket, and the valuable snuff-box Lord Sligo gave me, and two pelisses, are all I have saved—all the travelling-equipage for Smyrna is gone; the servants naked and unarmed; but the great loss of all is the medicine-chest, which saved the lives of so many travellers in Greece.

[When Lady Hester reached Damascus in 1813, she decided to visit Palmyra. Warned by the Arabs against attempting to cross the desert under military escort, she put herself under Arab protection and embarked for the ruins by herself. In a letter to General Oakes, dated January 25, 1813, she gives the following account of her first experiment upon the good faith of the Arabs:]

I went with the great chief, Mahannah el Fadel (who commands 40,000 men), into the desert for a week, and marched for three days with their camp. I was treated with the greatest respect and hospitality, and it was the most curious sight I ever saw; horses and mares fed upon camel's milk; Arabs living upon little else except rice; the space around me covered with living things; 1600 camels coming to water from one tribe only; the old poets from the banks of the Euphrates singing the praises of the ancient heroes; women with lips dyed bright blue, and nails red, and hands all over flowers and different designs; a chief who is obeyed like a great king; starvation and pride so mixed that really I could not have had an idea of it. . . . However, I have every reason to be perfectly contented with their conduct towards me, and I am the *Queen* with them all.

[In the intervening years, Lady Hester travelled a great deal, but finally settled for the remainder of her life in what was then known as Syria. By 1836, she had apparently fallen upon difficult times.]

LADY H. S. TO DR. M.

August 21st, 1836—I hope I shall not claim in vain the assistance of an old friend, at the moment I most require one I can depend upon, to settle the business of my debts, &c., now made public. Money has been left me, which has been concealed from me. I could hardly, at first, believe it, until I was assured of it by a young lawyer, who had the fact from one of my Irish relations. I should wish you to come as soon as you can possibly make it convenient to yourself, and return when the business is over.

An English traveller, who has written, as I am informed, a very learned work, told a person that when M. Lamartine's book first came out in England, the impression was so strong that many people, who did not personally know me, talked of coming here to investigate my affairs, and to offer their services, but that they were prevented. A woman, of high rank and good fortune,[1] who has built herself a *palais* in a remote part of America, has announced her intention of passing the rest of her life with me, so much has she been struck with my situation and conduct. She is nearly of my age; and, thirty-seven or thirty-eight years ago— I being personally unknown to her—was so taken with my general appearance, that she never could divest herself of the thoughts of me, which have ever since pursued her. At last, informed by M. Lamartine's book where I was to be found, she took this extraordinary determination, and in the spring I expect her. She is now selling her large landed estate, preparatory to her coming. She, as well as Leila, the mare, is in the prophecy. The beautiful boy has also written, and is wandering over the

---

[1] The Baroness de Feriat.

face of the globe, till destiny marks the period of our meeting.

Such wonders, doctor! Copy these signs upon another paper, and remain silent upon the subject. Bring with you your notes upon Palmyra, &c.—do not forget. Perhaps I may receive from you an answer to my former letter by the next steamboat; but, as it only remains an hour at Beyrout, this must be sent off to be in waiting there. God bless you!

[Not signed.]

[Lady Hester seems to have been interrupted in her writing, and breaks off; but she thus resumes again:]

The little black is not twelve years old, yet she does my bedroom, and answers the bell: she is the only good-tempered black I have seen; so I try to please her, poor thing! If you come, I should, therefore, wish (if not too expensive) that you should bring, as an encouragement, a pair of ear-rings, a string of beads, a pair of bracelets, and a thimble. Her ears, having been spoilt with boring and heavy ear-rings, were obliged to be bored again very high nearer the face—it is a beautiful ear.

Now, what I want for myself is six cups and saucers; the top, I think, four inches in diameter; height, four inches; foot, two inches. I had a cup I was so fond of; for tea and coffee tasted so good out of it! It was strong and good china, but it is gone: and one cup held enough for my breakfast—a moderate cup and a half. I want also a teapot, black or red, or what you like; two cream-jugs; four milk-jugs, in case two are broken,—being always in use—one for hot and one for cold milk; six plates; four glass things, for butter and honey; a toast-rack, not plated—a plated one for strangers; a dozen basins; some little phials and corks; a few common candlesticks, brass or something strong; a few common entangling combs; a few scrubbing-brushes for the kitchen—that is all.

I do not want any books, having no one to read to me: it even puts my eyes out to write this.

I have heard of your situation, and it pains me beyond expression. Here you might, I believe, have been happy, and I also comfortable, as I have confidence in your integrity; and, whilst you were regulating all as I should have wished, you would have pursued those avocations most pleasing to your taste. What advice can I give you that I have not already given fifty times?

Of myself, I can say but little which is amusing; for, from the time the Egyptian troops entered this country until now, I have been in hot water. After the siege,[2] all that remained of the wretched population fled here, and my house and the village were, for the space of three years, the tower of Babel. Indeed, it was only at the beginning of this year that I got rid of the last of eighteen persons of one family, all orphans and widows; and only a lad, who was not capable, from his want of education, of gaining anything for himself and family, remained. I had, at one time, seventy-five coverlets out for strangers, chiefly soldiers— the village full of families—and those at Sayda and other places coming and going for a little money to buy their daily bread.

I have saved many lives by my energy and determination, and have stood alone in such a storm! All trembled, Franks as much as the rest; and, if they pretended to act with a little spirit, they were sure to have folly, and not justice, on their side, and to be at last obliged to give in: but the most of them joined, heart and hand, with the usurpers, whom I have treated without mercy, and, in the end, carried all before me. God helped me in all; for, otherwise, I never could have got through with it, having no one of any sort of use to me.

Lunardi, Mr. Webb's man, whom you so strongly recommended to me, turned himself into a doctor, and was too much taken up with his new title to be of any use to me: yet, this useless Lunardi is a good-hearted fellow. Were you to see him now, however, you would hardly know him; his manners are so improved, as well as his understanding: I believe, also, that he is attached to me.

Anxiety, agitation, and fatigue, together with the violent passions I sometimes put myself in, caused me, only a year ago, to vomit blood enough several times to have killed a horse. In seven days it stopped; but yet I was obliged to be bled eleven times in four months and a half, fearing a return. Yesterday, I was working like a *fellah* [ploughman] in my garden. I am very thin, but contented about my health, as this gives proof of my natural strength. With the blood running out of my mouth, I was collected enough to give orders respecting a man, who, if he had

[2] Of Acre.

been caught, would have lost his head; and no soul in the family knew of this but one, who insisted on seeing me in the state I was in: and although I could hardly speak, I reflected much, and, thank God! settled all to my satisfaction.

Abdallah Pasha has behaved very ill at Constantinople—a vain, stupid fool, without heart and without common sense: but it is for the Sultan that I have worked, as I am really attached to him, he being a most superior character.

Your friend Urquhart will be very useful to Lord Ponsonby, who, though a sensible man, is idle. Should U. gain the confidence of the Turks, he may learn their opinion of me; but he must not repeat it to the Franks, as a great jealousy exists respecting my politics. I have long foretold the change that must take place in those of the French and English, and now say that Sultan Mahmood will be *mansóor* [victorious].

P.[3] has gambled away nearly five hundred dollars I gave him about four years ago for things that I wanted, and never sent me anything.

Do not be uneasy about my health; for an English medical man, who came here after my illness, said he never saw such a constitution in his life, and that my pulse was then a better pulse than his.

I am reckoned here the first politician in the world, and by some a sort of prophet. Even the Emir [Beshýr] wonders, and is astonished; for he was not aware of this extraordinary gift formerly: but yet, all say—I mean enemies—that I am worse than a lion when in a passion, and that they cannot deny I have justice on my side.

Write whenever you please; do not expect me to write, as it hurts my eyes too much, and I have no one to assist me.

[Signed]   H. L. S.

---

[3] An Italian.

8

HARRIET MARTINEAU
The Secrets of the Hareem

FROM
Eastern Life: Present and Past (1848)

Harriet Martineau was born in Norwich, England, in 1802, the daughter of a Heugenot manufacturer. When she came to America in 1834, almost totally deaf, she was already famous as the author of stories and articles on issues of the day. She lived in New York for a period and travelled through the South and the West before returning to England. Three books grew out of this overseas experience: Society in America *(1836), notable for its antislavery passages;* How to Observe *(1838); and* Retrospect of Western Travel *(also 1838). This remarkable burst of creativity provoked the editor of the* Edinburgh Review *into an unchivalric observation: "I dreamed I was chained to a rock and being talked to death by Harriet Martineau."*

After writing further books on economics, culture, history, philosophy, and travel, as well as novels, stories, and autobiography, she travelled to the Middle East and recorded her impressions in Eastern Life: Present and Past. *Though she encountered typical difficulties in publishing this volume, it was highly acclaimed when it appeared. In the following selection from that book, Harriet Martineau describes the hareem from an angle that contrasts revealingly with the romanticized version often given by male writers who most probably had never been inside one.*

I saw two Hareems in the East; and it would be wrong to pass them over in an account of my travels; though the subject is as little agreeable as any I can have to treat. I cannot now think of the two mornings thus employed without a heaviness of heart greater than I have ever brought away from Deaf and Dumb Schools, Lunatic Asylums, or even Prisons. As such are my impressions of hareems, of course I shall not say whose they were that I visited. Suffice it that one was at Cairo and the other at Damascus.

The royal hareems were not accessible while I was in Egypt. The Pasha's eldest daughter, the widow of Defterdar Bey, was under her father's displeasure, and was, in fact, a prisoner in her own house. While her father did not visit her, no one else could: and while she was secluded, her younger sister could not receive visitors: and thus, their hareems were closed. The one which I saw was that of a gentleman of high rank; and as good a specimen as could be seen. The misfortune was that there was a mistake about the presence of an interpreter. A lady was to have met us who spoke Italian or French: but she did not arrive; and the morning therefore passed in dumb show: and we could not repeat our visit on a subsequent day, as we were invited to do. We lamented this much at the time: but our subsequent experience of what is to be learned in a hareem with the aid of an intelligent and kind interpretess convinced us that we had not lost much.

Before I went abroad, more than one sensible friend had warned me to leave behind as many prejudices as possible; and especially on this subject, on which the prejudices of Europeans are the strongest. I was reminded of the wide extent, both of time and space, in which Polygamy had existed; and that openness of mind was as necessary to the accurate observation of this institution as of every other. I had really taken this advice to heart: I had been struck by the view taken by Mr. Milnes in his beautiful poem of "the Hareem"; and I am sure I did meet this subject with every desire to investigate the ideas and general feelings involved in it. I learned a very great deal about the working of the institution; and I believe I apprehend the thoughts and feelings of the persons concerned in it: and I declare that if we are to look for a hell upon earth, it is where polygamy exists: and that, as polygamy runs riot in Egypt, Egypt is the lowest depth of this hell. I always before believed that every arrangement and prevalent practice had some one fair side—some one redeeming quality: and diligently did I look for this fair side in regard to polygamy: but there is none. The longer one studies the subject, and the deeper one penetrates into it—the more is one's mind confounded with the intricacy of its iniquity, and the more does one's heart feel as if it would break.

I shall say but little of what I know. If there were the slightest chance of doing any good, I would speak out at all hazards; I would meet all the danger, and endure all the disgust. But there is no reaching the minds of any who live under the accursed system. It is a system which belongs to a totally different region of ideas from ours: and there is nothing to appeal to in the minds of those who, knowing the facts of the institution, can endure it: and at home, no one needs appealing to and convincing. Any plea for liberality that we meet at home proceeds from some poetical fancy, or some laudable desire for impartiality in the absence of knowledge of the facts. Such pleas are not operative enough to render it worth while to shock and sadden many hearts by statements which no one should be required needlessly to endure. I will tell only something of what I saw, and but little of what I thought and know.

At ten o'clock, one morning, Mrs. Y. and I were home from our early ride, and dressed for our visit to a hareem of a high order. The lady to whose kindness we mainly owed this opportunity, accompanied us, with her daughter. We had a disagreeable drive in the carriage belonging to the hotel, knocking against asses, horses and people all the way. We alighted at the entrance of a paved passage leading to a court which we crossed: and then, in a second court, we were before the entrance of the hareem.

A party of eunuchs stood before a faded curtain, which they held aside when the gentlemen of our party and the dragoman had gone forward. Retired some way behind the curtain stood, in a half circle, eight or ten slave girls, in an attitude of deep obeisance. Two of them then took charge of each of us, holding us by the arms above the elbows, to help us upstairs. After crossing a lobby at the top of the stairs, we entered a handsome apartment, where lay the chief wife—at that time an invalid. The ceiling was gaily painted; and so were the walls—the latter with curiously bad attempts at domestic perspective. There were four handsome mirrors; and the curtains in the doorway were of a beautiful shawl fabric, fringed and tasselled. A Turkey carpet not only covered the whole floor, but was turned up at the corners. Deewáns extended round nearly the whole room—a lower one for ordinary use, and a high one for the seat of honour. The windows, which had a sufficient fence of blinds, looked upon a pretty garden, where I saw orange trees and many others, and the fences were hung with rich creepers.

On cushions on the floor lay the chief lady, ill and miserable-looking. She rose as we entered; but we made her lie down again: and she was then covered with a silk counterpane. Her dress was, as we saw when she rose, loose trowsers of blue striped cotton under her black silk jacket: and the same blue cotton appeared at the wrists, under her black sleeves. Her headdress was of black net, bunched out curiously behind. Her hair was braided down the sides of this headdress behind, and the ends were pinned over her forehead. Some of the black net was brought round her face, and under the chin, showing the outline of a face which had no beauty in it, nor traces of former beauty, but which was interesting to-day from her manifest illness and unhappiness. There was a strong expression of waywardness and peevishness about the mouth, however. She wore two handsome diamond rings; and she and one other lady had watches and gold chains. She complained of her head; and her left hand was bound up: she made signs by pressing her bosom, and imitating the dandling of a baby, which, with her occasional tears, persuaded my companions that she had met with some accident and had lost her infant. On leaving the hareem, we found that it was not a child of her own that she was mourning, but that of a white girl in the hareem: and that the wife's illness was wholly from grief for the loss of this baby; a curious illustration of the feelings and manners of the place! The children born in large hareems are extremely few: and they are usually idolised, and sometimes murdered. It is known that in the houses at home which morally most resemble these hareems (though little enough externally) when the rare event of the birth of a child happens, a passionate joy extends over the wretched household: jars are quieted, drunkenness is moderated, and there is no self-denial which the poor creatures will not undergo during this gratification of their feminine instincts. They will nurse the child all night in illness, and pamper it all day with sweetmeats and toys; they will fight for the possession of it, and be almost heartbroken at its loss: and lose it they must; for the child always dies—killed with kindness, even if born healthy. This natural outbreak of feminine instinct takes place in the too populous hareem, when a child is given to any one of the many who are longing for the gift: and if it dies naturally, it is mourned as we saw through a wonderful conquest of personal jealousy by this general instinct. But when the jealousy is uppermost—what happens then?—why, the strangling the innocent in its sleep—or the letting it slip from the window into the river below—or the mixing poison with its food; the mother and the murderess, always rivals and now friends, being shut up together for life. If the child lives, what then? If a girl, she sees before her from the beginning the nothingness of external life, and the chaos of interior existence, in which she is to dwell for life. If a boy, he remains among the women till ten years old, seeing things when the eunuchs come in to romp, and hearing things among the chatter of the ignorant women which brutalise him for life before the age of rationality comes. But I will not dwell on these hopeless miseries.

A sensible looking old lady, who had lost an eye, sat at the head of the invalid: and a nun-like elderly woman, whose head and throat were wrapped in unstarched muslin, sat behind for a time, and then went away, after an affectionate salutation to the invalid. Towards the end of the visit, the husband's mother came in—looking like a little old man in her coat trimmed with fur. Her countenance was cheerful and pleasant. We saw, I think, about twenty more women—some slaves—most or all young—some good-looking, but none handsome. Some few were black; and the rest very light: Nubians or Abyssinians and Circassians, no doubt. One of the best figures, as a picture, in the hareem, was a Nubian girl, in an amber-coloured watered silk, embroidered with black, looped up in festoons, and finished with a black bodice. The richness of the gay printed cotton skirts and sleeves surprised us: the finest shawls could hardly have looked better. One graceful girl had her pretty figure well shown by a tight-fitting black dress. Their heads were dressed much like the chief lady's. Two, who must have been sisters, if not twins, had patches between the eyes. One handsmaid was barefoot, and several were without shoes. Though there were none of the whole large number who could be called particularly pretty individually, the scene was, on the whole, exceedingly striking, as the realisation of what one knew before, but as in a dream. The girls went out and came in, but, for the most part, stood in a half circle. Two sat on their heels for a time: and some went to play in the neighbouring apartments.

Coffee was handed to us twice, with all the well-known apparatus of jewelled cups, embroidered tray cover, and gold-flowered napkins. There were chibouques, of course: and sherbets in cut glass cups. The time was passed in attempts to have conversation by signs; attempts which are fruitless among people of the different ideas which belong to different races. How much they made out about us, we do not know: but they inquired into the mutual relationships of the party, and put the extraordinary questions which are always put to ladies who visit the hareems. A young lady of my acquaintance, of the age of eighteen, but looking younger, went with her mother to a hareem in Cairo (not the one I have been describing) and excited great amazement when obliged to confess that she had not either children or a husband. One of the wives threw her arms about her, intreated her to stay for ever, said she should have any husband she liked, but particularly recommended her own, saying that she was sure he would soon wish for another wife, and she had so much rather it should be my young friend, who would amuse her continually, than anybody else that she could not be so fond of. Everywhere they pitied us European women heartily, that we had to go about travelling, and appearing in the streets without being properly taken care of—that is watched. They think us strangely neglected in being left so free, and boast of their spy system and imprisonment as tokens of the value in which they are held.

The mourning worn by the lady who went with us was the subject of much speculation: and many questions were asked about her home and family. To appease the curiosity about her home, she gave her card. As I anticipated, this did not answer. It was the great puzzle of the whole interview. At first the poor lady thought it was to do her head good: then, she fidgetted about it, in the evident fear of omitting some observance: but at last, she understood that she was to keep it. When we had taken our departure, however, a eunuch was sent after us to inquire of the dragoman what "the letter" was which our companion had given to the lady.

The difficulty is to get away, when one is visiting a hareem. The poor ladies cannot conceive of one's having anything to do; and the only reason they can understand for the interview coming to an end is the arrival of sunset, after which it would, they think, be improper for any woman to be abroad. And the amusement to them of such a visit is so great that they protract it to the utmost, even in such a case as ours to-day, when all intercourse was conducted by dumb show. It is certainly very tiresome; and the only wonder is that the hostesses can like it. To sit hour after hour on the deewán, without any exchange of ideas, having our clothes examined, and being plied with successive cups of coffee and sherbet, and pipes, and being gazed at by a half-circle of girls in brocade and shawls, and made to sit down again as soon as one attempts to rise, is as wearisome an experience as one meets with in foreign lands. The weariness of heart is, however, the worst part of it. I noted all the faces well during our constrained stay; and I saw no trace of mind in any one except in the homely one-eyed old lady. All the younger ones were dull, soulless, brutish, or peevish. How should it be otherwise, when the only idea of their whole lives is that which, with all our interests and engagements, we consider too prominent with us? There cannot be a woman of them all who is not dwarfed and withered in mind and soul by being kept wholly engrossed with that one interest—detained at that stage in existence which, though most important in its place, is so as a means to ulterior ends. The ignorance is fearful enough; but the grossness is revolting.

At the third move, and when it was by some means understood that we were waited for, we were permitted to go—after a visit of above two hours. The sick lady rose from her cushions, notwithstanding our opposition, and we were conducted forth with much observance. On each side of the curtain which overhung the outer entrance stood a girl with a bottle of rose water, some of which was splashed in our faces as we passed out.

We had reached the carriage when we were called back: his Excellency was waiting for us. So we visited him in a pretty apartment, paved with variegated marbles, and with a fountain in the centre. His Excellency was a sensible-looking man, with gay, easy and graceful manners. He lamented the mistake about the interpreter, and said we must go again, when we might have conversation. He insisted upon attending us to the carriage, actually passing between the files of beggars which lined the outer passage. The dragoman was so excessively shocked by this degree of condescension, that we felt obliged to be so too, and remonstrated: but in vain. He stood till the door was shut, and the whip was cracked. He is a liberal-minded man; and his hareem is nearly as favorable a specimen as could be selected for a visit; but what is this best specimen? I find these words written down on the same day, in my journal: written, as I well remember, in heaviness of heart. "I am glad of the opportunity of seeing a hareem: but it leaves an impression of discontent and uneasiness which I shall be glad to sleep off. And I am not conscious that there is prejudice in this. I feel that a visit to the worst room in the Rookery in St. Giles's would have affected me less painfully. There are there at least the elements of a rational life, however perverted; while here humanity is wholly and hopelessly baulked. It will never do to look on this as a case for cosmopolitan philosophy to regard complacently, and require a good construction for. It is not a phase of natural early manners. It is as pure a conventionalism as our representative monarchy, or German heraldry, or Hindoo caste; and the most atrocious in the world."

And of this atrocious sytem, Egypt is the most atrocious example. It has unequalled facilities for the importation of black and white slaves; and these facilities are used to the utmost; yet the population is incessantly on the decline. But for the importation of slaves, the upper classes, where polygamy runs riot, must soon die out—so few are the children born, and so fatal to health are the arrangements of society. The finest children are those born of Circassian or Georgian mothers; and but for these, we should soon hear little more of an upper class in Egypt. Large numbers are brought from the south—the girls to be made attendants or concubines in the hareem, and the boys to be made, in a vast proportion, those guards to the female part of the establishment whose mere presence is a perpetual insult and shame to humanity. The business of keeping up the supply of these miserable wretches—of whom the Pasha's eldest daughter has fifty for her exclusive service—is in the hands of the Christians of Asyoot. It is these Christians who provide a sufficient supply, and cause a sufficient mortality to keep the number of the sexes pretty equal: in consideration of which we cannot much wonder that Christianity does not appear very venerable in the eyes of Mohammedans.

These eunuchs are indulged in regard to dress, personal liberty, and often the possession of office, domestic, military, or political. When retained as guards of the hareem, they are in their master's confidence—acting as his spies, and indispensable to the ladies, as a medium of communication with the world, and as furnishing their amusements—being at once playmates and servants. It is no unusual thing for the eunuchs to whip the ladies away from a window, whence they had hoped for amusement; or to call them opprobrious names; or to inform against them to their owner: and it is also no unusual thing for them to romp with the ladies, to obtain their confidence, and to try their dispositions. Cases have been known of one of them becoming the friend of some poor girl of higher nature and tendencies than her companions; and even of a closer attachment, which is not objected to by the proprietor of both. It is a case too high for his jealousy, so long as he knows that the cage is secure. It has become rather the fashion to extenuate the lot of the captive of either sex: to point out how the Nubian girl, who would have ground corn and woven garments, and nursed her infants in comparative poverty all her days, is now surrounded by luxury, and provided for for life: and how the Circassian girl may become a wife of the son of her proprietor, and hold a high rank in the hareem: and how the wretched brothers of these slaves may rise to posts of military command or political confidence; but it is enough to see them to be disabused of all impressions of their good fortune. It is enough to see the dull and gross face of the handmaid of the hareem, and to remember at the moment the cheerful, modest countenance of the Nubian girl busy about her household tasks, or of the Nubian mother, with her infants hanging about her as she looks, with face open to the sky, for her husband's return from the field, or meets him on the river bank.

It is enough to observe the wretched health and abject, or worn, or insolent look of the guard of the hareem, and to remember that he ought to have been the head of a household of his own, however humble: and in this contrast of what is with what ought to have been, slavery is seen to be fully as detestable here as anywhere else. These two hellish practices, slavery and polygamy, which, as practices, can clearly never be separated, are here avowedly connected; and in that connexion, are exalted into a double institution, whose working is such as to make one almost wish that the Nile would rise to cover the tops of the hills, and sweep away the whole abomination. Till this happens, there is, in the condition of Egypt, a fearful warning before the eyes of all men. The Egyptians laugh at the marriage arrangements of Europe, declaring that virtual polygamy exists everywhere, and is not improved by hypocritical concealment. The European may see, when startled by the state of Egypt, that virtual slavery is indispensably required by the practice of polygamy; virtual proprietorship of the women involved, without the obligations imposed by actual proprietorship; and cruel oppression of the men who should have been the husbands of these women. And again, the Carolina planter, who knows as well as any Egyptian that polygamy is a natural concomitant of slavery, may see in the state of Egypt and the Egyptians what his country and his children must come to, if either of those vile arrangements is permitted which necessitates the other.

It is scarcely needful to say that those benevolent persons are mistaken who believe that Slavery in Egypt has been abolished by the Pasha, and the importation of slaves effectually prohibited. Neither the Pasha nor any other human power can abolish slavery while Polygamy is an institution of the country, the proportion of the sexes remaining in Egypt what it is, there and everywhere else.

The reason assigned by Montesquieu for polygamy throughout the East has no doubt something in it: that women become so easily marriageable that the wife cannot satisfy the needs of the husband's mind and heart: and that therefore he must have both a bride and a companion of whom he may make a friend. How little there is in this to excuse the polygamy of Egypt may be seen by an observation of the state of things there and in Turkey, where the same religion and natural laws prevail as in Egypt. In Egypt, the difficulty would be great of finding a wife of any age who could be the friend of a man of any sense: and in Turkey, where the wives are of a far higher order, polygamy is rare, and women are not married so young. It is not usual there to find such disparity of years as one finds in Egypt between the husband and his youngest wife. The cause assigned by Montesquieu is true in connexion with a vicious state of society: but it is not insuperable, and it will operate only as long as it is wished for. If any influence could exalt the ideas of marriage, and improve the training of women in Egypt, it would soon be seen that men would prefer marrying women of nearly their own age, and would naturally remain comparatively constant: but before this experiment can be tried, parents must have ceased to become restless when their daughter reaches eleven years old, and afraid of disgrace if she remains unmarried long after that.

I was told, while at Cairo, of one extraordinary family where there is not only rational intercourse and confidence at home, and some relaxation of imprisonment, but the young ladies read!—and read French and Italian! I asked what would be the end of this: and my informant replied that whether the young ladies married or not, they would sooner or later sink down, he thought, into a state even less contented than the ordinary. There could be no sufficient inducement for secluded girls, who never saw anybody wiser than themselves, to go on reading French and Italian books within a certain range. For want of stimulus and sympathy, they would stop; and then, finding themselves dissatisfied among the nothings which fill the life of other women, they would be very unhappy. The exceptional persons under a bad state of things, and the beginners under an improving system must ever be sufferers—martyrs of their particular reformation. To this they may object less than others would for them, if they are conscious of the personal honour and general blessing of their martyrdom.

The youngest wife I ever saw (except the swathed and veiled brides we encountered in the streets of Egyptian cities) was in a Turkish hareem which Mrs. Y. and I visited at Damascus. I will tell that story now, that I may dismiss the subject of this chapter. I heartily dreaded this second visit to a hareem, and braced myself up to it as one does to an hour at the dentist's, or to an expedition into the City to prove a debt. We had the comfort of a good and pleasant interpreter; and there was more mirth and nonsense than in the Cairo hareem; and therefore somewhat less disgust and constraint: but still it was painful enough. We saw the seven wives of three gentlemen, and a crowd of attendants and visitors. Of the seven, two had been the wives of the head of the household, who was dead: three were the wives of his eldest son, aged twenty-two; and the remaining two were the wives of his second son, aged fifteen. The youngest son, aged thirteen, was not yet married; but he would be thinking about it soon. The pair of widows were elderly women, as merry as girls, and quite at their ease. Of the other five, three were sisters: that is, we conclude, half-sisters; children of different mothers in the same hareem. It is evident at a glance what a tragedy lies under this; what the horrors of jealousy must be among sisters thus connected for life; three of them between two husbands in the same house! And we were told that the jealousy had begun, young as they were, and the third having been married only a week. This young creature, aged twelve, was the bride of the husband of fifteen. She was the most conspicuous person in the place, not only for the splendour of her dress, but because she sat on the deewán, while the others sat or lounged on cushions on the raised floor. The moment we took our seats I was struck with compassion for this child—she looked so grave, and sad and timid. While the others romped and giggled, pushing and pulling one another about, and laughing at jokes among themselves, she never smiled, but looked on listlessly. I was determined to make her laugh before we went away; and at last she relaxed somewhat—smiling, and growing grave again in a moment: but at length she really and truly laughed; and when we were shown the whole hareem, she also slipped her bare and dyed feet into her pattens inlaid with mother-of-pearl, and went into the courts with us, nestling to us, and seeming to lose the sense of her new position for the time: but there was far less of the gaiety of a child about her than in the elderly widows. Her dress was superb; a full skirt and boddice of geranium-coloured brocade, embossed with gold flowers and leaves; and her frill and ruffles were of geranium-colored gauze. Her eyebrows were frightful—joined and prolonged by black paint. Her head was covered with a silk net, in almost every mesh of which were stuck jewels or natural flowers: so that her head was like a bouquet sprinkled with diamonds. Her nails were dyed black; and her feet were dyed black in chequers. Her complexion, called white, was of an unhealthy yellow: and indeed we did not see a healthy complexion among the whole company; nor anywhere among women who were secluded from exercise, while pampered with all the luxuries of eastern living.

Besides the seven wives, a number of attendants came in to look at us, and serve the pipes and sherbet; and a few ladies from a neighbouring hareem; and a party of Jewesses, with whom we had some previous acquaintance. Mrs. Y. was compelled to withdraw her lace veil, and then to take off her bonnet: and she was instructed that the street was the place for her to wear her veil down, and that they expected to see her face. Then her bonnet went round, and was tried on many heads—one merry girl wearing it long enough to surprise many new comers with the joke. My gloves were stretched and pulled all manner of ways, in their attempts to thrust their large, broad brown hands into them, one after another. But the great amusement was my trumpet. The eldest widow, who sat next me, asked for it, and put it to her ear; when I said "Bo!" When she had done laughing, she put it into her next neighbour's ear, and said "Bo!" and in this way it came round to me again. But in two minutes, it was asked for again, and went round a second time—everybody laughing as loud as ever at each "Bo!"—and then a third time! Could one have conceived it!—The next joke was on behalf of the Jewesses, four or five of whom sat in a row on the deewán. Almost everybody else was puffing away at a chibouque or a nargeeleh, and the place was one cloud of smoke. The poor Jewesses were obliged to decline joining us; for it happened to be Saturday: they must not smoke on the sabbath. They were naturally much pitied: and some of the young wives did what was possible for them. Drawing in a long breath of smoke, they puffed it forth in the faces of the Jewesses, who opened mouth and nostrils eagerly to receive it. Thus was the sabbath observed, to shouts of laughter.

A pretty little blue-eyed girl of seven was the only child we saw.

She nestled against her mother; and the mother clasped her closely, lest we should carry her off to London. She begged we would not wish to take her child to London, and said she "would not sell her for much money." One of the wives was pointed out to us as particularly happy in the prospect of becoming a mother; and we were taken to see the room in which she was to lie in, which was all in readiness, though the event was not looked for for more than half a year. She was in the gayest spirits, and sang and danced. While she was lounging on her cusions, I thought her the handsomest and most graceful, as well as the happiest, of the party: but when she rose to dance, the charm was destroyed for ever. The dancing is utterly disgusting. A pretty Jewess of twelve years old danced, much in the same way; but with downcast eyes and an air of modesty. While the dancing went on, and the smoking, and drinking coffee and sherbet, and the singing, to the accompaniment of a tambourine, some hideous old hags came in successively, looked and laughed, and went away again. Some negresses made a good back ground to this thoroughly Eastern picture. All the while, romping, kissing and screaming went on among the ladies, old and young. At first, I thought them a perfect rabble; but when I recovered myself a little, I saw that there was some sense in the faces of the elderly women. In the midst of all this fun, the interpretess assured us that "there is much jealousy every day"; jealousy of the favoured wife; that is, in this case, of the one who was pointed out to us by her companions as so eminently happy, and with whom they were romping and kissing, as with the rest. Poor thing! even the happiness of these her best days is hollow: for she cannot have, at the same time, peace in the hareem and her husband's love.

They were so free in their questions about us, and so evidently pleased when we used a similar impertinence about them, that we took the opportunity of learning a good deal of their way of life. Mrs. Y. and I were consulting about noticing the bride's dress, when we found we had put off too long: we were asked how we liked her dress, and encouraged to handle the silk. So I went on to examine the bundles of false hair that some of them wore; the pearl bracelets on their tattooed arms, and their jewelled and inlaid patterns. In answer to our question what they did in the way of occupation, they said "nothing": but when we inquired whether they never made clothes or sweetmeats, they replied "yes." They earnestly wished us to stay always; and they could not understand why we should not. My case puzzled them particularly. I believe they took me for a servant; and they certainly pitied me extremely for having to go about without being taken care of. They asked what I did: and Mrs. Y., being anxious to do me all honour, told them I had written many books: but the information was thrown away, because they did not know what a book was. Then we informed them that I lived in a field among mountains, where I had built a house; and that I had plenty to do; and we told them in what way: but still they could make nothing of it but that I had brought the stones with my own hands, and built the house myself. There is nothing about which the inmates of hareems seem to be so utterly stupid as about women having any thing to do. That time should be valuable to a woman, and that she should have any business on her hands, and any engagements to observe, are things quite beyond their comprehension.

The pattens I have mentioned are worn to keep the feet and flowing dress from the marble pavement, which is often wetted for coolness. I think all the ladies here had bare feet. When they left the raised floor on which they sat, they slipped their feet into their high pattens, and went stumping about, rather awkwardly. I asked Dr. Thompson, who has admission as a physician into more houses than any other man could familiarly visit, whether he could not introduce skipping-ropes upon these spacious marble floors. I see no other chance of the women being induced to take exercise. They suffer cruelly from indigestion—gorging themselves with sweet things, smoking intemperately, and passing through life with more than half the brain almost unawakened, and with scarcely any exercise of the limbs. Poor things! our going was a great amusement to them, they said; and they showed this by their intreaties to the last moment that we would not leave them yet, and that we would stay always. "And these," as my journal says, "were human beings, such as those of whom Christ made friends! The chief lady gave me roses as a farewell token. The Jewish ladies, who took their leave with us, wanted us to visit at another house: but we happily had not time. I am thankful to have seen a hareem under favourable circumstances; and I earnestly hope I may never see another."

I kept those roses, however. I shall need no reminding of the most injured human beings I have ever seen—the most studiously depressed and corrupted women whose condition I have witnessed: but I could not throw away the flowers which so found their way into my hand as to bespeak for the wrongs of the giver the mournful remembrance of my heart.

9

FREDERIKA BREMER
Pilgrimage to the Holy Land
FROM
Travels in the Holy Land, II (1862)

Frederika Bremer enjoyed an illustrious career as a traveller, a writer, and a feminist. Born in 1801 near Abo in Sweden, the daughter of an ironmaster, she received an excellent education and then retired to a life of good works as a nurse among the peasants on her father's estate. In her spare time, she turned to writing and produced a succession of novels and stories that were sentimental, naive, and moralistic, but also fresh in their approach to the everyday life of the common people among whom she lived. In translations, such titles as The H Family *(1829),* The President's Daughter *(1834),* The Home *(1839),* The Twins and Other Tales *(1843), and* The Bondmaid *(1844) earned her a devoted if modest following in America before she went there in 1849 on a visit. She was the first person to translate Ralph Waldo Emerson into a foreign language.*

The Homes of the New World *(1853), probably her best-known book today, is based on her travels in the New World, and selected letters from that book became* America of the Fifties *(1924). Her other books of travel were* Greece and the Greeks *(1852);* Life in the Old World *(1860), mainly about Switzerland and Italy; and* Travels in the Holy Land, *I and II (1862), from which the following selection is taken.*

Until her death in 1865, she remained interested in German romantic philosophy, in philanthropy, and in religion. Her later books advocated the emancipation of women.

By now, travel in the Holy Land is relatively safe and easy, and accounts about it tend to be boringly familiar. When Frederika Bremer made her pilgrimage almost a century and a quarter ago, the Bedouins were hostile to Western men and women alike, the roads were little more than rocky trails, and the only available transportation was saddlehorse. It took stamina, sophistication, and pluck for anyone, let alone a single woman who spoke no Arabic, to venture into that arid, challenging territory. Yet Frederika Bremer's narrative is short on complaints and full of delightful details about Oriental life, "from the splendid to the humble, from the low to the lofty." It stands as one of the earliest and most informative records by a Western woman of a journey through the land of the Bible.

The first remarkable place which the traveller reaches on this side of Nazareth is Cana, about an hour's distance. The portion of the village which is called the old is nothing but a ruin of blackened walls and stones; the newer is little better, and seems almost wholly desolate. But in the valley below—the village lies upon rock-terraces—fig-trees, olives, and pomegranates flourish most luxuriantly, apparently without cultivation. Vines grow altogether wild on the heights.

It was at Cana where, according to the Gospel of St. John, Jesus and his relatives sanctified the most important festival of family life—because it celebrates its commencement—and increased the beverage of earth's gladness by a miracle of His divine power, an evangel which should be presented to all those who appropriate to themselves the innocent good gifts of the earth, for no other purpose than selfish enjoyment.

Leaving the verdant valley of Cana, the country becomes more bald; you ride across an extensive, unwooded plain, the hills become more and more naked, and opening to the left reveal a desert region, dried up and yellow. The lofty, calm, gently-waving contours of the mountain-ranges of Lebanon, and anti-Lebanon on the north, give repose to the eye. After having passed some smooth, dangerous hills, not far from Nazareth, the path becomes good and level. The road is one continual descent, and the heat of the atmosphere increases the farther we advance towards the valley of the Jordan; whilst swarms of small flies, which resemble a sand-rain, settle down on your face, get into your eyes, nose, and ears, and make the journey tormenting. Luckily there was on this day a great deal of cloud, and now and then it rained; very unusual weather for this time of the year, but to me a real benefit. By degrees the country became totally devoid of wood; the yellow hills and fields produced hardly anything but briars and thistles, as well as a kind of stiff, prickly grass; the thistles, however, have often beautiful flowers. Human dwellings there are none, neither are there any animals, nor yet man; it is a burnt-up wilderness. In the distance however, before me, I see a lofty stretch of hills enveloped in a misty atmosphere, a living sign which tells me that I am approaching the valley of the Jordan and the Lake of Genesareth. But still I have yet a long ride over sunburnt ground, in a hot, stifling atmosphere.

I cannot describe the feelings which I experienced when the yellow, parched hills opened all at once, as by a stroke of magic, and revealed to me a clear blue lake embosomed amongst softly rounded hills. It was the Lake of Genesareth; and my eye rested upon it with unspeakable refreshment and joy. It seemed to me that I never had beheld any lake so heavenly blue before. But neither had I ever beheld any lake before in a setting of yellow and brown hills. I was yet, however, at the distance of an hour and half from it; but from this moment the journey became one of sheer interest and enjoyment, causing me to forget both heat and weariness. Hameth, who was accustomed to conduct Christian pilgrims on this road, knew what was interesting to them by the way, and told me the names of various remarkable places as we went along. There was the wilderness plain where Jesus fed the multitude who had come to hear him and were an hungered—a frightfully wild tract; here the hill where He preached His glorious Sermon of the Mount—a terrace-formed, isolated hill, a splendid natural cathedral.

The road now proceeds with long sweeps over the yellow, thistle-covered hills, ever increasing in steepness, and ever more beautifully expands the clear, heaven-reflecting lake, in a crescent form, before the enchanted eye. The lake itself resembles an eye glancing upward from a countenance deeply furrowed by age and labour.

The city of Tiberias lies like a lump of dark-coloured coral, a blackened ruin, without majesty or beauty, on the shore of Genesareth. It was not until I came nearer that I saw several beautiful palm-trees and small green gardens amongst the houses and ruins, for the ruins seemed to constitute the greater portion of the city from the walls to the dilapidated Turkish mosque, above which a beautiful palm-tree bends as if sorrowing. Judging from the arched arcades and towers of the other buildings, it may be concluded that they were at one time magnificent. Many earthquakes, and especially the last great one in 1837, have produced terrible devastation through the whole of this country.

A few minutes after I had ridden through the unpretending city gate of Tiberias I found myself, to my astonishment, in the most charming little locality, with a family of Greek Christians, and in the Christian quarter of the city. My muckaro [Hameth], who has a great inclination to play the part of my master and ruler, had conducted me, of his own head, to these his old acquaintance. I was at first satisfied with this arrangement. A palm-tree and a beautiful pomegranate stood by the clean little court, in which handsome and well-dressed children were at play, and the lady—a very handsome lady too—who wore a large gold plate on the back of her head, with blue silk tassels hanging from it.

I was conducted up into a little room furnished in Oriental taste with divans, red cushions, and many-coloured coverlets, all evidencing affluence; and, that which is more rare in the East, order and cleanliness. Close outside one of the windows a pomegranate was waving its branches laden with its brilliant flowers, whilst tall cane-plants formed a thick verdant screen outside the other; and from the roof or the piazza I had a free view across the lake. It was a pleasure to me to see from thence the sun take leave of the eastern mountains amidst a combat with shadows and cloud, as well as to watch the life which was going forward in the streets, and on the roofs round about me, for my dwelling lay high. It astonished me to see that the people who wandered amongst or were upon the ruinous grey houses were so handsome, and generally so well dressed; to see signs of prosperity, and sometimes even of affluence, in their dress and their demeanour; even the drivers of asses had an elegant costume. The women went about with their faces uncovered, and the white linen, or veil, which was thrown over their heads, was fastened close under the chin, and thrown behind over the shoulders, down the back, displaying the gold neck-bands and other ornaments with which they love to adorn themselves. This day was a festival, and I therefore saw the Christian population of Tiberias in its holiday attire.

The Jews' quarter was situated nearer to the lake, also on a hill where, too, I observed some larger and well-built houses. "The Jews here," said my host, Signor Elias, "are rich, proud, and abominable. The Turkish population is also very bad." I thought that perhaps the Jewish and Turkish populations said the same of the Christian. "For the rest," said my host, "everybody is well off; there are *no poor* in Tiberias."

What I saw of the life of the people in the city seemed to me to confirm his words.

It was amusing at sunset to see the inhabitants of the houses come up to the roofs, where small huts of straw or clay were erected; the women, in their bright, many-coloured garments, bringing up coverlets and carpets, which they spread out in the airy huts, where the night was to be spent. The men sate down outside of them, smoking and talking with each other, or caressing the little children whom the mothers brought to them. It was a scene of Oriental life which the pleasant, fresh evening air spiced as with ambrosia. Also upon my roof came the members of the family, and seated themselves; and there I too sate with a little black-haired Regina on my knee, until darkness and sleep summoned us all to rest. And I needed rest after the sleepless night in Nazareth, and the fatiguing day's journey.

They made a bed for me of red cushions by the open window, looking into the court; fine white sheets were spread on the cushions, and over the whole was displayed a grand new coverlet. My bed looked delicious; the twigs of the pomegranate came in through the open window, the stars shone through the crown of the lofty palm-tree, and the brightness of the new moon lit up the whole atmosphere. The night was so wonderfully beautiful and bright, that I thought, even if I should not be able to sleep through the night, I should yet enjoy its gloriousness. And thus I laid myself down on my bed by the window, and looked up at the beaming vault of heaven, and at the softly waving branches of the palm-tree.

But I discovered before long that I might just as soon expect to lie at peace in an ants' nest as in this room or on this bed. It was an actual nest of fleas, and I then remembered the dreadful saying which I had heard, that the king of the fleas had established his camp at Tiberias. I was obliged to call up the people of the house, who had also gone to rest, and beg of them to make me up a bed on the roof, or in the court in the open air—anywhere, only not in the house. They made me up a bed, therefore, on a large table under the pomegranate-tree in the court. The moon shone through its branches down upon my couch. I heard the soft sighing of the night-wind in the palm branches; light dewy clouds sailed over my head, and scattered me with their drops; the air was pleasant: it was altogether romantically beautiful; but ah! those little Bedouins—more terrible to me than the great ones—left me, even here, not a moment's rest. At three o'clock in the morning, I got up, and dipping one of my sheets in the basin of the fountain in the court, wrapped myself in this Graefenberg envelopment, and succeeded in obtaining a few hours' sleep. On the following day, however, I should have to pay by headache for this night's entertainment. It was not amusing, especially under present circumstances. I longed for a cup of tea, but had neglected to provide myself with any at Jaffa, and at Tiberias tea was not to be obtained. I was told, however, that probably they might have some at the Greek convent in the city. I therefore hastened thither.

The convent is beautifully situated down by the shore of the lake, and the view from its flat roof is glorious. The monk who opened to me the gate received my petition for a few grains from which I would obtain the beneficent Oriental beverage, and replied kindly that I should have all that they had left of their store; and accordingly, searching in an old cupboard, he brought forth a dirty piece of paper, in which was some brown-black dust—a relic, indeed, of something which once had been tea, but had now lost all fragrance of and resemblance thereto. The good intention was not, however, the less worthy of gratitude. The convent is a substantial building, but its interior, as well as the church (which is built on a spot where tradition places one of the miracles of Jesus), evinces poverty; so did likewise the good monk's dress and appearance.

Whether, however, it was the decoction of the tea relic, or the delicious air—which at this time was refreshed by the abundant rain—or whether it was my own great desire to be speedily well again, but towards the evening I began to feel myself perfectly restored, and I then removed to the proper and only hotel of the city, built by a Jew, Mr. Weisemann, and where I was assured I should have to encounter no nocturnal enemies. Here I found myself in the midst of the Jews' quarter. The house was large, well built, and lying high, had a splendid view from the roof over the city and the lake. Handsome Spanish Jewesses came up there to stare at me, as at some extraordinary foreign animal.

The sound of a tambour and the clapping of hands in dancing time was heard from a house in the neighbourhood. There was a wedding at the house, and my host inquired if I should like to go there. I assented, and was conducted thither by Mr. Weisemann, and into a room full of women, some of whom were sitting on benches round the walls, the rest on the floor, in a compact circle, singing and clapping their hands, whilst a young dancer whirled round in the centre of the room. At the sight of Mr. Weisemann the hand-clapping, singing, and dancing all ceased, and a dreadful uproar and outcry arose amongst the women against the bold masculine violator of law who had dared to intrude into the peaceful circle of the other sex. All eyes, voices, and gestures were directed towards him with the strongest disapprobation. He did not look very much horrified by the demonstration; nevetherless, he soon vanished, and left me alone amongst the ladies, who now conducted me with much kindness of manner through the crowd, and made room for me near the open windows; after which, the singing, thrumming, dancing, and hand-clapping began again.

The dancer was a pale young woman with delicate features and remarkably large, beautiful eyes with long dark eyelashes; dark painted shadows increased the beauty of the eyes. Her form was refined and perfect, the pose of the figure easy, and the bust especially lovely in the white spencer or vest, buttoned below the breast. She wore on her head a kind of turban. Her dancing was a softly gliding round and round, almost entirely upon one spot, with a variety of posture and raised arms and hands, which were bordered with paint of a rusty-red colour. She moved, as it were, in a dream, and the grave expression of her countenance, the action of the arms, more angular than circular, nevertheless graceful, the softly swaying movement of the body, gave a mystical character to this dance, which involuntarily riveted the attention. Yet the noisy music, a kind of kettle-drum, the singing, which was a screeching without melody, and the hand-clapping, which, however, kept good time, were perfectly out of harmony with the dancing; nevertheless, the animated glances of the hand-clapping ladies showed that a cheerful state of feeling prevailed. When the pale dancer in her red tattered slippers had, amidst great applause, brought her monotonous circular dance to a close, another young woman took her place, who executed the same dance, but with less grace. I was told that it was Arabic. The company did not seem to me of a high class, although gold glittered on the heads, necks, and dresses of several of them; but their finery was without taste, and was not ornamental. The entertainment began with a variety of sweetmeats, of which I was pressed very kindly to partake; but after having done so, I soon left the intensely hot, crowded room for the cool air and the free view from my roof, on a higher terrace.

The sun was approaching its setting, and it was an exquisite enjoyment to me to watch the lights and shadows on the surrounding scenery, and the life of the people in the city and on the roofs. And this was here much more various than in the Christian quarter, because here I was not far from the Mohammedan quarter, and could see many parts of the city and its population. On one roof in the neighbourhood a Mussulman was performing his evening prayer, whilst brown female slaves were preparing his couch in the night-hut with splendid carpets; on another roof handsome Jewesses were seated with their children clustered round their supper. The Bedouin smoked his pipe phlegmatically, sitting outside his door, whilst the Jew boys in fur caps endeavoured slily to fling stones from the street through the windows of the house where the wedding was being celebrated. Great herds of black goats were driven close together outside the city, and girls and old women with large vessels of white foamy milk tripped merrily through the streets. Cows and asses emulated them in finding their individual homes within the gates of the houses. Within the houses you saw splendid, many-coloured dresses shining out on men and women who were stretched at their ease on red divans. Children were playing round the sleeping-huts on the roofs, mothers were variously busied, the men were smoking, dogs and cats were running about, whilst an innumerable number of hens were cackling in the courts within. It was a mingling of the humble and the splendid, of the low and the lofty, of colour and form; in a word, it was true Oriental everyday life.

In the meantime the sun went down in beauty, and the ruined city, with its crooked streets and beautiful palm-trees amongst the ruins, and the clear blue lake, were enveloped in shadow, at the same time that a pure golden gleam extended over the purple-tinted hills of Bashan and Hauran, on the opposite side of the Sea of Tiberias. The heavy night-cloud which hung over the lake was absorbed by degrees; the moon rose and mirrored herself in the quiet lake; the heaven became clear and full of light; above Mount Lebanon, in the north, now merely rested some dark clouds.

No city, excepting Tiberias, which is called by the people of the country Tabaria, now rises on the shore of Genesareth. You are shown, northward, the spot on which anciently stood Bethsaida; some heaps of stones alone remain of Chorazin and Capernaum. These formerly proud cities over which Jesus uttered His warning "woe!" have totally disappeared. Far away, amongst the mountains of the north, you see rising the cupolas of Safed, an increasing trading town, where, as well as in Tiberias, the most Jewish of the Jews are said to have established themselves. It was at Safed and Tiberias that—at the time of the birth of Christ and afterwards—the learned Rabbinical schools flourished; those schools in which the Babylonian philosophy united itself to the sacred doctrines of the Jews, and gave birth to the so-called Judaic tradition, or *Mischna,* afterwards comprehended in the Talmud (the word signifies the doctrine), the chief book of the Jews of Palestine at the present day, and with many of them of higher authority than even the books of Moses. The author of the Talmud is said to have been the Rabbi Juda, surnamed the

Holy, who lived on the shores of Genesareth, in the middle of the third century after Christ. He was regarded by his disciples with a reverence which almost amounted to worship. He arranged, increased, and determined the Hebrew tradition, with its interpretations, legends, and stories, five thick volumes, in which much that is sensible and beautiful is mixed up with a great deal that is foolish and poor. The author of the far profounder *Kabbala* (the remains), or at least of its latter portion, the Book *Sohar* (brightness, glory), is said to have been the learned Rabbi Simeon Ben Jochai. Oriental philosophy and the Hebrew doctrine of revelation here unite in the formation of a spiritual doctrine of nature, or symbolism. The facts and realities of faith are shown as based on spiritual phenomena and natural laws. I have seen in this book thoughts and gleams of light which I shall never forget, and I wish that competent European inquirers and men of science would bring both these hidden treasures of Asia to the light more than they have hitherto done.

In the village of Meirom, not far from Tiberias, you are shown the graves of these two celebrated Jewish teachers and of several of their learned brethren, which causes it, at the present day, to be a place of pilgrimage for the Jews of Palestine, who celebrate here every year, in the month of May, a festival in commemoration of the masters.

These cities and their flourishing schools were laid waste by Mussulman oppression and since by devastating earthquakes. They have converted the country round the Lake of Genesareth—the country which Josephus described as an earthly paradise, rich in the noblest fruits of the earth, and with the most lovely climate—into a desert. Tiberias, as well as Safed and other places near Genesareth, were shaken on the first of January, 1837, by a dreadful earthquake, which overturned a number of houses and killed several thousand persons. . . .

Tiberias has begun by degrees to recover itself, and its inhabitants derive some wealth by trading between the East and the West. They are in continual dread, however, of a recurrence of earthquakes and of the Bedouins, who live by plunder, and swarming along the shores of the Jordan, are the means of repressing any greater spirit of enterprise, and prevent the inhabitants from rebuilding their city. Tiberias, indeed, will never again be that which it has been. My host thought that the climate and everything else in the country was good, were the people only better. But "the people are bad." The Jews especially were severely treated; they were not able to undertake the least cultivation or planting. Thus a portion of the Jews here were extremely poor; they had scarcely daily bread, and would perish of hunger if the more wealthy did not help them. The family where the wedding was held the evening before belonged to the class who needed even the necessaries of life; nevertheless they had had a wedding for the daughter who had married the son of a family as poor as her own.

At six o'clock in the morning I betook myself, attended by my muckaro, to the hot springs of Tiberias. White buildings, rising on a green bend of the shore at about half-an-hour's distance from the city, point out the situation of the bath. You walk to it along the shore. The morning was lovely, and a north wind blew deliciously cool over the quiet lake. A number of sea-birds, which seemed to me like spirits, lay by hundreds on the water, rocked by its motion and undisturbed by any sportsman. The shore was, as it were, strewn with ruins, low walls and heaps of stones, which showed that at some former period it had been closely built. Amongst these ruins stood, here and there, a shrub of oleander or agnus-castus, and bushes of the beautiful honeysuckle—perhaps descendants of former gardens which surrounded handsome villas. Thistles and the light-green thorny shrub which I have already mentioned, also grew there abundantly.

The hot springs issue from the sand in several places near the shore, and pour their waters into the lake. The water feels burning hot to the hand. The new bath-house, a large, splendid rotunda of white marble, was built by Ibrahim Pacha, during his short but active government in Palestine. A guard of from twenty to thirty mounted Baschi-bassuks, in the Bedouin dress, surround the building for the protection of those who come hither to bathe, against the rapacious Bedouins of the neighborhood.

I wished to take a bath, as a means of refreshment after the sleepless night which I had passed. The water in the large marble-basin, the temperature of which was reduced by cold water, looked very tempting; but there were no doors in the house, no female attendant was visible, wherever you went you had to go through steaming water which overflowed on all sides; outside the bath-house I saw only the Arab guard, and no possibility of having a bath in peace and quiet and afterwards dry clothing. I went on, therefore, to the so-called old bath. It was a small rotunda of grey stone, and the building looked old and ruinous. Here, too, an Arab guard was stationed. Within, however, I found it more comfortable than in the white-marble bath. The door of the bath-room might be fastened with a stone, and a brown-complexioned Arab matron sat on the edge of the bath. The expression of her countenance and her manner, as she saluted me showed a degree of culture, as well as a gentle and kind disposition. She poured the water over herself from the bath with a little metal bowl, then she went down into the water up to her neck. Although the water here was also cooled down, still I found it so hot that I could not keep my feet in it for any length of time. To go down into it with my whole body seemed an impossibility. I seated myself on the edge of the bath whilst I put down my feet into the water and then drew them up again, and in reply to the questioning glances of the Arab lady I replied with the Arab words *tschob, kitir tschob*—warm, very warm! The good matron comprehended my embarrassment, and kindly reached me the little bowl that I might pour the water over myself from it.

The cry of the guard outside now announced another bather; the stone at the door was pushed aside and a young Arab woman slipped in, and then as soon as she had again secured the door, proceeded hastily to undress, and without the least hesitation leaped down into the bath, and up to her neck as the old lady had done before. This last comer was a woman as lovely as a statue, with golden-yellow hair, fair skin, and blue eyes like a northern maiden—in form she was a perfect Venus. Her look and manners also betokened more than ordinary cultivation. The elderly and the young lady remained in the water for about half-an-hour, nearly immovable during the whole time.

I found the water to be bitterly salt, with a flavour which reminded me of the waters of the Dead Sea, although less nauseous. I continued seated on the edge of the bath, satisfying myself by laving the water over me, which I found to be extremely refreshing, notwithstanding its heat.

When I returned to the city, the inhabitants were busy on the outside of the walls killing goats and sheep. Nor have I ever seen fatter joints than those which were carried away, in large numbers, on the shoulders of the butcher-boys into the city. It seemed to me, from what I now saw, and from what I had seen the preceding evenings, as if good living were the principal object in life of the people of Tiberias. Was it much different in those days when the Saviour resided and walked here? Did not He also see these people thus satisfied with themselves and their own little world; see these home-scenes, this occupation with the petty pleasures and needs of every-day life, as if there were nothing else in existence of any importance? And yet He did not allow Himself to be disturbed by it.

Again at my hotel I breakfasted, and then, accompanied by the son of my host, went to see the place where his former house had stood. Another very errant whitewashed house stood now in its stead, upon the perpendicular edge of rock on the shore of the lake. Without any ceremony my guide led me into a well-lighted room, where a Rabbi, who looked like a learned but not a good man, was walking up and down with small slips of olive-wood bound upon his forehead and wrists. These ornaments, which are called phylacteries, and which symbolize, as I believe, the ark of the covenant, are placed upon the Hebrew when he would engage in especially earnest prayer. I was sorry to disturb the learned gentleman; but, however, he did not allow himself to be disturbed; cast at me a cold, absent glance, made no reply to my unlearned greeting *Salaam, Alicham!* but continued to pace up and down the room, muttering to himself half-aloud.

Some minutes later I was seated on horseback, and rode up the western hills of Tiberias. It was a glorious morning. For the first time since my stay at Tiberias had Lebanon thrown the hood of mist from his ancient brow, and the lofty Sunnin, the highest cupola—which resembles the back of an elephant—shone forth beautifully with his snowy furrows and flecks against the dark blue sky.

I felt light and cheerful of heart this morning; the bath had wonderfully refreshed me, my horse carried me as lightly as a breath up the heights, and with thankful glances I photographed upon my inner life the picture of the beautiful lake, with its shores and magnificent surroundings, and its immortal memory. The wood-crowned summit of Tabor showed itself above the hills to the westward before me, now entirely free from cloud, although its top is said to be generally veiled with cloud in the morning. A fresh wind blew from the north, and chased away the swarms of flies which I heard buzzing and piping in the air round my head. The journey seemed to me wonderfully easy to-day; I could scarcely believe my eyes when I again beheld the beautiful verdant valley of Cana. Here we and our horses drank from the fresh, flowing fountain, and I seated myself in a shady grove of fig-trees to take breakfast, as did also Hameth and Joseph. I plucked some leaves from a wild vine as mementoes for myself and several others in Sweden, and early in the afternoon I again found myself at *Casa Nova* in Nazareth.

Tall Jacob [the author's Christian host] had obeyed my exhortation and washed my room with plenty of water, so that I now passed such a night there as, compared with the three preceding, was like paradise compared with purgatory. The friendly care which here, as at Carmel, is taken of Christian pilgrims, of whatever profession they may be, cannot be gratefully enough acknowledged. . . .

Early the following morning I was on my way to ascend Mount Tabor, one of the most fatiguing and even dangerous excursions in this district. Not long since, a young French tourist, whilst ascending, fell with his horse and broke his leg; after which he was nursed and cured by the nuns of Nazareth. And if the traveller have not a safe and strong horse for climbing, he had better make the ascent on foot, however difficult it may be, for the stones along the path are often actual giant-steps.

I never made an ascent on horseback without experiencing considerable anxiety (which, however, I keep to myself), and if I perceive that my horse is not safe-footed, this anxiety continues during the whole ride. This feeling naturally embitters the journey, but it seasons or sweetens the rest afterwards, and makes me enjoy in twofold degree every journey brought to its close, every completed day of travel, as a danger luckily overpast. And so especially with the present day's journey. My white horse was not sure-footed, but stumbled and even fell on the smooth hill, or amongst stones, and more than once on the road I was obliged to pluck him up violently. On the day when I was intending to ascent Tabor he was discovered to be unfit for travel, from a tumour on his back; therefore I was obliged to take Hameth's horse, the horse of the cruel Abdullah, which was large and very fiery. Hameth obtained another for himself in the town. I was rather afraid of my large, spirited horse, and found also that his paces were very fatiguing. But when he began to climb, I saw every reason to be highly satisfied, for where in all probability my white horse would have stumbled and fallen, the brown one clomb up with strong and secure foothold.

The ride to Tabor occupied about three hours. Half an hour before the foot of the mountain is reached, the country becomes woody, and you have here the rare pleasure in Palestine of riding in the shade of trees. . . .

Critical travellers have maintained that Tabor could not be the mountain which the Evangelists wished to describe as the spot on which the Transfiguration took place; because, even before that time, as since, the summit has been built upon and fortified. But this criticism has little worth; for, whilst ascending the hill, which is done by a winding, spiral path, I observed that the mount has a number of little elevations and platforms, any one of which is sufficiently large to have been the scene of an unusual occurrence, without its having been necessarily witnessed by the dwellers on the summit, even if we accept the Transfiguration of Christ as a circumstance which would be seen by uninitiated eyes. These critics have asserted that not Tabor, but the Great Hermon, the Sheik of the Mountains, as the Arabs call it, is the mountain which the Holy Scriptures refer to. But, whether Hermon or Tabor be the scene of the Transfiguration, the environs and the views are not essentially different. They were to me a principal fact. Tabor is infinitely beautiful and picturesque, with its wealth of lovely wood and rock, and its magnificent views, which expand on all sides as you circle the mount in your ascent. In about an hour's time you are on the summit in the midst of a glorious natural park, and can wander about freely and look round you on all sides. On the south your eye commands Galilee and Samaria as far as the hills of Judea; on the north lies the mountainous region of the Lebanon, the northern barrier of Palestine; in the far east the softly-waving blue horizon line points out the hilly country beyond Jordan; and in the far west you are conscious of the Mediterranean, which yet, however, my eye could not discern. All around below Mount Tabor lies an elevated extent of fertile plains and hills, where, amongst isolated groups of rock, stands forth, here and there, a little village. Highest among these hills is the Lesser Hermon, at the feet of which are seen the villages of Endor and Nain; in another direction, a little place is pointed out which bears the name of Deborich, and is remarkable as the birthplace of the celebrated judge and heroine Deborah. Some years ago "Deborah's palm-tree" was shown there.

When I had alighted safe and sound from my tall horse, I felt myself unspeakably happy. It was Whitsunday, and the day was Orientally splendid and lovely. The morning sun shone gloriously above the grand, joyous picture. Near and afar off, an indescribable freshness and peace breathed around here, and everything was so large, so calm, so beautiful, my soul sang with David, "Tabor and Hermon shall rejoice in Thy name." Brightest, most delightful of all was to me the remembrance of the festival of light which once took place here.

I rambled about and rested for a full hour on the mount; partly amongst the ruins, partly under beautiful, umbrageous trees. You find many monuments of Roman and Saracenic architecture. A Russian priest of the Greek Church has built for himself a little dwelling and a little chapel amongst these ruins. I could almost have envied him this abode, its pure air, and glorious views over heaven and earth. He had clear, lively eyes, like one who could fully understand and appreciate the treasures of Mount Tabor. The worst of it was that I could not converse with him, as he spoke only Russian and Greek.

There is a deep cistern on the Mount containing deliciously fresh water. Of this I drank, eating to it a piece of bread, in the shadow of an oak, with a view over the sunshine-illumined Galilee. No breakfast could possibly have been more refreshing. Around me grew tall wild mallows, poppies, and honeysuckles; brilliant flowers shone out amongst the shadowy trees; and the wind breathed fresh and invigorating! I should have liked to linger a long time here, to build myself a hut, because here, upon this summit, "it seemed good to be." But I was obliged to return to the trivial and every-day concerns of earth. Supplied with flowers and plants, I therefore took my way on foot down the glorious Mount, which I shall never see again, but shall never forget. Tabor is a prince amongst the hills of Palestine, a glorious natural altar, crowned with perpetual verdure, consecrated by an immortal memory.

And now I am again in Nazareth, and write this with joy in my heart, inasmuch as I have seen Genesareth, Nazareth, and Tabor, and that I now possess these places in my soul, traced there with features as clear and definite as any spot in my native land. Formerly they were to me shadow-pictures, now they have become sun-pictures to my mind. Yet another day's journey to Caipha and Carmel, and then I hope to have ended for ever my travels on horseback, at which I shall be no little pleased.

The town of Nazareth has, like all other towns which I have seen in this country, a mass of mean houses built of grey stone, with flat roofs, narrow, dirty, ill-kept streets, with rubbish-heaps on the right and left, with very few buildings of the better class. Amongst the so-called "Holy Places" here, is a beautiful Greek convent built over the Fountain of the Virgin. The Maria Fountain, at some distance, may always be seen surrounded by a chattering, noisy crowd of young girls as little resembling the Madonna type as possible. So it was also in the evening. The girls, most of them quite young, came to fetch water in brown clay vessels and were very much decked out with diadems of silver coins, breast and neck ornaments of gold and silver, and other finery more showy than beautiful. Their countenances, and in particular their eyes, were handsome; but their appearance and their manners betrayed so much boldness, as to create disgust. Poor, neglected children, it was no fault of theirs.

On my return through the town Jacob took me to his home. The tall Jacob is an original, who would be worth both studying and painting; his Christianity is, I am afraid, only "a blotted-out Paganism." He is full of the credulity and superstition of his native land (Arabia). The idea had entered, I cannot tell how, his not remarkably lucid brain, that I was a lady very learned in the stars, and learned also in every kind of magical and mystical science; he therefore asked me very seriously this morning if I could discover where hidden treasures lay? I replied, smiling, that if I could do so, I should be richer than was now the case, and denied all knowledge of forbidden subjects. My friend Jacob, however, did not believe me, and returned again and again with new and equally idle questions, for example:—

"There was a monk in the Franciscan convent whom he could not bear; could I tell him whether this man would soon be coming back?"

"There was on this day a wedding in his family; could I say whether the young couple would be happy?" and so on.

Arrived at his house, therefore, he asked me to tell his children's fortunes. As I saw it was no use to oppose Jacob's fixed idea regarding myself as a mistress of the secret art, I took courage and began boldly to predict the children's fortunes, that of a girl and four little boys, and so doing astonished even myself at my own assurance and impudence. Yet I based all on prudent preliminaries. The step-child of the house, a little boy, of whom the father thought nothing could ever be made, I predicted would especially be a great man, and have great luck, only he must be treated very well, sent to school, and so on. The daughter, a perfect Arab beauty of twelve, who was to be married in a few weeks to a young tradesman in the town, would, I foretold, be very happy, if she became a good, prudent wife and mother—and so on.

Jacob and his wife—who was still a lovely woman of the same type as the daughter—were holding at their house to-day the wedding of a young relative. She had been married that morning; but, according to the custom of the place, was not to see nor yet be seen by the bridegroom during the whole day until evening, neither to leave the house. She now was sitting here, therefore, in full bridal state, very much adorned with silver and gold. She was eighteen; looked good and sensible, but not happy. Jacob's wife was preparing the wedding repast, and invited me to taste of the dishes, *Cucuzza*, a kind of gourd filled with boiled rice—a favourite Arab dish—minced meat mixed with rice, rolled in vine-leaves like small sausages; and thick, boiled, sour milk, *Lebben*, with rice, like a kind of porridge, also a principal Arab dish. Rice plays a conspicuous part in all Arab entertainments, with savoury, sour, or sweet dishes; at the beginning and at the end of the meal rice must always have its place. I am making no objection to it; I believe this species of food to be as wholesome as it is agreeable to the palate, and hold in all esteem the Arab art of cooking.

The Valley of Nazareth is, in the evening, full of harvest life and labour; reaping, thrashing, winnowing, all takes place in the fields, and all is done with the hands and feet. Camels and asses lie in the heaps of grain, and eat as much as they can.

Yet one more fatiguing day's journey and I am then at the end of my Palestine travels.

10

Lady Ann Blunt
Hyena and Locust for Dinner

FROM
A Pilgrimage to Nejd (1881)

Just over a hundred years ago, Lady Ann Blunt gained the distinction of becoming the first Western woman to penetrate the mysterious territory of Nejd in Saudi Arabia, long thought to be the cradle of the Bedouin people.

This intrepid explorer of desert wastes was born in 1840, the daughter of William Noel, the first Earl of Lovelace, and Ada Byron, Lord Byron's only legitimate daughter. She received a typical aristocratic education, and in 1869 married the poet and later antiimperialist Wilfred Scawen Blunt. After his retirement from the British diplomatic service, the couple went to live in Egypt. Captivated by the culture, the Blunts studied Arabic, and in 1878 undertook an expedition to the Euphrates for the purpose of buying Arab horses for their estate in England. While visiting the ruins of Palmyra in central Syria,[1] they met Mohammad Abadallah, the son of the local sheikh, who was preparing to set out for Nejd in search of a wife from his own ancestral tribe.

For the Blunts, here was a splendid chance to see the famed horses of Ibn Rashid and perhaps to explore the great central stretches of the Saudi peninsula, still largely unknown to the West.[2] Having persuaded Mo-

---

[1] See Lady Ann Blunt, *Bedouin Tribes of the Euphrates* (London: Frank Cass, 1879).

[2] Sir Richard Burton and three or four other Europeans had explored parts of Saudi Arabia, but few had managed to reach the central regions. Charles Doughty, whose *Travels in Arabia Deserta* (1888) was destined to become a classic, had left the Nejd area only a few months before the Blunts embarked on their journey. Between 1899 and 1913, Gertrude Bell journeyed to the Middle East;

hammad to let them go along, they began the trek to Hail, the capital of Nejd. Discarding her Victorian garb, Lady Ann donned a keffiyeh, threw a Bedouin cloak over herself, and with stoic grace, endured the various hazards of the torturous journey, from violent sandstorms to unconventional repasts of roasted hyena and fried locusts.

Thinking themselves to be the first Christians to reach that region, the Blunts were worried about how they would be received by Ibn Rashid, the ruler of Nejd. Their first meeting with him lasted only fifteen minutes. Later, however, they were invited to watch him dispense justice in the square of Hail. After spending several weeks among the natives of Nejd and the throngs of Persian pilgrims encamped outside the city, the Blunts made their way back to a more familiar civilization and the journey's end in Baghdad. The Blunts' travels through the Nejd were on the whole peaceful, but in the Wadi Sirhan, as they were resting, they were attacked by tribesmen who came charging down on them with lances. Lady Ann, who had sprained her knee, could not mount her horse fast enough to escape. As a horseman began to hit her husband on the head with his own rifle, Lady Ann pleaded that they meant no harm and would submit to the Bedouins. Fortunately, the sheikh who had accompanied them arrived on the scene, and the attackers, recognizing a member of a friendly tribe, departed, leaving the Blunts to resume their journey.

In 1881, the Blunts bought an estate in Egypt and thereafter divided their time between this home and Sussex, until they decided to separate in 1906. In 1917, Lady Ann became the Baroness Wentworth and effected a reconciliation with her husband. She died in Cairo in 1922.

Lady Ann's account of her journey appeared almost ten years before Charles Doughty's more poetic narrative. Asked to explain the meaning of her unorthodox title, **A Pilgrimage to Nejd,** she wrote:

> To us ... Nejd had long assumed the romantic colouring of a holy land; and when it was decided that we were to visit Jebel Shammar, the metropolis of Bedouin life, our expedition presented itself as an almost pious undertaking; so that it is hardly an exaggeration, even now that it is over, and we are once more in Europe, to speak of it as a pilgrimage. For pilgrimage then it is, though the religion in whose name we have travelled was only one of romance.

---

in 1913, she became the second woman (Western) to visit Hail. Though she wrote many books about her travels, only one of them gives a full account of her journey to the Nejd. She became expert enough in Middle Eastern affairs to be appointed to the Arab intelligence bureau during World War I.

The book enjoyed considerable popularity in its day, going into three editions in a short period, and it was the only reliable source of information about the interior of Saudi Arabia until Doughty's book appeared. In this excerpt from the second volume, the Blunts are preparing to leave Nejd.

"Come, Myrrha, let us go on to the Euphrates."

BYRON

February 6—We are tired of loitering with the Haj, and besides, do not care to see more of Ibn Rashid, who is expected to-day. It is always a good rule not to outstay your welcome, and to go when you have once said good-bye. So, finding no indication of a move in the pilgrim camp this morning, we decided on marching without them. We have not gone far; indeed, from the high ground where we are camped we can see the smoke of the camp rising up at the edge of the plain. There is capital pasture here; and we have a fine wide prospect to the south and west; Jebel Jildiyeh being now due south of us, and Jebel Aja west by south, Hail perhaps forty miles off; to the north the Nefûd, and behind us to the east from the ridge above our camp, we can look over a subbkha (dry lake) six or seven miles distant, with the oasis of Bekaa or Taybetism (happy be its name) round its shores. The place had always been called Bekaa, we are told, till a few years ago, when the name was thought unlucky, and changed, though I cannot quite understand why, for the word means a place where water can collect.

We flew our falcon to-day, and, after one or two disappointments, it caught us a hare. The wadys [dry river bed] are full of hares, but the dogs cannot see them in the high bushes, and this was the only one started in the open. We have encamped early, and are enjoying the solitude. The moon will be full to-night; and it is provoking to think how much of its light has been wasted by delay. The moon is of little use for travelling after it is full.

February 7—Though we did not move our camp to-day, we had a long ride, and got as far as the village of Taybetism, which is worth seeing. It is a very curious place, resembling Jobba as far as situation goes. Indeed, it seems probable that most of the towns of Nejd have in common this feature, that they are placed in hollows towards which the water drains, as it is in such positions that wells can be dug without much labour. Like Jobba, Taybetism has a subbkha, but the latter is altogether a more important oasis, for the palm-gardens reach nearly round the lake, and though not quite continuous, they must have an extent of four or five miles. The houses seem to be scattered in groups all along this length, and there is no special town.[3] The geology of the district is most interesting. At the edge of the subbkha the sandstone rocks form strange fantastic cliffs, none more than fifty feet high, but most fanciful in form. Some, shaped like mushrooms, show that the subbkha must at one time have been an important lake, instead of the dry semblance of a lake it now is. We measured the largest of these, and found it was forty feet in length by twenty-five feet in width at top, with a stalk of only five feet, the whole mass resting on a high pedestal. Other rocks looked as though they had been suddenly cooled while boiling and red hot, with the bubbles petrified as they stood. There were broad sheets of rose-coloured stone like strawberry cream with more cream poured into it and not yet mixed, streaked pink and white. Here and there, there were patches of Nefûd sand with the green Nefûd adr [a kind of lichen][4] growing on them, and clusters of wild palms and tamarisks with a pool or two of bitter water. The subbkha, although quite dry, looked like a lake, so perfect was the mirage, of clear blue water without a ripple, reflecting the palms and houses on the opposite shore. We went round to some of these, and found beautiful gardens and well-to-do farms with patches of green barley growing outside. These were watered from wells about forty-five feet deep, good water, which the people drew for our mares to drink. We passed, but did not go into a large square kasr [castle] belonging to Ibn Rashid, where a dozen or so of dervishes from the Haj were loafing about. They asked us for news—whether the Emir had come, and whether the Haj [the title given to a man who has made the pilgrimage to Mecca] was still waiting. These were most of them not Persian dervishes, though Shias, but from Bagdad and Meshhed Ali, people of Arab race.

On our way back we crossed a party of Shammar Bedouins,

---

[3]It was to Taybetism that Abdallah ibn Saoud fled ten years ago when he was driven by his brother out of Aared, and from it that he sent that treacherous message to Midhat Pasha at Bagdad which brought the Turks into Hasa and broke up the Wahhabi Empire.
[4]English translations that appear in brackets have been added by the editor.

with their camels come for water for the Nefûd, which is close by. They gave us some lebben [a yogurt beverage] to drink, the first we have tasted this year. There were women with them. We also met a man alone on a very thin delûl [a female camel]. Mohammed made some rather uncomplimentary remarks about this animal, whereupon the owner in great scorn explained that she was a Bint Udeyhan, the very best breed of dromedaries in Arabia, and that if Mohammed should offer him a hundred pounds he would not sell her, that she was the camel always sent by Ibn Rashid on messages which wanted speed. He then trotted off at a pace which, though it appeared nothing remarkable, soon took him out of sight.

Awwad and Ibrahim Kasir have been back to the Haj camp for water, and have brought news that the Emir has actually arrived, and a message from him, that if we go on to the wells of Shaybeh he will meet us there.

February 8—We have marched fifteen miles to-day from point to point, making a circuit round Taybetism and are now encamped at the top of the Nefûd. A Shammar boy of the name of Izzar with three delûls came back from the Haj camp yesterday with Awwad, and he undertakes to show us the way if we want to go on in front. He would sooner travel with us than with the Haj, as his beasts are thin, and he is afraid of their being impressed for the pilgrims. He wants to drive them unloaded to Meshhed, so that they may grow fat on the way, and then load them for the home voyage with wheat. He talks about six or seven days to Meshhed; but Wilfrid insists that we are not twenty miles nearer Meshhed than when we left Haîl, as we have been travelling almost due east, instead of nearly due north, and there must be four hundred miles more to go. This should take us twenty days at least. But the servants will not believe. We shall see who is right. They and Mohammed are very unwilling to go[5] on before the Haj, but now that we have got this boy Izzar we are determined not to wait. If we delay we shall run short of provisions, which would be worse than anything. Already, Awwad says, the pilgrims are complaining loudly that they shall starve if they are kept longer waiting in this way. They have brought provisions

---

[5] This does not seem to be a reference to Meshed in Iran, which is about twelve hundred miles from Nejd.

for so many days and no more, and there is no place now where they can revictual. "The Haj," added Awwad, "is sitting by the fire, very angry."

Our march to-day was enlivened by some hunting, though with no good result. Sayad and Shiekha coursed a herd of gazelles, and succeeded in turning them, but could not get hold of any, though one passed close to Mohammed, who fired without effect. They made off straight for the Nefûd. The falcon was flown at a houbara (frilled bustard), but the bustard beat him off, as he is only a last year's bird, and not entered to anything but hares. Rasham, however, is an amusement to us and sits on his perch at our tent door. This spot is pleasant and lonely, within a hundred yards of the edge of the Nefûd.

February 9—Having sent Izzar to a high point for a last look back for the Haj and in vain, we have given them up and now mean to march straight on without them. It is however annoying that we are still going east instead of north, coasting the Nefûd I suppose to get round instead of crossing it; but we dare not plunge into it against Izzar's positive assurance that the other is the only way. Soil sprinkled with jabsin (talc), and in places with the fruit of the wild poisonous melon. Passed the well of Beyud (eggs) thirty feet deep, and travelled six and a half hours, perhaps eighteen miles, to our present camp absolutely without incident. Looking at the stars to-night, Mohammed tells me they call Orion's belt "mizan" (the balance), and the pole star "el jiddeh" (the kid). We now have milk every day from Izzar's she-camel, a great luxury.

February 10—At eight o'clock we reached the wells of Shaybeh. There are forty of them close together in the middle of a great bare space, with some hills of white sand to the north of them. The wind was blowing violently, drifting the sand, and the place looked as inhospitable a one as could well be imagined, a good excuse for over-ruling all notions of stopping there, "to wait for the Emir."

Shaybeh stands on the old Haj road which passes east of Haîl, making straight for Bereydeh in Kaslm, and the reason of our travelling so far east is thus explained. Now we have turned at right angles northwards, and there is a well-defined track which it will be easy enough for us to follow, even if we lose our Shammar guide. After leaving the wells, we travelled for some miles between ridges of white sand, which the wind was shaping "like the snow wreaths in the high Alps." The white sand, I noticed, is always of a finer texture than the red, and is more easily affected by the wind. It carries, moreover, very little vegetation, so that the mounds and ridges are less permanent than those of the Nefûd. While we were watching them, the wind shifted, and it was interesting to observe how the summits of the ridges gradually changed with it, the lee side being always steep, the wind side rounded. We gradually ascended now through broken ground to the edge of a level gravelly plain, beyond which about four miles distant we could see the red line of the real Nefûd. We had nearly crossed this, when we sighted an animal half a mile away, and galloped off in pursuit, Mohammed following. I thought at first it must be a wolf or a wild cow, but as we got nearer to it, we saw that it was a hyæna, and it seemed to be carrying something in its mouth. The dogs now gave chase, and the beast made off as fast as it could go for the broken ground we had just left, and where it probably had its den, dropping in its hurry the leg of a gazelle, the piece of booty it was bringing with it from the Nefûd. The three greyhounds boldly attacked it, Sayad especially seizing it at the shoulder, but they were unable to stop it, and it still went on doggedly intent on gaining the broken ground. It would have escaped had not we got in front and barred the way. Then it doubled back again, and we managed to drive it before us towards where we had left our camels. I never saw so cowardly a creature, for though much bigger than any dog, it never offered to turn round and defend itself as a boar or even a jackal would have done, and the dogs were so persistent in their attacks, that Wilfrid had great difficulty in getting a clear shot at it, which he did at last, rolling it over as it cantered along almost under the feet of our camels. Great of course were the rejoicings, for though Mohammed and Awwad affected some repugnance, Abdallah declared boldly and at once, that hyæna was "khosh lahm," capital meat. So it was flayed and quartered on the spot. I confess the look of the carcass was not appetising, the fat with which it was covered being bright yellow, but hyænas in the desert are not the ghoul-like creatures they become in the neighbourhood of towns, and on examination the stomach was found to be full of locusts and fresh gazelle meat. Wilfrid pronounced it eatable, but I, though I have just tasted a morsel, could not bring myself to make a meal off it. I perceive that in spite of protestations about unclean food, the whole of this very large and fat animal has been devoured by our followers. I am not sure whether Mohammed kept his resolution of abstaining.

Locusts are now a regular portion of the day's provision with us, and are really an excellent article of diet. After trying them in several ways, we have come to the conclusion that they are best plain boiled. The long hopping legs must be pulled off, and the locust held by the wings, dipped into salt and eaten. As to flavour this insect tastes of vegetable rather than of fish or flesh, not unlike green wheat in England, and to us it supplies the place of vegetables, of which we are much in need. The red locust is better eating than the green one.[6] Wilfrid considers that it would hold its own among the *hors d'œuvre* at a Paris restaurant; I am not so sure of this, for on former journeys I have resolved that other excellent dishes should be adopted at home, but afterwards among the multitude of luxuries, they have not been found worth the trouble of preparation. For catching locusts, the morning is the time, when they are half benumbed by the cold, and their wings are damp with the dew, so that they cannot fly; they may then be found clustered in hundreds under the desert bushes, and gathered without trouble, merely shovelled into a bag or basket. Later on, the sun dries their wings and they are difficult to capture, having intelligence enough to keep just out of reach when pursued. Flying, they look extremely like May flies, being carried side-on to the wind. They can steer themselves about as much as flying fish do, and can alight when they like; in fact, they very seldom let themselves be drifted against men or camels, and seem able to calculate exactly the reach of a stick. This year they are all over the country, in enormous armies by day, and huddled in regiments under every bush by night. They devour everything vegetable; and are devoured by everything animal: desert larks and bustards, ravens, hawks, and buzzards. We passed to-day through flocks of ravens and

---

[6] Red is said to be the female and green the male, but some say all are green at first and become red afterwards.

buzzards, sitting on the ground gorged with them. The camels munch them in with their food, the greyhounds run snapping after them all day long, eating as many as they can catch. The Bedouins often give them to their horses, and Awwad says that this year many tribes have nothing to eat just now but locusts and camels' milk; thus the locust in some measure makes amends for being a pestilence, by being himself consumed.

February 11—Some boys with camels joined us last night, Bedouins from the Abde tribe of Shammar, on their way to meet the Haj, as they have been ordered up by Ibn Rashid. They have given us some information about the road. Ibn Duala is five days' journey on; but we shall find the Dafir, with their Sheykh, Ibn Sueyti, on the second day. Ibn Sueyti, they say, has a kind of *uttfa* [large cloak used to protect the wearer against the elements] like Ibn Shaalan's, but it is pitched like a tent when a battle is to be fought. The Ajman, near Queyt, have a real *uttfa* with ostrich feathers and a girl to sing during the fighting. They also narrated the following remarkable tale.

There is, they say, in the desert, five days' march from here to the eastwards, and ten days from Suk es Shiôkh on the Euphrates, a *kubr* or tomb, the resting-place of a prophet named Er Refay. It is called Tellateyn el Kharab (the two hills of the ruins), and near it is a birkeh or tank always full of water. The tomb has a door which stands open, but round it there sleeps all day and all night a huge snake, whose mouth and tail nearly meet, leaving but just room for anyone to pass in. This it prevents unless the person presenting himself for entrance is a dervish, and many dervishes go there to pray. Inside there is a well, and those who enter are provided ("min Allah") for three days with food, three times a day, but on the fourth they must go. A lion is chained up by the neck inside the kubr.

The birkeh outside is always full of water, but its shores are inhabited by snakes, who spit poison into the pool so that nothing can drink there. But at evening comes the ariel (a fabulous antelope), who strikes the water with his horns, and by so doing makes it sweet. Then all the beasts and birds of the desert follow him, and drink. The Sheykh of the Montefyk is bound to send camels and guides with all dervishes who come to him at Suk-es-Shiôkh to make the pilgrimage to Refay. The boys did not say that they had themselves seen the place.

We are not on the high road now, having left it some miles to the right, and our march to-day has been mostly through Nefûd. The same swarms of locusts everywhere, and the same attendant flocks of birds, especially of fine black buzzards, one of which Abdallah was very anxious to secure if possible, as he says the wing bones are like ivory, and are used for inlaying the stocks of guns and stems of pipes. But he had no success, though he fired several times. Wilfrid was more fortunate, however, in getting what we value more, a bustard, and the very best bird we ever ate. Though they are common enough here, it is seldom that they come within shot, but this one was frightened by the hawk, and came right overhead.

About noon, we came to a solitary building, standing in the middle of the Nefûd, called Kasr Torba. It is square, with walls twenty feet high, and has a tower at each corner. It is garrisoned by four men, soldiers of Ibn Rashid's, who surlily refused us admittance, and threatened to fire on us if we drew water from the well outside. For a moment we thought of storming the place, which I believe we could have done without much difficulty, as the door was very rotten and we were all very angry and thirsty, but second thoughts are generally accepted as best in Arabia, and on consideration, we pocketed the affront and went on.

Soon afterwards, we overtook a young man and his mother, travelling with three delúls in our direction. They were on the look-out, they said, for their own people, who were somewhere in the Nefûd, they didn't quite know where. There are no tracks anywhere, however, and they have stopped for the night with us. Very nice people, the young fellow attentive and kind to his mother, making her a shelter under a bush with the camel saddles. They are Shammar, and have been on business to Haîl.

February 12—Our disappointment about water yesterday, has forced us back on to the Haj road and the wells of Khuddra, thirteen or fourteen miles east of last night's camp. We had, however, some sport on our way. First, a hare was started and the falcon flown. The Nefûd is so covered with bushes, that without the assistance of the bird the dogs could have had no chance, for it was only by watching the hawk's flight that they were able to keep on the hare's track. It was a pretty sight, the bird above doubling as the hare doubled, and the three dogs below following with their noses in the air. We made the best of our way after them, but the sand being very deep they were soon out of sight. Suddenly we came to the edge of the Nefûd, and there, a few hundred yards from the foot of the last sand-bank, we saw the falcon and the greyhounds all sitting in a circle on the ground, watching a large hole into which the hare had just bolted. The four pursuers looked so puzzled and foolish, that in spite of the annoyance of losing the game, we could not help laughing. Hares in the desert always go to ground. Mohammed and Abdallah and Awwad were keen for digging out this one, and they all worked away like navvies for more than half an hour, till they were up to their shoulders in the sandy earth (here firm ground), but it was in vain, the hole was big enough for a hyæna, and reached down into the rock below. Further on, however, we had better luck, and having run another hare to ground, pulled out not only it, but a little silver grey fox, where they were both crouched together. I do not think the hares ever dig holes, but they make use of any they can find when pressed. We also coursed some gazelles.

There are fourteen wells at Khuddra, mere holes in the ground, without parapet or anything to mark their position, and as we drew near, we were rather alarmed at finding them occupied by a large party of Bedouins. It looked like a ghazú [an attack], for there were as many men as camels, thirty or forty of them with spears; and the camels wore shedads [a flat seat used when camels went into battle] instead of pack saddles. They did not, however, molest us, though their looks were far from agreeable. They told us they were Dafir waiting like the rest for the Haj; that their Sheykh, Ibn Sueyti, was still two days' march to the eastwards, beyond Lina, which is another group of wells something like these; and they added, that they had heard of us and of our presents to the Emir, the rifle which fired twelve shots, and the rest. It is extraordinary how news travels in the desert. I noticed that Mohammed when questioned by them, said that he was from Mosul, and he explained afterwards that the Tudmur people had an old standing blood feud with the Dafir in consequence of some ghazú made long before his time, in which twenty of the latter were killed. This has decided us not to pay Ibn Sueyti the visit we had intended. It appears that there has been a battle lately between the Dafir and the Amarrat

(Anazeh), in which a member of the Ibn Haddal family was killed. This proves that the Anazeh ghazús sometimes come as far south as the Nefûd. These wells are seventy feet deep, and the water when first drawn smells of rotten eggs; but the smell goes off on exposure to the air.

The zodiacal light is very bright this evening; it is brightest about two hours after sunset, but though I have often looked out for it, I have never seen it in the morning before sunrise. It is a very remarkable and beautiful phenomenon, seen only, I believe, in Arabia. It is a cone of light extending from the horizon half-way to the zenith, and is rather brighter than the Milky Way.

February 13—We have travelled quite twenty-four miles today, having had nothing to distract our attention from the road, and have reached the first of the reservoirs of Zobeydeh.

To my surprise this, instead of being on low ground, is as it were on the top of a hill. At least, we had to ascend quite two hundred feet to get to it, though there was higher ground beyond. It is built across a narrow wady of massive concrete, six feet thick, and is nearly square, eighty yards by fifty. The inside descends in steps for the convenience of those who come for water, but a great rent in the masonry has let most of this out, and now there is only a small mud-hole full of filthy water in the centre. We found some Arabs there with their camels, who went away when they saw us, but we sent after them to make inquiries, and learnt that they were Beni Wáhari, a new artificial compound tribe of Sherârat, Shammar and others, made up by Ibn Rashid with a slave of his own for their Sheykh. They are employed in taking care of camels and mares for the Emir. They talk of eight days' journey now to Meshhed Ali, but Wilfrid says it cannot be less than fifteen or sixteen. [After two or more weeks of more or less uneventful travel, the Blunts reached their destination safely.]

PART III
The Far East

11

IDA PFEIFFER
Travelling Through China

FROM
A Lady's Voyage Round the World (1852)

Ida Laura Pfeiffer was born in Vienna about 1797, the lone daughter among seven children of a wealthy merchant named Reyer. According to her son's account, she grew up in tomboy fashion (no dresses until she was thirteen), her father cultivating in her the qualities of "courage, resolution, and contempt of danger" through a Spartan upbringing and a rather eccentric course of home education.

In 1806, Mr. Reyer died, leaving behind an eligible daughter and a considerable fortune. Pressed by her mother to marry, Ida accepted a proposal from one Dr. Pfeiffer, an elderly lawyer from Lemberg. The relationship was cordial, but in 1835, after fifteen years together, she moved with their two sons to Vienna (he remained in Lemberg). Once they were secure in their professions, she felt free to carry out her childhood dream of travel to exotic lands.

She decided to travel alone. In 1842, she embarked upon her first venture, a trip to the Middle East and Italy. She carefully kept a diary, which became a book, Journey of a Viennese Lady to the Holy Land *(1843).*

In 1845, she visited the geysers and hot springs of Iceland and wrote Voyage to the Island of Iceland *(1847). Money from the sale of the book led to a more ambitious adventure: In 1846, she left Hamburg and sailed around the world, travelling en route through primitive parts of South America, China, India, Iraq, Iran, and Russia. Her journey up the Pearl River in China, described in this selection, was regarded as a daring exploit for a single woman, no less perilous than her expedition across Mesopotamia and Persia. The book based on her journey,* A

Lady's Voyage Round the World *(1852)*, *brought her name before appreciative English readers.*

In 1851, this indefatigable woman undertook a second globe girdling, exploring this time the country of the cannibalistic Battas of Sumatra, who had never before permitted a European to come among them. From there she sailed to California, where she joined the gold miners and slept in the wigwams of the Yuba Indians before returning in 1855 to Vienna.

In the following year, she published My Second Journey Round the World. *Before she had finished cataloguing the biological specimens and ethnographical objects she had brought back with her, she had conceived a plan to explore the island of Madagascar. Despite the representations of Alexander von Humboldt, she could not be dissuaded from risking her health again. This time she was unlucky: She contracted Madagascar fever, and after a prolonged illness, died in the home of her brother in Vienna in 1860.* The Last Travels of Ida Pfeiffer *(1861) is a record of that journey, with an autobiographical memoir by the author and a biographical epilogue by her son Oscar.*

Mrs. Pfeiffer was elected to the Geographical Society of Berlin, and of Paris, but was refused the honor by the London organization on the grounds that she was a woman. Her translator, Mrs. Percy Sinnett, paid her a tribute that rings true today: She was a woman who "emancipated herself in earnest—not from the fashions of gowns and petticoats, but from indolence, and vanity, and fear."

A year ago I should have little thought there was any chance of my becoming acquainted with this remarkable country, not merely from books but in my proper person; that the shaven heads and long tails and cunning little eyes, as we see them in pictures and on tea-chests, would have presented themselves in living forms before me. But scarcely was our anchor dropped before several Chinese already stood upon our deck, while numbers of others appeared in boats surrounding us, and displaying in pretty order fruits, pastry, and various kinds of beautiful works, so that the space round the ship looked like a fair. Some among them lauded in broken English the treasures they had brought, but after all they got but little for their trouble, for our crew bought only fruit and cigars.

Captain Jurianse now hired a boat and we rowed ashore, but on landing the first thing we had to do was to pay half a Spanish dollar each to a mandarin. I heard that this abuse was shortly after abolished. We had to go to one of the Portuguese houses of business, and in doing so passed through a great part of the town; for Europeans, women as well as men, can now go about freely here, without as in other Chinese towns being exposed to the danger of being stoned. In those streets which are exclusively inhabited by Chinese, things looked very lively and bustling. The men were sitting in groups playing dominoes in the streets, and in the shops of the locksmiths, tailors, shoemakers, &c., there was working, gossiping, gambling, and dancing going on at once. I was greatly amused at the Chinese mode of eating with two little sticks, which they manage with great adroitness; it is only in eating rice that they seem to labor under difficulties, as it will not hold together. The plan is therefore to bring the vessel containing it as near as possible to the mouth, which is held in readiness wide open, and then dexterously shove a heap into the expectant aperture. In performing this operation it happens of course often that a portion falls back again into the dish, but that is of no consequence; with fluid food they make use of China spoons. My stay at Macao proved to be an exceedingly short one, for as our captain found there was no chance of doing any business there, he resolved to go to sea the next day, but he kindly offered to take me with him as a guest. His invitation was so much the more welcome to me, as I had not a single letter of introduction to Macao, and the opportunities of going to Hong Kong are not at all frequent.

The distance from Macao to Hong Kong is about sixty leagues, and as you are continually passing bays, gulfs, and groups of islands, the voyage is varied and interesting.

The English obtained the island of Hong Kong from the Chinese in 1842, and founded upon it the seaport of Victoria, which already contains many palace-like buildings of freestone. Merchants receive land gratis from the government, on condition of building upon it, and many, on the first occupation of the island, began buildings on a grand scale, which they would now gladly sell for half their cost price, since trade has been far less profitable than was expected; nay, in some instances, they would be willing to give up their land and the foundations laid upon it, merely to be released from the necessity of completing the buildings. The situation of Victoria is not very pleasing, as it is surrounded by naked hills; it has a decidedly European aspect, so that if it were not for the Chinese workmen and small dealers in the streets and booths, you could hardly believe yourself on Chinese ground. No Chinese woman was to be seen in the streets, so that I was not sure it might not be unsafe for me to wander about as I did. I never experienced, however, the smallest insult, and even the curiosity of the people was by no means troublesome.

. . . It happened after a few days that an opportunity presented itself for me to go to Canton, but in a Chinese junk. Mr. Pustan, a merchant of Victoria, who had received me in a very friendly manner, strongly dissuaded me from trusting myself without any protection to the Chinese, and thought I should either hire a boat for myself, or get a place in the steamer; but for my limited means these plans were too expensive, as neither would have cost less than twelve dollars, while the price on the junk was only three. The appearance and manner of the Chinese, too, was not such as to occasion me any fear, so I put my pistols in order, and went quietly on board the junk. It was raining violently, and just getting dark, and I therefore went down into the cabin to amuse myself by looking at my Chinese fellow-voyagers. The company was certainly not select, but not at all indecorous in behavior, so that I had no fear of remaining among them; some were playing at dominoes, and others on a sort of mandolin with three strings, which uttered most dismal music, and nearly all were smoking and gossiping, and drinking tea without sugar, out of little cups, which were offered to me from all sides: no Chinese, either rich or poor, drinks either water, or anything stronger, but constantly unsugared weak tea.

I did not go into my cabin till rather a late hour, and then I made the unpleasing discovery that it was not water-tight, and that the rain was coming in. Immediately, however, that the captain of the junk was made aware of this, he found me another place, in company with two Chinese women, who, as well as the men, were smoking tobacco, and out of pipes not larger than thimbles, which required to be stuffed afresh every four or five whiffs. My neighbors soon remarked that I had no *head-stool,* and they would not desist from their entreaties till I accepted one from them. These stools, made of bamboo or strong pasteboard, and about eight inches high, are made use of instead of pillows, and are really more comfortable than might be supposed.

Early in the morning I hastened on deck to see the entrance into the mouth of the Yang-Tsi Kiang (also called the Tiger River), but we were already so far up that there was no more mouth to be seen; I saw it, however, on my return: it is one of the largest rivers of China; and at a short distance from its entrance into the sea it has a breadth of nearly eight miles, but at the actual mouth it is so hemmed in by rocks, that it loses half its breadth. The country is beautiful, and some fortifications on the summit of a hill give it a very romantic effect. At Hoo-man, or Whampoa, the stream divides into several arms, of which the one leading to Canton is called the Pearl river, and here ships drawing much water have to anchor. Along the banks of the Pearl river extend immense rice plantations, intermingled with fruit-trees and bananas: the latter often form beautiful arcades; but they are planted more for utility than ornament, as they consolidate the ground, and prevent its being entirely washed away by the abundant irrigation required for the rice. Pretty country-houses, in the true Chinese style, with fantastic jagged and peaked roofs, and colored tiles, come into view from time to time, lying in the shade of groups of trees; and various kinds of pagodas, from three to nine stories high, rise on small hills near the villages, and draw attention from a great distance. There were many fortifications, but they looked more like great unroofed houses than any thing else.

As you advance toward Canton, the villages begin to follow each other very closely; but they have a miserable appearance, and are mostly built on stakes close on the river, and lying before them are numerous boats, many of them also serving as dwellings. The river now becomes more and more animated, and covered with vessels of all sizes and of the strangest forms. There were junks, the back part of which rose two stories above the water, and which looked like houses with lofty windows and galleries, and covered by a roof; they are often of immense size, and several thousand tuns burthen. Then came the Chinese ships of war, flat, broad, and long, and carrying twenty or thirty guns: mandarins' boats, with their painted doors and windows, carved galleries, and colored silk flags; and, best of all, the flower-boats decorated with wreaths and garlands, and pretty arabesques. The interior of these flower-boats consists of a saloon and several cabinets, furnished with looking-glasses, silk hangings, glass lustres, and colored lanterns, between which are suspended ornamental baskets filled with fresh flowers, so that they have quite a fairy-land aspect. The flower-boats remain at anchor night and day, and serve for places of entertainment; plays are acted in them, and dancing and conjuring tricks performed. Women of good character are never to be seen in them; the entrance of Europeans is not exactly prohibited, but they would not be likely to receive a very flattering reception, should they make their appearance, and might even meet with serious ill-treatment. Besides all these, there were thousands of shampans, some anchored, some cruising, and darting about; fishermen casting their nets; people of all ages bathing and swimming; and children romping and tumbling about in the boats, so that one dreaded every moment to see them fall overboard: but careful parents tie the little ones to hollow gourds, or bladders filled with air, so that if they fall into the water they may not sink. All these varied occupations, this unwearied life and activity, affords such picturesque effects as can hardly be conceived without being witnessed.

Since these few years past, the entrance into, and residence in the factories of Canton has been permitted to European women, so that I did not feel much hesitation in landing from the junk. I required consideration, however, by what means I was to reach the abode of Mr. Agassiz,[1] to whom I was recommended. I could, as yet, speak no Chinese word, and had to make myself understood by signs; I succeeded, however, in making my captain comprehend that I had no money with me, but that if he would take me to the factory, I would pay him, and he agreed to accompany me thither.

When Mr. Agassiz saw me come in in this unceremonious manner, and heard the mode of my journey, and of my having walked from the junk to his house, he appeared excessively surprised; and it was then that I first learned how much risk I

---

[1] Editor's note: This is the famous Louis Agassiz, the Swiss-American zoologist who was in China on one of his many scientific expeditions.

had run in venturing into the streets of Canton, in company only with a Chinese: I was told I might regard it as quite a peculiar piece of good fortune that I had not been grossly insulted, and even stoned by the populace, and in such a case my Chinese escort would infallibly have taken to flight, and left me to my fate.

I had certainly remarked that on my way from the ship to the factory, that old and young had called and hooted after me, and pointed their fingers,—that the people had run out of the shops, and that by degrees we had quite a procession following us. But there was nothing to be done but to put a good face on the matter, and I therefore marched fearlessly on; no harm happened to me. Since the last war with the English, the hatred against Europeans has been on the increase, and it has been embittered against the women by a Chinese prophecy, which declares that a woman shall one day conquer the Celestial Empire. I feared, therefore, that it would be to little purpose for me to remain in Canton, and was beginning to consider whether I might not do better to go to the north of China, where the people and the nobles are easier of access; but I fortunately became acquainted with a German, a Mr. Von Carlovitz, who had passed some years in Canton, and who offered to become my Mentor, if I would only wait with patience for the arrival of the European post, which was expected in a few days: during this period the minds of merchants are so excited, that they have not leisure for any other thought than that of their correspondence. I had to wait eight days—until the steamer arrived and again departed—but the reception I met with was so very kind and cordial, that the time did not appear at all long: especially as I had thus an opportunity of studying a little the mode of life of the European residents.

Very few Europeans bring their families to China, and fewer still to Canton, where women and children live almost as prisoners, and can at the utmost only leave the house in a closed litter. Besides this, every thing is so excessively dear that you might live as cheaply in London. An apartment of six rooms and a kitchen costs from seven to eight hundred dollars. Servants require from four to eight dollars a month, and female servants nine or ten, for no Chinese woman will serve a European without being very highly paid for it. Since, too, custom requires a separate servant for every different kind of work, you have to keep a great number.

A family of not more than four persons will need twelve or more. In the first place, every member of the family must have one servant exclusively to himself,—then there must be cooks, waiting-women, nurses, and coolies for the commoner kinds of work, such as cleansing rooms, and carrying wood and water; and with all this crowd you are badly served, for if one goes out, and you happen to want his particular kind of service, you must wait till he comes back, for no other will supply his place.

The daily manner of life of the Europeans settled here is the following. A cup of tea is taken immediately after rising, then a cold bath. About nine follows the more substantial breakfast, consisting of fried cutlets, cold roast meat, eggs, bread and butter, and tea. Every one then departs to his employment till dinner, which is generally at four o'clock. The general dishes are turtle soup, highly-seasoned curries, roast meat, ragouts, and pastry. All the dishes, curry and rice excepted, are dressed in the English mode by Chinese cooks. Cheese and fruit are taken after dinner, pine-apples, mangoes, *long-yen,* and *lytschi:* which latter fruit the Chinese esteem as the most delicious in the world; it is about the size of a nut, has a reddish-brown, rough shell, very white and tender pulp, and a black kernel. The *long-yen* is something like it, but rather smaller, and somewhat watery in flavor; I did not think either very good. The pine-apples are larger than those reared in European forcing-houses, but inferior I thought to them in sweetness and aroma.

The liquors drank are Portuguese wine, and English beer. Ice broken into small pieces, and wrapped in a napkin, is offered with both; though this is rather an expensive article, as it is brought from America. In the evening tea is again drank.

A large punka is kept constantly going during the meals by a cord carried through the room, like a bell-wire, by means of which a servant works the punka in an ante or lower room.

Living is very dear for Europeans—for the cost of a small establishment can not be reckoned at less than 6,000 dollars yearly—a large sum considering what is got for it; neither carriages nor horses are kept; there are no public amusements; the solitary recreation of many gentlemen consists in a boat, for which they pay seven dollars a month, or in a small pleasure-garden laid out by the Europeans of Canton, where they walk occasionally of an evening. It lies opposite the factory, surrounded by a wall on three sides, the fourth is washed by the Pearl river. The Chinese, on the other hand, live at very small expense; a man can subsist very well on 60 cash a day—(1,200 cash make a dollar). He can hire a boat for half a dollar a day, which will bring him in enough for a family of from six to nine persons to live on. It must be confessed however, that the Chinese are not fastidious in the matter of eating; they devour dogs, rats, and mice, the blood of every animal, the entrails of birds; and even, I have been told, silk-worms, grubs, and animals that have died a natural death; but rice is their chief food, and serves them not only as a dish, but as bread. It is very cheap, from one and three fourths to two and a half dollars the pikul, of 125 pounds.

The dress of both sexes, of the lower classes, consists of wide trowsers and a long upper robe, generally disgustingly dirty; indeed a Chinese is no friend to washing either his garments or his person, and generally wears his trowsers till they fall to pieces. The upper robe is made of silk or nankeen, dark blue, brown, or black. In the colder season, they put one summer garment over another, and bind them together with a girdle.

As great pride is taken in the length and thickness of the tail of hair, it is often increased by false or black silk interwoven. When they are at work, the tail is coiled round the neck, but it must always be let down on entering a room, as it is contrary to all Chinese notions of propriety to appear with it twisted up. The women comb their hair back from their foreheads, and bind it round their heads in a very artist-like style; it must take a good deal of time to construct the edifice, but is seldom done more than once a week. Both men and women cover their heads occasionally with hats of thin bamboo, often three feet in diameter, which are admirable protectors from the sun and rain, excessively light and almost indestructible. The poorer classes go barefoot; their houses, of brick or wood, are miserable hovels, and the inside is worthy of the out—a wretched table, a few chairs, and bamboo mats, head-stools, and old coverlets form the whole furniture; a few flower-pots, however, are never wanting. The cheapest of all dwellings is a boat: one half of which is reserved for the family, and the other let out either as a ferry or excursion-boat, generally under the management of the wife. Notwithstanding the limited space, for the whole boat is scarcely twenty-five feet in length, it is usually kept extremely clean. Every nook is put to use, and place for a diminutive altar always found: all the cooking and washing for the family is done in their half of the boat, yet no disagreeable sight shocks the temporary possessor of the other half, and rarely is a whimper from the poor little ones heard. The mother steers, with her youngest child tied to her back; the elder children have often similar burdens, with which they climb and jump about without taking any heed of the unfortunate infants. I was often pained to see the head of a newly-born baby flung from side to side with every caper of its juvenile nurse, or exposed wholly unsheltered to the burning sun. One who has not seen can hardly form an idea of the poverty and privations of a boat-dwelling Chinese family.

It is exceedingly difficult, almost impossible, for a foreigner to give any very accurate information of Chinese habits and customs, but I saw all I possibly could, never missed an opportunity of mingling with the people, and carefully noted down all I saw. One morning, as I was going out, I met fifteen criminals all bearing the *Cang-gue,* or wooden yoke, in which they are led about the streets as a spectacle to the people. The *Cang-gue* consists of two large pieces of wood fitting into each other and having one to three openings, through which the head and one or both hands are drawn, according to the greatness of the crime. Such a yoke weighs from fifty to a hundred pounds, and weighs so heavily upon the back and shoulders that the poor criminal is unable to feed himself, and must wait till some compassionate person lifts the food to his mouth: such a punishment is inflicted for periods varying from a few days to several months, and in the latter case it is almost always fatal.

Another punishment, beating with a bamboo stick, if given on a tender part of the body, often causes death after the fifteenth stroke. Some of the punishments are of such hideous severity that our capital punishments of strangling or beheading seem mild in comparison: the Chinese endeavor to obtain the ends of justice by flaying alive, crushing the limbs, cutting the sinews of the feet, &c., and I was told that in certain cases criminals are sawed in two or starved to death. In the first case the poor wretch is pressed between two planks and sawed lengthways, in the second buried up to his chin in the earth and so left till death puts an end to his sufferings, or the *Cang-gue* is put on him and from day to day less and less food given him, till at last it is reduced to a single grain of rice.

The population of China consists of many and very different races, whose characteristics I am, unfortunately, unable to give, on account of the shortness of my stay in China. The people whom I saw in Canton, Hong Kong, and Macao were of middling stature; the countryman, the porter, the workman, is much sunburnt; the upper classes, generally white-skinned. The face is broad, the eyes small, oblique, far apart, the nose broad, and the mouth wide. The fingers of many I found to be extraordinarily long and thin. Aristocratic nails are generally half an inch long; one man I saw who had them above an inch in length, but only on the left hand: with this hand he was unable to lift a flat object without laying the hand flat upon it and clutching it between the fingers. Women of rank are generally inclined to corpulence, which is greatly admired in man or woman.

Although I had heard so much of the little feet of the Chinese women, the first sight of one excited my highest astonishment. The sight of these feet *in naturâ* was procured me by a missionary's wife, Madame Balt. The four smaller toes seemed to me grown into the foot; the great toe was left in its natural position. The forepart of the foot was so tightly bound with strong broad ligatures that all the growth is forced into height instead of length and breadth, and formed a thick lump at the ankle; the under part measured scarcely four inches long and an inch and a half wide. The foot is constantly bound up in white linen or silk and strong broad ribbons, and stuck in a very high-heeled shoe.

To my surprise these crippled fair ones tripped about with tolerable quickness; to be sure they waddled like geese, but they did manage to get up and down stairs without the help of a stick.

The boat-dwellers being the poorest, are the only class of Chinese who do not cultivate this peculiar species of beauty. In families of rank all the girls are condemned to it, in the lower classes only the eldest daughter. The value of a bride depends upon the smallness of her foot.

The crippling process is not begun before the completion of

the first, sometimes not till the third year: and the foot is not pressed into an iron shoe, as some have asserted, but only tightly bound with very strong ligatures.

Although the religion of the Chinese permits several wives, they are far behind the Mohammedans in their use of the privilege; the rich have seldom more than from six to twelve, and the poor are content with one.

It is well known that the seas of Canton swarm with pirates, yet nothing is ever done either to punish them or diminish their numbers, as the mandarins do not think it beneath their dignity to go shares with them. The commerce with opium is forbidden, yet so much is smuggled into the country every year that its value exceeds that of the tea exported. The merchants come to an understanding with the mandarins and public officers, a certain sum is paid for every pikul, and not unfrequently the mandarin will bring the whole cargo to land under his own flag.

It is said that an extensive establishment for coining false money is known to exist near Hong Kong, which carries on its operations quite undisturbed simply by paying tribute to the mandarins in authority. A short time ago some pirate ships ran aground near Canton and the commanders were captured. Their companions wrote to the government to free them, and threatened, in case of refusal, to set some towns on fire: every one was convinced that a sum of money had been sent with the letter, for shortly after it was announced that the pirates had escaped.

. . . I ventured upon many excursions, in which Mr. Von Carlovitz had the kindness and the patience to accompany me, and exposed himself to many dangers on my account; he bore with the greatest indifference the abuse of the mob, when they followed us and gave vent to their wrath at the boldness of the European woman; and I saw, under his kind protection, more than any woman ever saw in China before.

Our first visit was to the celebrated temple Honan, said to be one of the finest in China. This temple with its numerous subsidiary buildings and extensive gardens is surrounded by a high wall. We entered a large outer court, at the extremity of which a colossal gate led into an inner court: under the arch of this portal stand two statues of war-gods, eighteen feet high, in threatening attitudes and with frightfully distorted faces; they are to guard the entrance from evil genii. A second similar portal, under which the four heavenly kings are placed, leads to a third court, in which is the chief temple, 100 feet long, and of equal width. The flat roof, from which depend a multitude of glass lustres, lamps, artificial flowers, and colored ribbons, rests on rows of wooden pillars. The numerous statues, altars, censers, vases of flowers, candelabras, and other ornaments, reminded us involuntarily of a Catholic church.

In the foreground stand three altars, behind which are three statues, representing Buddha as the past, the present, and the future, of colossal size, and in a sitting posture. By chance a service was going on when we entered,—a kind of mass for the dead, celebrated at the charge of the mandarin for his deceased wife. Before the right and left altar stood priests, whose robes, as well as the ceremonial observance, strikingly resembled that of Roman Catholics.

Beside this chief temple there are a number of small ones, all decorated with statues of gods. The twenty-four gods of mercy and Kwanfootse, a demi-god of war, seemed to enjoy particular reverence. The former have four, six, and even eight arms. All these divinities, including Buddha himself, are made of wood gilded and painted in gaudy colors. In the Temple of Mercy we had like to have met with a disagreeable adventure; a bonze offered me and my companions a couple of wax tapers to light in honor of their god; we were about to comply as a matter of civility, when an American missionary who accompanied us, snatched them out of our hands angrily, and gave them back to the priests, declaring that our compliance would be an act of idolatry. The priest took up the affair seriously, immediately closed the door and called to his brethren, who came flocking from all sides, and abused us terribly, all the while pressing upon us in an alarming manner. With considerable difficulty we fought our way through the crowd, and got out of the temple.

When the scuffle was over, our guide led us to the house of the Sacred Swine, a handsome stone hall; but in spite of all the care bestowed upon these singular objects of reverence, their odor was so offensive that we could only approach them with compressed noses. These creatures are fed and cherished so long as they live, and are suffered to die a natural death. We saw only one pair of these fortunate grunters, and were told the number rarely exceeded three pairs. The dwelling of a bonze which we visited pleased me better than the swine-palace; there were but two rooms, a sitting and bed-room, but they were neatly and conveniently arranged. The walls of the sitting-room were ornamented with wood carving, the furniture was old and elegantly wrought, a small altar stood against the further wall, and the floor was paved with large stone slabs.

We found here an opium smoker; he lay stretched on the ground on a mat, and had beside him some tea-cups, some fruit, a small lamp, and several pipes, the heads of which were smaller than thimbles; out of one he was imbibing the intoxicating vapor. I was told that there were persons who smoke from twenty to thirty grains a day. As he had not yet reached the unconscious state, he dragged himself up with some difficulty and laid his pipe aside; his eyes were fixed and vacant, his face deadly pale—it was a depressing and pitiable spectacle. In conclusion, we were taken into the garden, where the bodies of the bonzes are burnt after death—a particular distinction, other persons being simply buried. A plain mausoleum about thirty feet square, and a few small private monuments, is all there is to be seen; and neither were handsome. The large one contained the bones of the consumed bodies; in the smaller, rich Chinese were buried, whose friends must pay enormously for the honor of such a burial-place. At a little distance stands a tower, eighteen feet high, and about eight in diameter, in the floor of which is a small hollow where the fire is kindled; over the hollow stands an arm-chair, wherein the deceased bonze is placed in full costume. Wood and dry twigs are then heaped round, kindled, and the door fast closed. After some hours it is re-opened, the ashes scattered round the tower, and the bones laid aside till the mausoleum is opened, which is only done once a year.

Our second excursion was to the Halfway Pagoda, so called by the English, because it is situated halfway between Canton and Whampoa. We went thither by the Pearl river. The pagoda stands on a little eminence in the midst of extensive rice-fields, has nine stories, and a height of 170 feet. The circumference is not great, and the size all the way up being nearly the same, it has the appearance of a tower. It was formerly one of the most celebrated in China, but has been long disused: the interior was quite empty, and no intermediate ceiling prevented the eye from losing itself at the summit of the building. On the outside, narrow balconies, without any kind of balustrade, and attainable by excessively steep stairs run round each story. As these projecting balconies are formed of colored tiles, and floored with brightly painted clay, the effect is very pretty. The edges of the tiles arranged obliquely in rows, with each edge raised about four inches above the next, have, at a distance, the effect of fret work; and from the beauty of its color, and fineness of the clay made use of, they might easily be mistaken for porcelain.

While we were looking at the pagoda the people of the village gathered about us, and as they seemed tolerably quiet, we ventured upon a visit to the village itself. The houses, or rather huts, were built of a kind of brick, with flat roofs, but had nothing peculiar in their construction. There was no interior ceiling; the only covering was the roof of the house, the floor of beaten clay, and the partition wall chiefly composed of bamboo matting; there was very little furniture, and that little exceedingly dirty. In the midst of the village stood some small temples, with a few dim lamps burning before the chief idol.

The most remarkable thing about this village was the enormous number of domestic birds in and about the houses. It really required considerable care to avoid treading on the creatures as they walked; they are artificially hatched, as in Egypt. As we were leaving the village, we saw two shampans approach the shore, out of which leaped a number of brown, half naked, and mostly armed men, who rapidly traversing the rice-fields, came straight toward our party. We took them for pirates, and awaited their approach with some anxiety: if they meant mischief, we were lost; for here, at a distance from Canton, and surrounded by Chinese, who would unquestionably have lent them a helping hand, it would be easy to dispatch us, if they were so inclined.

But the leader, accosting us in broken English, announced himself as the captain of a Siamese ship-of-war. He said that he had brought over the Governor of Bankok, who was going thence to Pekin, and by degrees we recovered from our fright, so far as even to accept the captain's invitation to go on board his ship. He took us into his boat, which he steered himself, and did the honors of his vessel in person. There was nothing very attractive in it: the crew were a rude, wild-looking set, and all alike so ragged and dirty, that it was impossible to distinguish officers from men. The ship mounted twelve guns; the crew was sixty-eight in number. The captain entertained us with English beer and Portuguese wine; and it was late in the evening when we reached home.

The farthest excursion it is permitted to make from Canton extends to about eighty miles up the Pearl river. Mr. Agassiz was so good as to procure me this pleasure. He hired a handsome boat, furnished it amply with provisions, and requested a missionary, who had made the voyage several times, to accompany me and Mr. Von Carlovitz. A missionary is the best escort one can have in China; for they speak the language of the country, become acquainted with the people, and, within certain limits, go about in tolerable freedom and security.

In this excursion I had an opportunity of observing the manner in which the missionaries manage their peculiar business. The gentleman who had been so obliging as to accompany us, made use of this voyage to scatter some of the good seed. He had packed five hundred tracts in our boat, and as often as another boat approached ours, which happened pretty frequently, he leaned as far over the side as he could, held up his hand, furnished with half a dozen tracts, and shouted and gesticulated for the people to come nearer and receive the prize. If they did not comply with the invitation, we rowed close to them, the missionary showered down his tracts by dozens, and rejoiced in anticipation at the good that was to result from this proceeding. When we reached a village the business was done on a yet more liberal scale: the servant was laden with a whole pack of tracts; in a few minutes we were surrounded by curious lookers-on, and as quickly the cargo was discharged among them.

Every Chinese took what was offered—it cost him nothing; and if he could not read (the tracts were written in the Chinese language), he had at least a stock of paper. Our friend returned home glowing with satisfaction. He had distributed 500 copies of his book among the Chinese! What delightful intelligence for the Missionary Society! what a splendid announcement for the religious periodicals!

My wish to take a walk round the walls of Canton, an attempt no woman had yet ever ventured to make, was gratified by the kindness of the missionary; but under the condition that I should put on male attire. We passed through a number of narrow streets paved with broad stones. In every house we saw in some niche a small altar, from one to two feet high, before which lamps were burning: the quantity of oil wasted in this way must be enormous. By degrees the shops were opened, which resembled pretty little booths, as the front wall was entirely removed. The goods were contained partly in open chests, and partly displayed on tables, behind which the owners sat at work. In one corner a small flight of steps led to the upper part of the house.

As in the Turkish towns, each trade has a street to itself, the dealers in glass in one street, the silk merchants in another, &c.: the physicians, who are also the druggists, have their street apart also. Between the houses we saw many little temples, of which, however, the gods contented themselves with the ground floor, the upper ones being occupied by ordinary mortals.

The life and movement in the streets were very great, especially in those where provisions were sold. Women and girls of the lower class were walking about, making their purchases as in Europe. They were all unveiled, and many waddled like geese; for, as I have before observed, the custom of crippling some of the women prevails in all classes. The throng was greatly increased by the number of porters carrying huge baskets laden with provisions on their shoulders, and shouting continually, now in praise of their wares, now bidding people get out of their way; sometimes the wary will be stopped by the sedans of the wealthier inhabitants, which take up the whole width of the streets.

The care with which the Chinese cultivate every spot of earth is well known; as they have few cattle it follows that they have little manure, and hence the extreme care with which they seek for the article furnished by any and every living creature. The most disagreeable incident of the streets is meeting, as you do in every street—I had almost said at every step—persons bearing vessels full of all sorts of ordure.

All these little streets were built along the wall; and all doors, closed in the evening, lead into the interior of the city which no foreigner dare profane.

Some few sailors and others, in their rambles about the wall have passed through these doors without knowing whither they were going, till made aware of their mistake by a shower of stones.

After we had walked at least some miles, forcing our way through these close alleys, we emerged again into the open air and from a small elevation near the wall gained a tolerable view over the town. The wall is about sixty feet high, in many places overgrown with grass, bushes, and parasite plants. The town looked, from the hill, a confused mass of little houses, with a few trees growing among them, for we could discern no wide streets or squares, nor any building of architectural importance, with the exception of one pagoda of five stories.

The road led us over a hilly but fertile country, and well cultivated fields and meadows. Many of these hills serve as cemeteries, and are covered with mounds, against which were laid gravestones about two feet high: some had inscriptions, and there were also family vaults excavated in the hillside, and marked out by masonry in the form of a horse-shoe.

The Chinese do not bury all their dead. The coffins are sometimes placed on wooden benches, two feet in height, within small stone buildings, consisting of two side walls and a roof, the other two sides being left open. The coffins are hollowed trunks of trees, and very massive.

All the hamlets we passed through were populous, but the inhabitants looked very poor and very dirty. In passing through some of the streets we were obliged to hold our noses, and would willingly have closed our eyes also, so nauseous were the disgusting sights of sick people, whose bodies were covered with eruptions, boils, and tumors.

When we were nearly at the end of our walk we met a funeral procession. Its approach was announced by horrible discordant sounds, intended for music; and we had hardly time to get out of the way when the train came by, in as much haste as if they had been running away from something. First ran the worthy musicians, then followed the mourners, then two empty sedan chairs, and lastly came the coffin,—a trunk of a tree hollowed,—the priests, and a crowd of idlers.

The high-priest wore a sort of white fool's cap, with three points; the mourners, all men, had each a white cloth, either wrapped round the head or the arm,—white being the mourning color in China.

I was fortunate enough to see some of the summer palaces and gardens of the upper classes; that of the mandarin Hauquau was the handsomest. The house was tolerably large, with very broad stately terraces: the windows were turned toward the interior, and the roof like those of Europe, except that it was somewhat flatter. The projecting roofs, with zigzag edges and points, with the numerous little bells and painted tiles and bricks, are used for pagodas and summer pavilions, but not for dwelling-houses. On the principal door two figures of gods were painted, to guard the entrance from evil spirits.

The forepart of the house contained several reception rooms, with one side entirely open to the garden on the ground floor; in winter these sides are hung with matting; the upper one opened on a magnificent terrace, adorned with flowers, and commanding a splendid view of the thronged river, the country around, and the suburbs of Canton.

As we had been so fortunate as to reach the house without being stoned, we took courage to visit the extensive pleasure-grounds belonging to the mandarin, situated about three miles from the house, on a canal connected with the Pearl river. We had scarcely entered the canal, however, than our boatmen attempted to turn back, for they saw a mandarin boat lying within with all its flags flying—a sign that the mandarin himself was on board; and they were afraid of incurring punishment from him, or being stoned by the people, if they rowed past with Europeans. However, we would not hear of such a thing, but boldly passed the mandarin's boat, landed, and pursued our way on foot. In a few minutes we had a crowd after us, and the people began to push the children against us, in order to irritate us. But we armed ourselves with patience, quietly walked on, and succeeded in reaching the gardens, the gate of which was instantly closed behind us.

The gardens were in perfect order, but laid out with very little taste. On all sides, pavilions, kiosks, and bridges were to be seen; and every path and corner was encumbered with pots of all sizes, containing flowers and dwarfed fruit-trees of various kinds.

The Chinese are masters in the art of crippling trees, which they prefer thus treated to the finest in a state of nature. The taste that called forth these Lilliputian woods is not be admired; but the quantity and beauty of the fruit their miniature branches bore was really something remarkable. Among these dwarfs we found playthings of another kind: plants tortured into the shapes of fish, birds, ships, pagodas, &c., the eyes of the animals being represented by eggs stuck in their heads, with a black spot in the middle.

There was no want either, of rock-work, singly and in masses, all crowded with figures of birds, beasts, and flower-pots, which can be removed at pleasure, and formed into different groups— a favorite amusement of the Chinese ladies; another, an equal favorite with both sexes, is flying kites, which they divert themselves with for hours together: and the garden of every Chinese of rank contains one or more open spaces for the pursuit of this pastime.

12

ISABELLA BIRD

Among the Aino

FROM
*Unbeaten Tracks in Japan: An Account of
Travels on Horseback in the Interior* (1880)

Isabella Lucy Bird, the daughter of a devout Church of England clergyman, was born in 1831. She travelled within the British Isles as a child and read most of the published accounts about travels in America and Asia before she herself undertook the journeys that resulted in a series of popular books.

In 1856, she completed The Englishwoman in America, *a vivid and forceful narrative describing her journey across the then still-raw continent. After the Civil War, she returned to America and wrote* A Lady's Life in the Rocky Mountains *(1879). Two years later, she married an Edinburgh physician, John Bishop, but the marriage lasted only the five remaining years of his life. Her subsequent travels, like those in America, were on her own. Her reputation (though not her popularity) was based on her interests in Asia rather than in North America, and it was such books as* Unbeaten Tracks in Japan *(two volumes, 1880),* The Golden Chersonese *(1883),* Journeys in Persia and Kurdistan *(two volumes, 1891),* Among the Tibetans *(1894),* Korea and Her Neighbors *(1898),* The Yangtze Valley and Beyond *(1899), and* Chinese Pictures *(1900) that justified her election as the first woman Fellow of the Royal Geographical Society. Before her death in 1904, she founded several hospitals in China and Korea.*

The following selection is taken from what is perhaps her most readable book: Unbeaten Tracks in Japan. *It is about her sojourn among the "hairy Ainus" (or Ainos), the aboriginal people of Japan who had been forced by invaders from Asia to retreat to the islands of Hokkaido* and Sahkalin. She was, insofar as we know, the first European woman to face the hazards of such a journey alone.

According to historian Andrew Hill Clark, Isabella Bird was both intellectually and socially a true snob (and this judgment may seem borne out by the often pungent, even jarring observations she makes on American and Ainu manners and customs). Yet this excerpt proves that her mental acuity was substantial. The sharpness of her views, in the words of Clark, "gives us a superb limning of dozens of characters," adding piquancy to her account.

AINO HUT, BIRATORI, *August 23*—I am in the lonely Aino land, and I think that the most interesting of my travelling experiences has been the living for three days and two nights in an Aino hut, and seeing and sharing the daily life of complete savages, who go on with their ordinary occupations just as if I were not among them. I found yesterday a most fatiguing and over-exciting day, as everything was new and interesting, even the extracting from men who have few if any ideas in common with me, all I could extract concerning their religion and customs, and that through an interpreter.

I have reserved all I have to say about the Ainos till I had been actually among them, and I hope you will have patience to read to the end. Ito is very greedy and self-indulgent, and whimpered very much about coming to Biratori at all,—one would have thought he was going to the stake. He actually borrowed for himself a sleeping-mat and *futons,* and has brought a chicken, onions, potatoes, French beans, Japanese sauce, tea, rice, a kettle, a stew-pan, and a rice-pan, while I contented myself with a cold fowl and potatoes.

We took three horses and a mounted Aino guide, and found a beaten track the whole way. It turns into the forest at once on leaving Sarufuto, and goes through forest the entire distance, with an abundance of reedy grass higher than my hat on horseback along it, and as it is only twelve inches broad and much overgrown, the horses were constantly pushing through leafage soaking from a night's rain, and I was soon wet up to my shoulders. The forest trees are almost solely the *Ailanthus glandulosus* and the *Zelkowa keaki,* often matted together with a white-flowered trailer of the Hydrangea genus. The undergrowth is simply hideous, consisting mainly of coarse reedy grass, monstrous docks, the large-leaved *Polygonum cuspidatum,* several umbelliferous plants and a "ragweed" which, like most of its gawky fellows, grows from five to six feet high. The forest is dark and very silent, threaded by this narrow path, and by others as narrow, made by the hunters in search of game. The "main road" sometimes plunges into deep bogs, at others is roughly corduroyed by the roots of trees, and frequently hangs over the edge of abrupt and much-worn declivities, in going up one of which the baggage-horse rolled down a bank fully thirty feet high, and nearly all the tea was lost. At another the guide's pack-saddle lost its balance, and man, horse, and saddle went over the slope, pots, pans, and packages flying after them. At another time my horse sank up to his chest in a very bad bog, and as he was totally unable to extricate himself, I was obliged to scramble upon his neck and jump to *terra firma* over his ears.

There is something very gloomy in the solitude of this silent land, with its beast-haunted forests, its great patches of pasture, the resort of wild animals which haunt the lower regions in search of food when the snow drives them down from the mountains, and its narrow track, indicating the single file in which the savages of the interior walk with their bare, noiseless feet. Reaching the Sarufutogawa, a river with a treacherous bottom, in which Mr. Von Siebold [a German explorer who had lived among the Ainos the year before] and his horse came to grief, I hailed an Aino boy, who took me up the stream in a "dug-out," and after that we passed through Biroka, Saruba, and Mina, all purely Aino villages, situated among small patches of millet, tobacco, and pumpkins, so choked with weeds that it was doubtful whether they were crops. I was much surprised with the extreme neatness and cleanliness outside the houses; "model villages" they are in these respects, with no litter lying in sight anywhere, nothing indeed but dog troughs, hollowed out of logs, like "dug-outs," for the numerous yellow dogs, which are a feature of Aino life. There are neither puddles nor heaps, but the houses, all trim and in good repair, rise clean out of the sandy soil.

Biratori, the largest of the Aino settlements in this region, is very prettily situated among forests and mountains, on rising ground, with a very sinuous river winding at its feet and a wooded height above. A lonelier place could scarcely be found. As we passed among the houses the yellow dogs barked, the women looked shy and smiled, and the men made their graceful salutation. We stopped at the chief's house, where, of course, we were unexpected guests; but Shinondi, his nephew, and two other men came out, saluted us, and with most hospitable intent helped Ito to unload the horses. Indeed their eager hospitality created quite a commotion, one running hither and the other thither in their anxiety to welcome a stranger. It is a large house, the room being 35 by 25, and the roof 20 feet high; but you enter by an ante-chamber, in which are kept the millet-mill and other articles. There is a doorway in this, but the inside is pretty dark, and Shinondi, taking my hand, raised the reed curtain bound with hide, which concealed the entrance into the actual house, and leading me into it, retired a footstep, extended his arms, waved his hands inwards three times, and then stroked his beard several times, after which he indicated by a sweep of his hand and a beautiful smile that the house and all it contained were mine. An aged woman, the chief's mother, who was splitting bark by the fire, waved her hands also. She is the queen-regnant of the house.

Again taking my hand, Shinondi led me to the place of honour at the head of the fire, a rude, movable platform six feet long, by four broad, and a foot high, on which he laid an ornamental mat, apologising for not having at that moment a bearskin wherewith to cover it. The baggage was speedily brought in by several willing pairs of hands; some reed mats fifteen feet long were laid down upon the very coarse ones which covered the whole floor, and when they saw Ito putting up my stretcher they hung a fine mat along the rough wall to conceal it, and suspended another on the beams of the roof for a canopy. The alacrity and instinctive hospitality with which these men rushed about to make things comfortable were very fascinating, though comfort is a word misapplied in an Aino hut. The women only did what the men told them.

They offered food at once, but I told them that I had brought my own, and would only ask leave to cook it on their fire. I need not have brought any cups, for they have many lacquer bowls, and Shinondi brought me on a lacquer tray a bowl full of water from one of their four wells. They said that Benri, the chief, would wish me to make his house my own for as long as I cared to stay, and I must excuse them in all things in which their ways were different from my own. Shinondi and four others in the village speak tolerable Japanese, and this of course is the medium of communication. Ito has exerted himself nobly as an interpreter, and has entered into my wishes with a cordiality and intelligence which have been perfectly invaluable; and though he did growl at Mr. Von Siebold's injunctions regarding politeness, he has carried them out to my satisfaction, and even admits that the mountain Ainos are better than he expected; "but," he added, "they have learned their politeness from the Japanese!" They have never seen a foreign woman, and only three foreign men, but there is neither crowding nor staring as among the Japanese, possibly in part from apathy and want of intelligence. For three days they have kept up their graceful and kindly hospitality, going on with their ordinary life and occupations, and though I have lived among them in this room by day and night, there has been nothing which in any way could offend the most fastidious sense of delicacy.

They said they would leave me to eat and rest, and all retired but the chief's mother, a weird, witch-like woman of eighty, with shocks of yellow-white hair, and a stern suspiciousness in her wrinkled face. I have come to feel as if she had the evil eye, as she sits there watching, watching always, and for ever knotting the bark thread like one of the Fates, keeping a jealous watch on her son's two wives, and on other young women who come in to weave—neither the dullness nor the repose of old age about her; and her eyes gleam with a greedy light when she sees *saké*, of which she drains a bowl without taking breath. She alone is suspicious of strangers, and she thinks that my visit bodes no good to her tribe. I see her eyes fixed upon me now, and they make me shudder.

I had a good meal seated in my chair on the top of the guest-seat to avoid the fleas, which are truly legion. At dusk Shinondi returned, and soon people began to drop in, till eighteen were assembled, including the sub-chief, and several very grand-looking old men, with full, grey, wavy beards. Age is held in much reverence, and it is etiquette for these old men to do honour to a guest in the chief's absence. As each entered he saluted me several times, and after sitting down turned towards me and saluted again, going through the same ceremony with every other person. They said they had come "to bid me welcome." They took their places in rigid order at each side of the fireplace, which is six feet long, Benri's mother in the place of honour at the right, then Shinondi, then the sub-chief, and on the other side the old men. Besides these, seven women sat in a row in the background splitting bark. A large iron pan hung over the fire from a blackened arrangement above, and Benri's principal wife cut wild roots, green beans, and seaweed, and shred dried fish and venison among them, adding millet, water, and some strong-smelling fish-oil, and set the whole on to stew for three hours, stirring the "mess" now and then with a wooden spoon.

Several of the older people smoke, and I handed round some mild tobacco, which they received with waving hands. I told them that I came from a land in the sea, very far away, where they saw the sun go down, so very far away that a horse would have to gallop day and night for five weeks to reach it, and that I had come a long journey to see them, and that I wanted to ask them many questions, so that when I went home I might tell my own people something about them. Shinondi and another man, who understood Japanese, bowed, and (as on every occasion) translated what I said into Aino for the venerable group opposite. Shinondi then said "that he and Shinrichi, the other Japanese speaker, would tell me all they knew, but they were but young men, and only knew what was told to them. They would speak what they believed to be true, but the chief knew more than they, and when he came back he might tell me differently, and then I should think that they had spoken lies." I said that no one who looked into their faces could think that they ever told lies. They were very much pleased, and waved their hands and stroked their beards repeatedly. Before they told me anything, they begged and prayed that I would not inform the Japanese Government that they had told me of their customs, or harm might come to them!

For the next two hours, and for two more after supper, I asked them questions concerning their religion and customs, and again yesterday for a considerable time, and this morning, after Benri's return, I went over the same subjects with him, and have also employed a considerable time in getting about 300 words from them, which I have spelt phonetically of course, and intend to go over again when I visit the coast Ainos.

The process was slow, as both question and answer had to pass through three languages. There was a very manifest desire to tell the truth, and I think that their statements concerning their few and simple customs may be relied upon. I shall give what they told me separately when I have time to write out my notes in an orderly manner. I can only say that I have seldom spent a more interesting evening.

About nine the stew was ready, and the women ladled it into lacquer bowls with wooden spoons. The men were served first, but all ate together. Afterwards *saké,* their curse, was poured into lacquer bowls, and across each bowl a finely-carved *"saké-stick"* was laid. These sticks are very highly prized. The bowls were waved several times with an inward motion, then each man took his stick and, dipping it into the *saké,* made six libations to the fire, and several to the "god," a wooden post, with a quantity of spiral white shavings falling from near the top. The Ainos are not affected by *saké* nearly so easily as the Japanese. They took it cold, it is true, but each drank about three times as much as would have made a Japanese foolish, and it had no effect upon them. After two hours more talk one after another got up and went out, making profuse salutations to me and to the others. My candles had been forgotten, and our *séance* was held by the fitful light of the big logs on the fire, aided by a succession of chips of birch bark, with which a woman replenished a cleft stick that was stuck into the fire-hole. I never saw such a strangely picturesque sight as that group of magnificent savages with the fitful firelight on their faces, and for adjuncts the flare of the torch, the strong lights, the blackness of the recesses of the room and of the roof, at one end of which the stars looked in, and the row of savage women in the background—eastern savagery and western civilisation met in this hut, savagery giving, and civilisation receiving, the yellow-skinned Ito the connecting-link between the two, and the representative of a civilisation to which our town is but an "infant of days."

I found it very exciting, and when all had left crept out into the starlight. The lodges were all dark and silent, and the dogs, mild like their masters, took no notice of me. The only sound was the rustle of a light breeze through the surrounding forest. The verse came into my mind, "It is not the will of your Father which is in Heaven that one of these little ones should perish." Surely these simple savages are children, as children to be judged; may we not hope as children to be saved through Him who came "not to judge the world, but to save the world"?

I crept back again and into my mosquito net, and suffered not from fleas or mosquitoes, but from severe cold. Shinondi conversed with Ito for some time in a low musical voice, having previously asked if it would keep me from sleeping. No Japanese ever intermitted his ceaseless chatter at any hour of the night for a similar reason. Later, the chief's principal wife, Noma, stuck a triply-cleft stick in the fire-hole, put a potsherd with a wick and some fish-oil upon it, and by the dim light of this rude lamp sewed until midnight at a garment of bark cloth which she was ornamenting for her lord with strips of blue cloth, and when I opened my eyes the next morning she was at the window sewing by the earliest daylight. She is the most intelligent-looking of all the women, but looks sad and almost stern, and speaks seldom. Although she is the principal wife of the chief, she is not happy, for she is childless, and I thought that her sad look darkened into something evil as the other wife caressed a fine baby boy. Benri seems to me something of a brute, and the mother-in-law obviously holds the reins of government pretty tight. After sewing till midnight she swept the mats with a bunch of twigs, and then crept into her bed behind a hanging mat. For a moment in the stillness I felt a feeling of panic, as if I were incurring a risk by being alone among savages, but I conquered it, and after watching the fire till it went out, fell asleep till I was awoke by the severe cold of the next day's dawn.

When I crept from under my net, much benumbed with cold, there were about eleven people in the room, who all made their graceful salutation. It did not seem as if they had ever heard of washing, for when water was asked for, Shinondi brought a little in a lacquer bowl, and held it while I bathed my face and hands, supposing the performance to be an act of worship! I was about to throw some cold tea out of the window by my bed, when he arrested me with an anxious face, and I saw what I had not observed before, that there was a god at that window, a stick with festoons of shavings hanging from it, and beside it a dead bird. The Ainos have two meals a day, and their breakfast was a repetition of the previous night's supper. We all ate together, and I gave the children the remains of my rice, and it was most amusing to see little creatures of three, four, and five years old, with no other clothing than a piece of pewter hanging round their necks, first formally asking leave of the parents before taking the rice, and then waving their hands. The obedience of the children is instantaneous. Their parents are more demonstrative in their affection than the Japanese are, caressing them a good deal, and two of the men are devoted to children who are not their own. These little ones are as grave and dignified as Japanese children, and are very gentle.

I went out soon after five, when the dew was glittering in the sunshine, and the mountain hollow in which Biratori stands was looking its very best, and the silence of the place, even though the people were all astir, was as impressive as that of the night before. What a strange life! knowing nothing, hoping nothing, fearing a little, the need for clothes and food the one motive principle, *saké* in abundance the one good! How very few points of contact it is possible to have! I was just thinking so, when Shinondi met me, and took me to his house to see if I could do anything for a child sorely afflicted with skin disease, and his extreme tenderness for this very loathsome object made me feel that human affections were the same among them as with us. He had carried it on his back from a village, five miles distant, that morning, in the hope that it might be cured.[1] As soon as I entered, he laid a fine mat on the floor, and covered the guest-seat with a bearskin. After breakfast he took me to the lodge of the sub-chief, the largest in the village, 45 feet square, and into about twenty others all constructed in the same way, but some of them were not more than 20 feet square. In all, I was received with the same courtesy, but a few of the people asked Shinondi

[1]Mrs. Bird neglects to tell the reader the fate of the sick child.

not to take me into their houses, as they did not want me to see how poor they are. In every house there was the low shelf with more or fewer curios upon it, but besides these, none but the barest necessaries of life, though the skins which they sell or barter every year would enable them to surround themselves with comforts, were it not that their gains represent to them *saké* and nothing else. They are not nomads. On the contrary, they cling tenaciously to the sites on which their fathers have lived and died. But anything more deplorable than the attempts at cultivation which surround their lodges could not be seen. The soil is little better than white sand on which without manure they attempt to grow millet, which is to them in the place of rice, pumpkins, onions, and tobacco, but the look of their plots is as if they had been cultivated ten years ago, and some chance-sown grain and vegetables had come up among the weeds. When nothing more will grow, they partially clear another bit of forest, and exhaust that in its turn.

In every house the same honour was paid to a guest. This seems a savage virtue which is not strong enough to survive much contact with civilisation. Before I entered one lodge, the woman brought several of the finer mats, and arranged them as a pathway for me to walk to the fire upon. They will not accept anything for lodging, or for anything that they give, so I was anxious to help them by buying some of their handiwork, but found even this a difficult matter. They were very anxious to give, but when I desired to buy they said they did not wish to part with their things. I wanted what they had in actual use, such as a tobacco-box and pipe-sheath, and knives with carved handles and scabbards, and for three of these I offered 2½ dollars. They said they did not care to sell them, but in the evening they came saying they were not worth more than 1 dollar 10 cents, and they would sell them for that; and I could not get them to take more. They said it was "not their custom." I bought a bow and three poisoned arrows, two reed-mats, with a diamond pattern on them in reeds stained red, some knives with sheaths, and a bark cloth dress. I tried to buy the *saké*-sticks with which they make libations to their gods, but they said it was "not their custom" to part with the *saké*-stick of any living man—however, this morning Shinondi has brought me, as a very valuable present, the stick of a dead man! This morning the man who sold the arrows brought two new ones, to replace two which were imperfect. I found them punctiliously honest in all their transactions. They wear very large earrings with hoops an inch and a half in diameter, a pair constituting the dowry of an Aino bride, but they would not part with these.

A house was burned down two nights ago, and "custom" in such a case requires that all the men should work at rebuilding it, so in their absence I got two boys to take me in a "dug-out" as far as we could go up the Sarufutogawa, a lovely river, which winds tortuously through the forests and mountains in unspeakable loveliness. I had much of the feeling of the ancient mariner—

> We were the first
> Who ever burst
> Into that silent sea.

For certainly no European had ever previously floated on the dark and forest-shrouded waters. I enjoyed those hours thoroughly, for the silence was profound, and the faint blue of the autumn sky, and the soft blue veil which "spiritualised" the distances, were so exquisitely like the Indian summer. . . .

Yesterday morning we all breakfasted soon after daylight, and the able-bodied men went away to hunt. Hunting and fishing are their occupations, and for "indoor recreation" they carve tobacco-boxes, knife-sheaths, *saké*-sticks, and shuttles. It is quite unnecessary for them to do anything; they are quite contented to sit by the fire, and smoke occasionally, and eat and sleep, this apathy being varied by spasms of activity when there is no more dried flesh in the *kuras,* and when skins must be taken to Sarufuto to pay for *saké.* The women seem never to have an idle moment. They rise early to sew, weave, and split bark, for they not only clothe themselves and their husbands in this nearly indestructible cloth, but weave it for barter, and the lower class of Japanese are constantly to be seen wearing the product of Aino industry. They do all the hard work, such as drawing water, chopping wood, grinding millet, and cultivating the soil, after their fashion; but to do the men justice, I often see them trudging along, carrying one and even two children. The women take the exclusive charge of the *kuras,* which are never entered by men.

I was left for some hours alone with the women, of whom there were seven in the hut, with a few children. On the one side of the fire the chief's mother sat like a Fate, for ever splitting and knotting bark, and petrifying me by her cold, fateful eyes. Her thick, grey hair hangs in shocks, the tattooing round her mouth has nearly faded, and no longer disguises her really handsome features. . . .

The younger women were all at work; two were seated on the floor weaving without a loom, and the others were making and mending the bark coats which are worn by both sexes. Noma, the chief's principal wife, sat apart, seldom speaking. Two of the youngest women are very pretty—as fair as ourselves, and their comeliness is of the rosy, peasant kind. It turns out that two of them, though they would not divulge it before men, speak Japanese, and they prattled to Ito with great vivacity and merriment; the ancient Fate scowling at them the while from under her shaggy eyebrows. I got a number of words from them, and they laughed heartily at my erroneous pronunciation. They even asked me a number of questions regarding their own sex among ourselves, but few of these would bear repetition, and they answered a number of mine. As the merriment increased the old woman looked increasingly angry and restless, and at last rated them sharply, as I have heard since, telling them that, if they spoke another word, she should tell their husbands that they had been talking to strangers. After this not another word was spoken, and Noma, who is an industrious housewife, boiled some millet into a mash for a mid-day lunch. During the afternoon a very handsome young Aino, with a washed, richly-coloured skin and fine clear eyes, came up from the coast, where he had been working at the fishing. He saluted the old woman and Benri's wife on entering, and presented the former with a gourd of *saké*, bringing a greedy light into her eyes as she took a long draught, after which, saluting me, he threw himself down in the place of honour by the fire, with the easy grace of a staghound, a savage all over. His name is Pipichari, and he is the chief's adopted son. He had cut his foot badly with a root, and asked me to cure it, and I stipulated that it should be bathed for some time in warm water before anything more was done, after which I bandaged it with lint. He said "he did not like me to touch his foot, it was not clean enough, my hands were too white," etc.; but when I had dressed it, and the pain was much relieved, he bowed very low and then kissed my hand! He was the only one among them all who showed the slightest curiosity regarding my things. He looked at my scissors, touched my boots, and watched me, as I wrote, with the simple curiosity of a child. He could speak a little Japanese, but he said he was "too young to tell me anything, the older men would know." He is a "total abstainer" from *saké*, and he says that there are four such besides himself among the large number of Ainos who are just now at the fishing at Mombets, and that the others keep separate from them, because they think that the gods will be angry with them for not drinking.

Several "patients," mostly children, were brought in during the afternoon. Ito was much disgusted by my interest in these people, who, he repeated, "are just dogs;" referring to their legendary origin, of which they are not ashamed. His assertion that they have learned politeness from the Japanese, is simply baseless. Their politeness, though of quite another and more manly stamp, is savage, not civilised. The men came back at dark, the meal was prepared, and we sat round the fire as before; but there was no *saké*, except in the possession of the old woman; and again the hearts of the savages were sad. I could multiply instances of their politeness. As we were talking, Pipichari, who is a very "untutored" savage, dropped his coat from one shoulder, and at once Shinondi signed to him to put it on again. Again, a woman was sent to a distant village for some oil, as soon as they heard that I usually burned a light all night. Little acts of courtesy were constantly being performed; but I really appreciated nothing more than the quiet way in which they went on with the routine of their ordinary lives.

During the evening a man came to ask if I would go and see a woman who could hardly breathe; and I found her very ill of bronchitis, accompanied with much fever. She was lying in a coat of skins, tossing on the hard boards of her bed, with a matting-covered roll under her head, and her husband was trying to make her swallow some salt fish. I took her dry, hot hand, such a small hand, tattooed all over the back; and it gave me a strange thrill. The room was full of people, and they all seemed very sorry. A medical missionary would be of little use here; but a medically-trained nurse, who would give medicines and proper food, with proper nursing, would save many lives and much suffering. It is of no use to tell these people to do anything which requires to be done more than once: they are just like children. I gave her some chlorodyne, which she swallowed with difficulty, and left another dose ready mixed, to give her in a few hours; but about midnight they came to tell me that she was worse; and on going I found her very cold and weak, and breathing very hard, moving her head wearily from side to side. I thought she could not live for many hours, and was much afraid that they would think that I had killed her. I told them that I thought she would die; but they urged me to do something more for her; and as a last hope I gave her some brandy, with twenty-five drops of chlorodyne, and a few spoonfuls of very strong beef-tea. She was unable, or more probably unwilling, to make the effort to swallow it, and I poured it down her throat by the wild glare of strips of birch bark. An hour later they came back to tell me that she felt as if she was very drunk; but going back to her house, I found that she was sleeping quietly, and breathing more easily; and creeping back just at dawn, I found her still sleeping, and with her pulse stronger and calmer. She is now decidedly better, and quite sensible, and her husband, the sub-chief, is much delighted. It seems so sad that they have nothing fit for a sick person's food; and though I have made a bowl of beef-tea with the remains of my stock, it can only last one day.

I was so tired with these nocturnal expeditions and anxieties, that on lying down I fell asleep, and on waking found more than the usual assemblage in the room, and the men were obviously agog about something. They have a singular, and I hope an unreasonable, fear of the Japanese Government . . . but I really think that the *Kaitaikushi* Department means well by them, and, besides removing the oppressive restrictions by which, as a conquered race, they were fettered, treats them far more humanely and equitably than the U.S. Government, for instance, treats the North American Indians. However, they are ignorant; and one of the men who had been most grateful because I said I would get Dr. Hepburn to send some medicine for his child, came this morning and begged me not to do so, as, he said, "the Japanese Government would be angry". . . .

The sub-chief then spoke, and said that I had been kind to their sick people, and they would like to show me their temple, which had never been seen by any foreigner; but they were very much afraid of doing so, and they asked me many times "not to tell the Japanese Government that they showed it to me, lest some great harm should happen to them." The sub-chief put on a sleeveless Japanese war-cloak to go up, and he, Shinondi, Pipichari, and two others accompanied me. It was a beautiful but very steep walk, or rather climb, to the top of an abrupt acclivity beyond the village, on which the temple or shrine stands. It would be impossible to get up, were it not for the remains of a wooden staircase, not of Aino construction. Forest and mountain surround Biratori, and the only breaks in the dense greenery are glints of the shining waters of the Sarufutogawa, and the tawny roofs of the Aino lodges. It is a lonely and a silent land, fitter for the *hiding* place than the *dwelling* place of men.

When the splendid young savage, Pipichari, saw that I found it difficult to get up, he took my hand and helped me up, as gently as an English gentleman would have done; and when he saw that I had greater difficulty in getting down, he all but insisted on my riding down on his back, and certainly would have carried me, had not Benri, the chief, who arrived while we were at the shrine, made an end of it by taking my hand and helping me down himself. Their instinct of helpfulness to a foreign woman strikes me as so odd, because they never show any courtesy to their own women, whom they treat (though to a less extent than is usual among savages) as inferior beings.

On the very edge of the cliff, at the top of the zigzag, stands a wooden temple or shrine, such as one sees in any grove, or on any high place on the main island, obviously of Japanese construction, but concerning which Aino tradition is silent. No European had ever stood where I stood, and there was a solemnity in the knowledge. The sub-chief drew back the sliding doors, and all bowed with much reverence. It was a simple shrine of unlacquered wood, with a broad shelf at the back, on which there was a small shrine containing a figure of the historical hero Yoshitsuné, in a suit of inlaid brass armour, some metal *gohei*, a pair of tarnished brass candlesticks, and a coloured Chinese picture representing a junk. Here, then, I was introduced to the great god of the mountain Ainos. There is something very pathetic in these people keeping alive the memory of Yoshitsuné, not on account of his martial exploits, but simply because their tradition tells them that he was kind to them. They pulled the bell three times to attract his attention, bowed three times, and made six libations of *saké,* without which ceremony he cannot be approached. They asked me to worship their god, but when I declined on the ground that I could only worship my own God, the Lord of Earth and Heaven, of the dead and of the living, they were too courteous to press their request. As to Ito, it did not signify to him whether or not he added another god to his already crowded Pantheon, and he "worshipped," *i.e.* bowed down, most willingly before the great hero of his own, the conquering race.[2]

While we were crowded there on the narrow ledge of the cliff, Benri, the chief, arrived, a square-built, broad-shouldered, elderly man, strong as an ox, and very handsome, but his expression is not pleasing, and his eyes are bloodshot with drinking. The others saluted him very respectfully, but I noticed then and since that his manner is very arbitrary, and that a blow not infrequently follows a word. He had sent a message to his people by Ito that they were not to answer any questions till he returned, but Ito very tactfully neither gave it nor told me of it, and he was displeased with the young men for having talked to me so much. His mother had evidently "peached." I like him less than any of his tribe. He has some fine qualities, truthfulness among others, but he has been contaminated by the four or five foreigners that he has seen, and is a brute and a sot. The hearts of his people are no longer sad, for there is *saké* in every house to-night.

---

[2]Editor's note: The Ainu religion, before the coming of the Japanese, centered on the cult of the bear. A captive bear was sacrificed annually and it was believed by the Ainu that his spirit guarded their settlements.

13

KATE MARSDEN
On a Mission to the Lepers

FROM
On Sledge and Horseback to Outcast Siberian Lepers (1892)

Kate Marsden was born in England in 1859. As a young lady, serving as a nurse during the Russo-Turkish War of 1877–78, she heard that there was an herb to be found in northern Siberia that reputedly alleviated the suffering caused by leprosy. It was supposedly so secret that information would be given only to those who could prove to its possessors that they were working to benefit those who had the disease. According to Kate Marsden, some doctors did not care enough to risk health and life and others had neither the time nor the money to spend months and perhaps years visiting the lepers and testing the properties of the herb in a systematic way.

She conceived the idea of going to Siberia herself, where she would try to persuade the local shamans to reveal all that they knew to a woman. She presented her proposal to Her Majesty the Queen in 1890 and the Queen enlisted the approval and the assistance of the Empress of Russia. (It was not a simple matter, even in those days, to travel without restrictions in Russian territory.)

Before departing, she visited the Middle East in order to acquaint herself with the conditions of the lepers there, and saw enough misery in Jerusalem and Constantinople to strengthen her resolution. She arrived in Moscow late in 1890 and from there embarked upon a perilous mission across the Siberian wastes to the lepers of the Yakutsk region, travelling mainly by sledge and enduring every degree of discomfort. She remained with the lepers for about three months, but before she could discover whether a secret remedy existed, she herself was taken seriously ill and had to be carried back to Saint Petersburg. Upon returning to

England, she was elected a Fellow of the prestigious Royal Geographical Society, an honor that was bestowed on twenty-one other "well-qualified ladies" between 1892 and 1894. A group of the Society's Fellows successfully challenged the future appointment of women (no others were elected until 1913), and Kate Marsden was refused a ticket to the anniversary dinner in 1894 on the ground that she would be the "only lady among 200 [men] nearly all of them smoking."

That Kate Marsden richly deserved the honor of membership in that organization is demonstrated beyond doubt by this account of her journey.

We left Yakutsk for Viluisk June 22nd, 1891, to begin our long journey of three thousand versts (2000 miles) on horseback, for the purpose of visiting the lepers living in forests unknown, even to the Russians. Our cavalcade was somewhat curious, consisting of about fifteen men and thirty horses; all those around me were talking in a language which I could not understand, though Mr. Petroff did, who also knew a little French. The photographer in Yakutsk took our photograph; but someone moved before it was finished, and therefore it was a failure. It might have given an idea of our costumes. As to mine, it was not very elegant: a sun-hat, over it a network arrangement as a protection from the mosquitoes, a jacket with very long sleeves, with the badge of the red cross on my left arm. Very full trousers down to my knees, and high boots above my knees. A revolver, a whip, and a little travelling bag. I was obliged to ride as a man for many reasons. First, because the Yakutsk horses were so wild that it was impossible for me to ride otherwise; second, no woman could ride on a lady's saddle for 3000 versts; and thirdly, as there were no roads, the horse constantly stumbles on the roots that are in the forest, threatening to throw the rider over its head; then it sinks into the mud till the rider's feet are on earth; having somehow recovered its footing, it rushes along between the branches of the trees and shrubs, utterly regardless of the fact that they were tearing and making mincemeat of the rider's dress. The first day we did five versts (3⅓ miles); the second, fifteen (10); the third, twenty (13⅓); and after that, 80 versts without stopping for sleep. One's sufferings were far worse than even when travelling in the tarantass; the stiffened position of my body being altogether contrary to its usual free and easy habit; and the jerky movements of the untrained horse gave me dreadful pain.

We were obliged to take food with us for three months; some black and white dried bread, some dried prunes, some tea and sugar, and other indispensable articles for so long a journey; for, excepting at Viluisk, you can get absolutely nothing, not even bread and tea.

Before leaving Yakutsk, His Grace the Archbishop asked us to go to his house, that he might give us his blessing. When we went, His Grace, dressed in all his most brilliant robes, blessed us and pronounced over us his benediction. All the time I was in Yakutsk he took care of me like a father, tenderly and lovingly. We left there very quietly, so as not to attract attention. I had a very great objection to make any parade of our starting to my work, for it was serious; and it is my desire that it should be finished as it was begun, with the blessing of God on us at every step, whether that step be difficult or easy.

When you are travelling through marshes in which your horse, without a moment's warning, sinks up to his stomach, you are obliged to hold on by the reins and by your knees and hands and every way, as best you can. The only thought in my mind at the time was to keep on and not fall off, and to keep my horse on his feet, for if my horse fell I must fall with it, and find myself in the mud. The first ten marshes it was not so difficult; but after we had passed hundreds of them all the body ached; I felt as though I had spent fifty years on the tread-mill. It was then, that, to keep in the saddle, was a feat worthy of a hero.

On the official maps there is a road traced leading from Yakutsk to Viluisk, but in reality there is no such road—so do not be misled by official maps if you should go there. You will have to pass through unnamed marshes, and never find any such road.

During the summer the mosquitoes are frightful, both in the night and in the day; and when you arrive at a yourta, which serves as a post-station, the dirt and vermin and smell are simply disgusting; bugs, lice, fleas, etc., cover the walls, as well as the benches on which you have to sleep. Even on the ground you will find them, and, as soon as a stranger comes in, it seems as if the insects make a combined assault on him in large battalions; and, of course, sleep is a thing never dreamed of. After a few days the body swells from their bites into a form that can neither be imagined nor described. They attack your eyes and your face, so that you would hardly be recognised by your dearest friend. Yet with all these pains and penalties we had still to continue riding from forty to eighty versts in one day; we did even 100 versts without sleep. The fatigue, and the want of rest were dreadful. Cows and calves were in the same yourta with us, and the smell from them and from everything else was horrible. We would, indeed, have made very funny pictures of miserable travellers. As there is only one yourta at a post-station, ladies and gentlemen are obliged to sleep all together, and any traveller that may be present at the same time; a gentleman might put up with it, but it is impossible for a lady. After riding on horseback for the first time, my body was in constant pain, and complete rest with the possibility of undressing was indispensable; but as they say in French, "*à la guerre comme à la guerre.*" As undressing was not possible, I was obliged to rest the best way I could. The Cossack was also ill that day, and Mr. Petroff and myself had our heads bound up so as to ease the pain a little, having been badly burnt by the sun. To have even five minutes' rest we were obliged to have a fire made up of cowdung in this disgusting yourta, and, to prevent the smoke from escaping, as that is the only way to have any rest, we were obliged to cover the opening of the chimney. The mosquitoes left us alone; but as to our eyes, they were so irritated by the smoke that they were bathed in tears; and my head suffered even worse. The other animals, however, did not cease to attack us all the time. I would indeed have presented an original picture. To remain five minutes longer within was not possible, we could do nothing at all because of the smoke; and this continued all day.

Really, I think the sufferings of this journey have added twenty years to my age. But I would willingly do it ten times over to aid my poor lepers who are placed in the depths of these unknown forests.

You are always running the risk of being attacked by bears here, so that we always kept our revolvers ready at our side or under our heads; and two Yakuts as sentinels, with large fires at each end of the little encampment.

Soon after we started on our journey, we were obliged to

travel in the night, because our horses had no rest in the day time from the terrible horse-flies that were quite dangerous there. They instantly attacked the wretched beasts, so that it was an awful sight to see our horses with the blood running down their sides, many of them becoming so exhausted that they were not able to carry our luggage.

At one place the bears might have attacked us with impunity. It was a very dangerous spot, as we were in the depths of a thick forest; we could hardly see two yards off, and the Yakuts saw eleven bears as we passed. Before starting, we all grasped our revolvers and guns, and we always had a large box filled with stones, which made a great clatter as we travelled; the bells also of some of our horses made a considerable noise. One of the Cossacks was in front of me, Mr. Petroff was on one side, the other Cossack and the rest of the escort, the horses and luggage, being behind. In the less dangerous parts of the forest everyone used to sing, making noise enough to frighten fifty bears. The horses are in such a fearful dread of the bears that they smell them afar off; and, as soon as they know they are near, they become almost unmanageable, dragging you through the forests, between the trees, flying like the wind. One thing was perfectly clear, that had the bears come near, it is quite certain some of us would have been killed, if not by the bears, then by the horses, who were almost mad.

One further danger must be related, so that readers of this document may have some notion of the many trials that had to be endured. After having left Viluisk one night we entered an immense forest, where the horses made a peculiar noise with their feet, as if they were walking over hollow ground. Having asked what it meant, I was told that we were near a place where the forest was burning. In about half an hour there was seen in the distance a small body of flames; but on getting nearer it seemed almost a picture of the infernal regions, so terrible was it to the sight, and yet we were obliged to go right into it. Far as could be seen there were flames and smoke rising from the ground, which was everywhere, apparently, burning. One of the Yakuts was in front; I was next, my horse picking its way; but sometimes it would get into a hole where there was fire, when it became terrified, throwing itself from right to left, becoming restive and wild till one became almost exhausted; for, in addition to this, there was the effort to distinguish the path through the smoke with eyes smarting and almost blinded with the glare of the fire. However, we travelled on, but all at once we heard a dreadful noise behind us. Nothing could be seen through the flames and smoke, but the noise steadily kept coming nearer; our horses began to get still more restless, and before we could have any idea where the sound came from, a horse with some luggage on it, mad with fright at the flames and the smoke, rushed into our midst. Mr. Petroff, who was behind, had just time to give it a slash with his whip, which made it turn a little to the right, otherwise it would have been on me, and certainly I would have been killed. It was quite mad, and dashed right into the flames, as it was impossible to stop it, having so much to do to manage our own horses.

This was the most terrible experience of the journey, and it was only through God's mercy that we were kept alive.

In Viluisk I consulted with several persons as to the condition of the lepers in that province, and I was assured that it was dreadful, that they were thrust out by the community into immense forests, without anything with which to cover themselves; and the yourtas, or huts, in which they live are so small that they were packed in them more like animals than human bengs. We were said to have gone 2500 versts (1666 miles) on horseback; but as the Yakuts have no idea of the length of a verst, I am sure we must have gone over 3000; for frequently, when we were told that there were only ten versts to such and such a place, we found there were twenty.

The community, having heard that I had come to help them (non-officially), were so grateful and happy that they cleared a road in the forest for 1500 versts, where, otherwise, it would have been impossible to pass. They also built small bridges over the most dangerous marshes; but to accomplish this, they had to put aside all their agricultural work for the summer, which was certainly a loss to them. It was all the more gratifying to hear that they did it of their own free will. Everywhere along the road they showed me every possible kindness, begging me most earnestly to help their lepers.

A great difficulty I experienced was that I did not understand either the Russian or Yakutsk language, and being accompanied only by about thirty men, all of whom spoke in a language unknown to me. It was indeed most awkward for a lady to be alone under such circumstances in a foreign country. Mr. Petroff spoke a little French, so it was only through him that I could make myself understood.

The 3rd (15th) July, 1891, the ispravnick, the doctor (feldsher), two soldiers, Mr. Petroff and myself, left Viluisk for the leper dwellings in the Mastach district, near the lake Abungda, where the largest colony of them is situated.

We descended the river Viluie for about twenty versts, where we were met by the chief of the starostas and the Yakuts, about twenty men, with thirty horses; all were waiting to conduct us to the place to which we were going.

After we had some tea we entered the forests, and having gone up the hill for about twenty versts we stopped on seeing a fire, which is always a sign of someone being near, and inquired how far we had still to go before we could find drinkable water, and grass for our horses. As Mr Petroff was talking, I noticed something moving between the trees of the forest. I asked what it was, and was told that it was a leper-child who wanted to ask me to help him. I dismounted and went towards him; but the poor child, thinking that I would be frightened at his disease, as the Yakuts are, kept going backwards, and it was difficult to make him understand that I wanted to speak with him, and even touch him. I then spoke to his mother and brother, who told me the history of this poor child.

The community, having affirmed that he was a leper (and it must be understood that in this community there was not a single Russian, nor any man that had any idea of medicine), ordered this child to live alone in the forests in a yourta, that had been built for him about ten versts away from his mother, and, further, that he was to remain there for the rest of his life. Thank God, his mother took pity on him in his solitude, and built a tiny shed behind her yourta, where the child used to come secretly, as soon as it was dark, to sleep. But had the society found this out, the mother would have been punished by also being thrust into the depths of the forest and separated from the rest of the community.

This touching story proved the truth of all the cruelties that I had been told were practised on the poor lepers. We gave him every possible help, and the ispravnick took the child under his protection, which will prevent a repetition of such cruelties.

As for the consequences of this journey for all of us, but especially for me—a lady alone, who up to that time had never ridden on horseback, and was now obliged to ride like a man, the Yakut horse being unmanageable otherwise (indeed, along this dreadful road there was no possibility of riding otherwise)—the many difficulties, the fatigue, and want of proper and clean food, the danger from the bears that abound in the Viluisk province, the dangers of travelling in the night through dark forests, the roots of the trees interlacing the roads so that the horse is constantly stumbling against them, the cold at night, and the heat during the day, the strain on your eyes in trying to peer through the darkness, the dampness, the absence of any habitation near, and often only disgusting water to drink—all this will perhaps give you a little idea of some of our sufferings.

But I will not speak much about them, as the object of my task is not to tell what we endured, but to bear witness to the sufferings of the wretched lepers, and, with God's blessing, to put into this work all my strength, all my heart, and all my life; and I pray in the name of the Lord that every Christian will help them by his prayers, and his money, in their terrible condition.

About sixty versts (forty miles) from Abungda the priest of the district met us. We rested at his house, and then conducted us to Abungda. As we neared the dwellings of the lepers, the road got more difficult and impassable, for the lepers are always located in the farthest and loneliest places, those least frequented, and the most difficult of access, in order to prevent them returning to their former homes. We travelled along the lake, and as we came out of the forest we saw the yourtas where the lepers live.

They were expecting us, and as soon as they saw us we were saluted. After giving them every help and assistance we could, we all prayed together; and Her Majesty the Empress was not forgotten. I know that these prayers will be heard. It was terribly sad to listen to the feeble voices of these weak lepers; to see them on their knees making the sign of the Cross with their poor maimed hands, often without fingers and without strength, so that they could hardly lift up their arms; their faces frightfully disfigured by this disease; in their eyes you could read that all hope was lost. Their feet were toeless, so that some could not walk at all, and could only drag along their bodies with the help of a low stool. This picture of a dying life, without any consolation, touched us so deeply that the remembrance of it will remain with us all our days. In this place there were two yourtas about thirty yards apart; and between them seven graves, as if to take away the possibility of these poor creatures forgetting for one moment that death always follows them, and is always near.

When a leper dies he remains in the same yourta, with the living, for three days. Will you just look into the interior of this yourta? It is so small that the inmates are obliged to sleep on the benches along the wall, without any mattress, and so near to each other that the feet of one leper touch the head of the next, whilst the others have to sleep on the bare earth, these yourtas having no floors. There is a frightful odour from this disease, and the cold in the winter is so terrible that when the door is opened for a minute one is almost frozen. The cows are in the same hut, and the dead bodies have to remain there on the benches, adding to the frightful stench of the lepers. When the coffin is brought a leper is obliged to go out in the terrible cold, and drag as best he can the coffin into the hut, put the corpse into it, and, after that, put it on an old sledge and drag it for some yards to the grave. Indeed, these people have been cruelly forsaken and forgotten; but it is hoped that a brighter time is about to dawn for them, and that the greatest bitterness of their sorrow will soon be of the past.

When they had the small-pox there no one visited them, neither the doctors nor any of the Yakuts; they were obliged to bear the sufferings of this disease also quite alone, without any one to aid them; no beds for their suffering bodies, and almost without clothes, with the exception of the disgusting shoubas (fur cloaks), which only augmented the irritation so terrible in this disease. What they endured no one will ever know.

There was a girl of eighteen in this yourta, who had lived all her life with the lepers, though she was in perfect health. Her mother had been a leper, therefore the community ordered her to remain always with them. After consulting with the ispravnick, the priest, the doctor, and Mr. Petroff, we decided not to leave the place until this girl was freed. The kind ispravnick said that when she was washed and dressed in other clothes, he would willingly take her into his own house; and before we left Viluisk we saw the girl settled with him.

At Abungda the lepers had cows; and certainly this was the best place we visited, although even here the yourta in which they lived was only six yards long and four yards broad; and there were eleven lepers in it. Such conditions are quite unsuitable for these poor creatures, as they have to spend eight or nine months of the year in this place, or in another just as bad. All the other leper settlements we visited were worse and worse.

At one place, Djikinda, there was a man, a woman, and two children almost naked. In another place, Ilgidjan, there were six people almost naked. The men, women, and children live all together more like animals than human beings.

In another place, Abalack Kel, I saw a woman who had been condemned by the community to live all alone for the rest of her life; she had already been isolated for four years. She saw no one but her husband regularly, who brought her food and firing. She very rarely saw her children—then only at a long distance, as they never dared go near her. Thus, in this perfect, endless solitude, she has to live always. Her work in winter was to drag her body along the snow the best way she could, as she was not able to walk, to fetch the food that was taken to her by her husband, and left at some yards away from the hovel. If she had any strength she kindled a fire; if not, she had to remain in the cold.

Again, at another place, Harialach-Kell, there were three men who lived alone. They told me that the bears often frightened them by coming close to the yourta; but, luckily, they had a very clever dog, who used to bark incessantly at them till he chased them back into the forest, often returning without any voice left. Had it not been for this dog the bears would have entered the yourta, as the poor lepers have neither guns nor revolvers.

At a place named Honkeil, there was a man who had come a long distance to ask for my help; he said that the bears were his only companions, and that he had also a dog to protect him; he was likewise condemned to live alone in the forest.

Neither man, woman, nor child are exempt from this cruelty. Once the community decides that anyone is a leper he is thus condemned; even if he himself is not a leper, but if his parents have been lepers, or he has lived with lepers, it is the same; for life he is condemned to isolation.

In some places the yourtas are small, even for two people; but we found as many as eight and ten people in them. The dirt, the frightful odour from the lepers, the absence of any sanitary place, their food, chiefly consisting of fish, and often rotten fish, butter and grease that they drink, and bark of trees, and their disgusting clothes, will hardly give you an idea of the miserable conditions under which they barely exist. It is true what Father John of Viluisk says, that in all the world you will not find people in a more lost condition than they are. The terror the Yakuts have of this disease is remarkable; nothing in the world would make them touch or go near them. Be it father, mother, or child, they are torn away from their family, and condemned to live alone to the end of their life.

I will give you another instance of the cruelties practised in the name of disease. About twenty versts from Viluisk at the other side of the river Viluie, there was an orphan child, who had an inheritance of some four cows. His parents were dead, and his uncle had charge of him, who, wishing to take possession of these cows, informed the community that his nephew was a leper.

They told him that he was to be isolated like the rest, and they ordered the uncle to have charge of him. The uncle built him a tiny shed—the doctor who saw it said it was not large enough for a dog; the uncle then took the child into the forest where the shed was, and he left him there without providing any food or drink. After some time the child was found dead; he had died from starvation and cold. His uncle had buried him without a coffin, and when the doctor opened his body, he found nothing but a little clay in his stomach. What this poor child must have suffered from terror, hunger, thirst, and cold, no one will ever know. To prevent the possibility of a repetition of a similar case I asked the advice of the Committee, as well as their help, and that of many others.

In another place there was a woman-leper, who used to go

near the dwellings of the healthy Yakuts for stealing purposes; the starosta ordered that all her clothes were to be taken away from her so as to prevent her leaving her yourta. However, one day she ventured out without clothes, and her body was found frozen and dead.

We visited the lepers in thirteen different places; but at last I was too ill to go any farther, and neither the ispravnick, Mr. Petroff, nor the doctor, would take the responsibility of letting me go on; so I was obliged to remain in the tent.

At Sredni Viluisk a man was suspected of having leprosy; but as at last it was proved that he really had the disease, they ordered him to be sent thirty versts away, where there were other lepers belonging to the same community. He had neither fingers nor toes, and was so terribly disfigured that I asked them how he was going to be sent. I was answered, "Oh, very well, quite easily." But knowing full well that they consider that the worst things are quite good enough for the lepers, I wanted to be certain as to the manner in which he would be conveyed there. It was only after a great deal of trouble that I could get to the truth; first, I was told that he could walk; but I said, "No, that is impossible;" then they said, "We will put him on a bull." I again said, "No, that is also impossible." Then they said, "On a horse;" but to this I objected; and, at last, after a great deal of discussion, they consented to put him on a sledge, with some hay to lie upon.

Now, I do not think that they even thought that their first propositions were cruel, the Yakuts being so accustomed to walk and ride themselves; but we can well understand that the sufferings of this leper were indeed terrible—the poor man being so ill and so disfigured, needing the best care possible—and the Yakuts wanted to add to his sufferings, as he could not have held himself on a horse. And now, having seen all these things on the spot, I want every one to consider in what way we can ameliorate their condition.

Having witnessed all these horrors, I am going straight to Irkutsk to collect money, with the help of the Committee and others, for a hospital. After that I hope to have the honour of presenting myself to Her Majesty the Empress at Gatchina, and to lay at her feet all these details, with the list of names of those persons who have given money for the hospitals; and I am more than sure that Her Majesty, who is so gracious and tender-hearted, will take all the sufferings of the sick and of the poor to heart, and sustain me in this work. As for myself, I will put all my strength, my health, my life into it, so that the existence of these wretched lepers may be bettered, and that they may have a hospital. But the result of this rests absolutely with the Lord; and it is in His name that I beg Christians everywhere to help them.

14

MRS. ERNEST HART

The Customs of Burma

FROM
Picturesque Burma (1897)

Before world events brought Burma into the limelight, it was for most people a place populated by tigers and celebrated in song by Rudyard Kipling. Hardly anyone but the rankest romantic supposed that it was possible for a Western woman to explore that distant prospect. However, Mrs. Ernest Hart was not one to be put off by what others considered barriers to new enterprise; a faithful wife-companion (a prevalent type among English women travellers), she steamed up and down the reaches of the Irrawaddy River on a three-decker mailboat and became the first Western woman to write a book about Burma.

Born Alice Marion Rowlands in about 1850 in Lower Sydenham, she was, like Kate Marsden, trained in the arduous profession of nursing. In 1872, she married Dr. Ernest Hart, the noted surgeon and medical journalist, and despite fierce opposition to the then-shocking proposal, helped her husband to found the Cremation Society. In 1874, with his assistance, she established the Donegal Industries Fund to develop the home industries of the Irish cottagers. In 1894, they undertook a tour of the Far East, visiting in addition to Burma, China and India. In Karachi, her husband, who was Jewish, lectured to Moslems on sanitation in holy places.

When they got back to England, she published her first book, Diet in Sickness and Health *(1895), and embodied her impressions of Burma in some articles that appeared in* Cornhill Magazine, The Saturday Review, *and* The Queen. *Not until some time later, when she learned how little was known in England about that beautiful if backward land, did she undertake the task of writing a book on the subject. Both an*

English and an American publisher showed interest in it, and Picturesque Burma *(Dent in London, Lippincott in Philadelphia) appeared in 1897, the year before her husband's death.*

As the following excerpt reveals, the book is based on the careful observation and study of Burmese customs rather than on casual conversations. It foreshadows the work of a later generation of trained anthropologists exemplified by Margaret Mead and Ruth Benedict, women who made valuable contributions to our understanding of other peoples in the world.

Women in Burma are probably freer and happier than they are anywhere else in the world. Though Burma is bordered on one side by China, where women are held in contempt, and on the other by India, where they are kept in the strictest seclusion, Burmese women have achieved for themselves and have been permitted by their men to attain, a freedom of life and action that has no parallel among Oriental peoples. The secret lies, perhaps, in the fact that the Burmese woman is active and industrious while the Burmese man is indolent and often a recluse. Becoming, therefore, both by taste and by habit the money-earner, the bargainer and the financier of the household, she has asserted and obtained for herself the right to hold what she wins and the respect due to one who can and does direct and control. Things are strangely reversed in Burma, for here we see man as the religious soul of the nation and woman its brain. Burmese women are born traders, and it is more often the wife than the husband who drives the bargain with the English buyer for the paddy harvest, or at any rate, she is present on the occasion and helps her easygoing husband to stand firm. So highly is trading esteemed, that a daughter of well-to-do parents, and even a young married woman, will set up a booth in the bazaar, and dressed in a bright silk tamein (skirt) and white jacket, with a flower jauntily stuck into her coiled black tresses, she will start every morning with a tray of sweetmeats, fruits, or toys on her head, and, with a gaiety and grace born of the sunshine and the bounteousness of the land, will push a brisk trade all through the short and sunny day. The earnings thus made are the woman's own, and cannot be touched by her husband.

English officials told me that contracts for army forage and for timber were often made with women-traders, and that they well understood the art of "holding up the market."

The education of women was in times gone by *nil*, and all that is thought necessary to teach them at present is to read and write. To be pretty, to be religious, to be amiable and gay-hearted, and to have a good business instinct, are all that is demanded of a woman in Burma; presently, when she comes to learn the advantages which education confers in dealing with the ubiquitous foreigner, she will doubtless demand it as her right. At present she fulfils all expectations. To charm is her openly avowed aim, and few things human are more charming than a group of Burmese women going up to the pagoda to worship at a festival. With her rainbow-tinted silk tamein fastened tightly round her slender figure, her spotlessly clean short jacket modestly covering the bosom, and with her abundant black tresses smoothly coiled on the top of her head, in the braids of which nestles a bouquet of sweet-smelling flowers, the Burmese young woman knows full well she is an object to be admired.

Perfectly well pleased with herself and contented with her world as it is, she gaily laughs and chats with her companions while puffing from time to time at an immense green cheroot. Amiable she is, as a matter of course, for are not the laws of Manu and Burma very particular in their denunciation of all who speak harshly and who use abusive words? Besides, what is there to vex her soul? She has not the thousand and one cares which harass the poor European housewife. Her home, built of bamboo and plaited mats, costs but a few rupees to erect, and can easily be restored if burnt down in a fire or shaken down in an earthquake. Her household goods can be numbered on her five fingers, and could be carried on her back. Her boys are taught free at the monastery, and till her girls are old enough to have their ears bored, clothing for them is an item of the smallest expenditure, for little children are generally seen wearing nothing but a "necklace and a smile." Her stall at the bazaar will give her earnings enough to buy the brightest silk tamein to wear at the next pagoda festival or boat race, and perhaps the money to win "merit" by purchasing packets of gold leaf to plaster on the stately statue of the holy Gautauma at the next full moon. Her husband treats her well; if not, if he neglects her, fails to provide for her, is unkind or abusive, she has but to go before the nearest magistrate and state her case, and he will grant a divorce, and she can depart with all her possessions and earnings. She has every reason to be happy, and to laugh gaily from pure light-heartedness as she carries her tray of goods to the bazaar, or her offering of fruit and flowers and gold-leaf to the pagoda.

Marriage in Burma is an affair of the heart. More often than not a Burmese girl chooses her own husband, but she is frequently aided in the selection by her parents, or by a go-between called an *oung bwé*. There are plenty of opportunities given for the meeting of young people of both sexes at the pagoda festivals, at the pwés or public plays, and at friends' houses on the occasions of marriages and funerals. Courting takes place in the evening, and a suitor for a girl's hand visits her at her father's house generally after eight o'clock. He does not come alone, but with his friends and supporters. The girl receives her lover alone or accompanied by a friend, and dressed in her best. The parents retire to another room, but though not present at the interview, a bamboo house does not admit of secrecy, and the mother probably sees and hears all that goes on. Presents are exchanged, but not kisses and caresses, as these would be thought highly improper. When the young people have made up their minds to marry, the parents' consent is asked, and is almost invariably given, even though the intended husband may be very young, and not yet in a position to support a wife. But the happy-go-lucky Burman has great sympathy with love's young dream, and arrangements are made to take the young couple into the house of the parents, either of the bride or the bridegroom, for the first few years, till the husband can afford to start a separate establishment. The marriage ceremony is not religious, the celibate Buddhist monks taking no part in such mundane affairs; but a great feast is given by the bride's parents, and the public pledging of troth is virtually the marriage ceremony. It is said that these marriages of boy and girl in the heyday of life and love are generally happy; warm family affection is one of the national traits of character, and kindness to one another is a religion and a habit.

Marriage in Burma is easily contracted. A girl cannot marry before she is twenty without the consent of her parents or guardians. Should she not, however, obtain this consent, the marriage is considered valid after three elopements. Marriage is viewed by the Burmans in the light of a partnership in which the wife has equal rights with the husband; theoretically the husband is lord of his wife, and has the control of the household, the children, and the family property, but this power cannot be exercised arbitrarily without consultation with the wife, and as she is often the bread-winner, her wishes are naturally deferred to.

The equality of women in marriage is particularly shown in the disposition of property. Property is divided into personal and joint. There has been no need in Burma for a Married Woman's Property Act, for all property belonging to a woman before marriage remains hers absolutely when she becomes a wife. The joint property consists of bequests by the parents or husband at the time of marriage for joint purposes, all profits arising since marriage from the employment or investment of the separate property of either husband or wife, and all property acquired by their mutual skill and industry. The husband cannot sell or alienate the joint property of himself and his wife without her consent or against her will, except when he manages the business or acts as her agent; also during the continuance of marriage neither the husband nor wife has the right to the exclusive possession of the joint property. The fact, that in Burma all the male population pass through the phongyee kioungs or monasteries, and must for a certain time don the yellow robe and become monks, and also that an immense number of men remain monks and lead celibate lives, has led to women taking a very active part in business, and hence has arisen the idea of an equal partnership in marriage. If, however, the wife is not engaged in business, it is acknowledged that she fulfils her part in the partnership by bearing the children and attending to the domestic comfort, and she still retains her control over the joint property.

Divorce is obtained with facility. Buddhist law recognises the fallibility of man, and the fact that in marriage, as in everything else, he may act in error, and should therefore have the opportunity given of retrieving his mistake. To obtain divorce in Burma, it is simply necessary for the parties to agree together that their marriage or partnership should be dissolved. The marriage is thereupon annulled; each takes their separate property; they divide the joint property equally; the husband takes the male children and the wife the female. There is no scandal, and no opprobrium is incurred. Should only one party insist on separation, and there is no fault on the other side, the party who does not wish to separate retains the joint property. Marriage cannot, however, be put an end to simply at the caprice of one of the parties. Polygamy is allowed by the Buddhist law, though the practice is regarded with disfavour by the Burmese people. The taking of a lesser wife is not of itself considered a sufficient cause of divorce by the first wife. Desertion is a valid reason; if a husband leaves his wife for three years and does not maintain her, or a wife her husband for one year because she has no affection for him, then "they shall not claim each other as husband and wife; let them have the right to separate and marry again."

Exceptions are made in the case where the husband absents himself to trade, to fight, or to study, in which cases the wife has to wait eight, seven, or six years respectively before she can marry again. If a married man enters a monastery, the marriage is dissolved. Constant ill-treatment on the part of a husband is sufficient cause for divorce, but not petty quarrels. A husband may put away his wife or take another if she has no children or has only female children; if she has leprosy or disease, if her conduct is bad, and if she has no love for her husband. If a husband is a drunkard, gambler, or better, or is immoral, and has three times in the presence of good men made a written engagement to reform and yet continues these evil practices, his wife may put him away. If the divorce is due to the fault of one party, he or she is not entitled to any share in the joint property. The partition of the property is the actual test of divorce, for according to the Dhamma, "If a husband and wife have separated and no division of property has taken place, neither shall be free to live with another man or woman. But if the property has been divided they may do so. Thus Manu has decided." In every case the husband takes the male children and the woman the female.

Marriages so easily made and so easily broken must inevitably lead to a certain looseness as regards the marriage tie; but there are several points of view in the Buddhist law which may be commended to Western peoples, namely, the equal status of women in marriage, the equal control and partition of the joint property, the division of the children of the marriage among the parents, and also the possibility of obtaining divorce without public scandal. As a matter of fact, marriages are happy in Burma, as a rule, and, whatever may be said to the contrary, illegitimate children are rare, except as the Eurasian offspring of Christian fathers, whose example is bitterly deplored by those who desire to see the Burmans take a higher standard.

Up to the age of ten the costume of a Burmese child consists at most of a piece of silk or cotton bound round the hips and falling to the knees, but the vast majority of the children of the people are absolutely naked and not ashamed; for not even the infantile costume of a string and a rupee, which passes muster in Bengal, is thought necessary in Burma. When a girl reaches, however, the age of twelve or thirteen, she passes from childhood to young womanhood, and the crossing of the Rubicon is marked by a ceremony of vital importance, and which is in no case ever omitted—namely, that of the boring of the ears.

On a certain day, selected by the astrologers as peculiarly lucky, all the friends and relatives of the family are invited, and musicians are engaged. The little maid, dressed in her best, awaits the great event with trepidation and anticipation, for will not the stab of the boring needle free her from the thraldom of childhood, and open to her the gay pleasures of maidenhood, and the privileges of flirtation, leading in the end to the consummation of marriage? At a given moment the professional ear-borer plunges sharp needles of gold through the lobes of her ears, and the loud music of the band drowns the cries of the little girl.

The process of enlarging the aperture is then begun, and has to be continued every day till the hole is large enough in diameter. Bundles of delicate stems of elephant-grass are passed into the opening, the number of which is increased every day, till a large and unsightly hole is produced in the dilated lobes of the ears. This is then filled either by tubes of glass of different colours, or by short circular pieces of silver with filigree ornamentation, or even by long rods of silver of considerable weight. I bought out of the ears of a Kachin woman, within sight of King Theebaw's throne, a pair of massive silver ear-tubes curiously worked. Royal ladies and ladies of the court used to have the sole right of wearing ear-tubes of gold set with jewels. Amber plugs are so highly valued that I would not pay the price asked for them in the bazaar at Mandalay. Ear-tubes of every conceivable colour and pattern, made of German glass, are exposed for sale in every bazaar, and the choice of a dainty ear-tube is a matter on which much care is expended by the Burmese coquette. The hole in the ear is sometimes so big that a large green cheroot can be easily carried in it, and I have been amused when travelling by rail to see a woman deposit her railway ticket for safety in the gaping space.

In the same way as boring the ears marks the age of puberty in a girl, so tattooing the legs is the sign in a boy that he is growing into manhood. When watching the coolies engaged in lading and unlading the boats on the Irrawaddy, one cannot fail to observe that every man seems to wear dark blue tights from the waist to the knee. These breeches are not, however, external, but are in the skin itself, and are the result of careful and skilful tattooing. On close inspection, it is found that all kinds of animals, but chiefly tigers, monkeys, and elephants, as well as beloos or devils, are cleverly tattooed on the skin in red and blue, each figure being encircled by a border of letters and words. A Burman would think it unmanly not to have his thighs tattooed, and the custom is universal. The operation is a painful one, so that only a little is done at a time, and during the process the boy is usually kept under the influence of an opiate.

The Shans are the best tattooers, but none of the Burmese are equal to the Japanese in the realisation of the artistic possibilities of the art. In Burma the reds usually fade out, while the dark blue dyes remain; but in Japan the figure of a dragon, or of a woman dressed in a flowery kimono, will be tattooed on the skin in delicate shades of blue and red, and will remain indelible and unchanged throughout the whole of the person's life. The Burmese tattooers are now learning to decorate the limbs of English sailors with pictures from the *Graphic* and the illustrated papers.

Marriage, though highly estimated among the Burmese, is not consecrated by a religious ceremony. The phongyees, or monks, accept celibacy with such earnestness of conviction, as being the highest state of mankind, that they cannot be expected to give their blessing on an occasion when happiness is sought by taking a step diametrically opposed to their views of life and its obligations. As there are no priests in Burma, the wedding ceremony is consequently purely secular.

A marriage having been arranged between a girl and her lover, the friends of the engaged couple are, on an auspicious day, bidden by the bride's parents to a great feast. The house is thronged with guests, all dressed in their gayest tameins and pasohs. Musicians and dancers are engaged, and a booth is erected where a pwé, or play, is given representing some love-story of a king's son. In the presence of the assembled guests, the bride and bridegroom eat out of the same dish; the bridegroom then presents his bride with a packet of pickled tea, which gift is returned. This constitutes the ceremony of marriage. The publicity of the avowed intention of the young people to marry, and the public giving of the girl to the man by her parents, are considered sufficient to tie the connubial knot as firmly as the Burmans think in all reason it should be tied. The bride is, as a rule, about seventeen or eighteen years of age, and the bridegroom the same age, or a little older. The young husband is generally taken to live with his wife's parents, where he has to contribute his share to the household work and expenses. It is he also who is expected to provide the marriage dower, not the bride or the bride's father.

In fact, Burma is perhaps the only country where it is recognised that a woman honours a man by marrying him, for the laws of Manu (said to have been composed 1280 B.C.) are still the laws of Burma, and there it is especially stated that "women are to be esteemed and honoured by their fathers, brothers, husbands, and fathers-in-law, if the latter wish to be happy themselves. The gods rejoice when women are honoured; where it is not done sacrifices avail nothing. When the women are ill-treated the family goes to ruin; when the contrary happens, it flourishes forever. A Burmese bride enters the married state certain of kind consideration and good treatment; if her experience is otherwise, the law gives her quick and sure redress.

There is an ancient tradition in Burma that when the earth was originally peopled from the heavens, nine of the spiritual beings gradually became human owing to their having partaken of gross food. Four became women and five men. Four of the men then took the four women to wife, but one man was left out in this pairing of couples, and was perforce a lonely bachelor. Enraged at the happiness of the married couples, he pelted them with stones on their marriage night. In sympathy with this primeval bachelor, and following immemorial custom, the young men of the neighbourhood collect after a wedding, and all through the night throw stones and pieces of wood on the roof of the house which shelters the happy couple; a custom which is so disagreeable and annoying, that in Lower Burma the bridegroom is fain to bribe his troublesome neighbours to forego a ceremony "more to be honoured in the breach than in the observance."

The Burman thoroughly enjoys a funeral. It would seem indeed to be sometimes a matter of regret that he cannot be there to participate in his own obsequies, for a poor man when dead will receive more gifts than he ever had when alive, and money, which would have kept him for a long time living in comfort, is squandered on his corpse. Burmans both bury and cremate their dead, and in each case the ceremonies are long, and are most punctiliously observed.

As soon as the person is dead, the body is washed, wrapped in a new white cloth, and dressed in the richest clothing the deceased possessed. The face is left uncovered, and between the teeth is put the coin of gold or silver which is supposed to pay for the passage across the river of death. Messages are then sent to the monastery and the musicians are summoned. The music selected on these occasions is mournful, and dirges are played outside the house without ceasing. The body is then placed in a wooden coffin of very flimsy construction; in the case of nobles, the coffins are gilded. Relatives and friends arrive at the house in great numbers as soon as it is known that a death has occurred, and they bring with them gifts or money. At the end of two, or at the most three days, the body is borne to the grave with great pomp and ceremonial. The coffin, which is painted red, is carried by eight persons, friends of the deceased, under a large canopy, gaily decorated with tinsel and paintings. Over the coffin is thrown the richest clothes which had been worn by the dead person. In the procession the alms intended for the monks are carried first, followed by nuns bearing baskets of betel and pickled tea. The monks come next, walking two and two, and carrying broad-leafed fans in their hands; after them walks the band of singers. The bier follows, and then a great crowd of relatives and friends, all dressed in white, making loud lamentations, and calling upon the dead to answer numerous questions.[1] At the cemetery the coffin is placed on the ground, and the senior monk delivers a sermon, which is simply a recitation of the great commandments and precepts of Buddha, after which the monks retire. The chief mourner then pours water slowly out of a cocoa-nut shell, saying, "May the deceased and all present share the merit of the offering made and the ceremonies now proceeding." The coffin is swung three times backwards and forwards over the open grave and lowered. Every visitor throws in a handful of earth and the grave-diggers fill up the grave. The alms and gifts are then distributed to the monks and the poor. No headstone marks the grave.

When the body is burnt, the pyre is kindled by the nearest relatives. Three days later the relations, dressed in white, return to search for and collect the bones that remain. These are carefully washed in cocoa-nut milk and placed in an earthenware pot, which is either kept in the house or buried. Sometimes a solid pagoda is raised over the bones of a great person as a monument; at others they are ground to powder, mixed with wood oil, and moulded into a little figure of Buddha, which is taken home and treasured in a sacred spot in the house.

For a week after the funeral a kind of Irish wake goes on. A great concourse of friends are incessantly coming to the house of mourning day and night, and are engaged in talking, eating,

---

[1] I have seen a similar Chinese funeral procession in the streets of Hong-Kong.

and drinking. Friends contribute towards the heavy expense of a funeral, but it often results, nevertheless, that the whole fortune left by the deceased is squandered on his obsequies.

When carrying a dead body, the procession must not move to the north or to the east; hence Burmese cemeteries are placed to the west of a city outside the gates. All bodies are carried out of the west gate, which is therefore called the gate of mourning.

15

FANNY BULLOCK WORKMAN
Bicycling Through India
FROM
Through Town and Jungle (1904)

Fanny Bullock Workman was the foremost American woman explorer of the nineteenth century. Born in 1859 in Worcester, Massachusetts, she was the daughter of Alexander Hamilton Bullock, once governor of Massachusetts, and Elvira Hazard Bullock. She was educated in private schools in New York, Dresden, and Paris. After her studies she returned to Worcester and married William Hunter Workman, a prominent physician.

In 1886, the Workmans visited Scandinavia and northern Europe, and then settled in Germany for about nine years. From there they took jaunts to Algiers, Greece, and Palestine. Later travels carried them— frequently on bicycle—through India, Ceylon, Java, Sumatra, and Cochin-China.

Mrs. Workman's career as an explorer began in earnest in 1899 when she made her first ascent of the Himalayas. On subsequent expeditions, she achieved a world mountaineering record for women (1906). She also made numerous first ascents, climbed a number of peaks of more than twenty thousand feet, discovered watersheds, explored glaciers, and mapped previously unsurveyed territory.

Because she had command of several languages, she was able to speak before learned societies in both America and Europe and she was the first woman to lecture before the Sorbonne in Paris. Ten European geographical societies honored her with their highest awards. During World War I, she lived in France. She died in Cannes in 1925.

Among the books she wrote, usually in collaboration with her husband, are Algerian Memories *(1895),* In the Ice World of the Hima-

210

layas *(1900)*, Peaks and Glaciers of the Nun Kun *(1909)*, The Call of the Snowy Hispar *(1910), and* Two Summers in the Icy Wilds of Eastern Karakorum *(1917)*. *These accounts are distinguished by a historical perspective on these far-off lands, but they often lack the depth of a sociological understanding of the inhabitants that a later generation of travel writers sought.*

Through Town and Jungle (1904), based on a bicycle trip the couple took in the late 1890s through the south of India, was written by Fanny Workman alone and appears to have a greater appreciation of people than the previous books produced in collaboration. The report on the aborigine Toda tribe may be the first of its kind, and with its cool reporting and minute, careful observations, it remains a readable book.

On the 25th of January we left Madras at daybreak en route to Ootacamund in the Nilgiri Hills, some three hundred and fifty miles to the south-west. On this day we rode seventy-five miles to Ranipat over roads that were partly lumpy and only fair at best. The bungalow here was a spacious building with brick floor, but destitute of furniture of any kind. One portion was occupied by a young lieutenant on duty, who was away on our arrival.

We took possession of the other half, but without much prospect of comfort, as the *chaukidar* had nothing in which to boil water, and our servant had gone ahead with our main baggage to the place we expected to reach on the morrow. The *chaukidar* advised us to apply to a retired English officer living near by for cots to sleep on, which advice we followed. He and his wife, on learning of the plight we were in in the unfurnished bungalow, kindly sent over not only the cots but sheets, pillows, a table, and washstand. The servants who brought the furniture were followed by a bearer with afternoon tea, which was most refreshing after the dust and heat of the day.

The lieutenant soon returned, and courteously invited us to dine with him, and allow his servants to attend to our wants. He played the part of host admirably, and we had a jolly meal together. All in all, owing to the kindness of our two benefactors, we passed as comfortable a night as we should have done in a well-appointed dak bungalow.

The lieutenant expressed surprise, that we had come from

Madras in one day, and said he had planned to cycle back there, but it had not occurred to him to make less than three étapes, sending tents ahead to meet him at night. Although accustomed to what he considered much exercise, he confessed he did not feel equal to cycling in the sun for so many hours. He further remarked that a woman, who could cycle seventy-five miles in a day in the Madras Presidency, need fear no heat she might meet in other parts of India. This was consoling.

The roads of South India are as a rule much better shaded than those of the middle and north. The trees here are chiefly banyans, mangoes, and tamarinds, which grow to a great size and cast a dense shade. In many cases their interlacing branches form a leafy arch over the road, which for miles completely shuts out the sun's rays. On roads thus shaded one may ride in comfort in the dry season even at a temperature of 90° Fahr. . . .

Monkeys were seen continually on this route. They were extremely shy, and never waited for us to come near them. If we stopped to look at them, they retreated immediately to a safe distance, but, if we did not appear to notice them, they would remain among the lower branches of the trees, peeking out at us from behind them. They seemed to prefer the tamarind trees, the fruit of which they ate with evident relish. When we stopped under these trees, they pelted us with the pods they were picking, grinning as if they enjoyed the sport.

On this day we sat under a spreading tamarind-tree to eat our tiffin. Shortly half a dozen rather small, dark brown monkeys climbed into the branches over us, and watched us attentively. At last one, more venturesome and perhaps more intelligent than the rest, cautiously descended, and sat on a small branch about ten feet above us. After a few moments he began to open and shut his mouth rapidly, looking directly at us, evidently intending to indicate that he wished some of our food. As we did not appear to notice his appeal, to emphasise it and show us he was in earnest, with an expression of great determination he seized the branch with both hands, and shook it several times with all his strength, much as an excited child might do. Was not the karma of that monkey about fitted for its next transmigration into a human being?

The temple at Vellore, while smaller than those at Madura

and Seringham, is of finer workmanship and earlier date. In front of the graceful seven-storied gopura stand two blue granite dwarpals, which faintly remind one of similar temple guardians in Java. The madapam is the chef-d'œuvre of the place with double flexioned cornice and admirably executed compound pillars, each of different design. The yalis and rearing horsemen on the columns of the portico are most spirited, and far removed from the ponderous conventional creatures seen in some Dravidian temples. Artists, and very good ones too, seem to have been employed here, where everything is carved, even to the fantastic fruit ceiling with its circle of lightly poised parrots.

Coming from the south one is impressed by the fine open work on many columns. It is the first suggestion of what the Chalukyas employed so effectively at Hulabid and elsewhere, and is particularly interesting from the fact, that the building dates of this and the Chalukyan temples differ by less than a century, that of this being about 1300. The temple stands within the eleventh century fort. It is worth while to ascend the bat-infested stairway to the top of the gopura for the view, which combines a sweep of distant sunglint plain, flanked by azure hills, with a near coup d'œil of beige ramparts, offset by a sluggish moat. In the distance the sun blazing with noon-day power transforms the landscape into brilliant almost palpitating form in the heat haze, while a soft cloud sheathing an arc of the sky overhead shrouds the near scene in solemn half-tones.

We came upon a number of women engaged in repairing the road under the direction of a tall, fine-looking man draped in spotless white. The women were bringing water to wet down the road in large earthen chattis, balanced on their heads. Their fine figures were well set off by their bright-coloured saris, and the freedom and grace of their movements were admirable.

We found the South Indians usually polite, and willing to render us any assistance in their power. We were surprised to find how large a number of them spoke English, particularly in the Madras Presidency. We seldom passed through a village of any size, where Indians were not to be found with considerable knowledge of English. Undoubtedly missionary work, which has been undertaken here to a greater extent than in many parts of India, is partly responsible for this, but by no means wholly, for large numbers of Hindus, who have not come under missionary influence, speak English well, so that instruction under Government auspices must be allowed credit also.

Those Madrasis who have nominally embraced Christianity are usually baptized with, or have adopted Biblical names, such as Jacob, Paul, Peter, Abraham, Methuselah, &c. The sincerity of their Christian professions seems to be doubted not only by the native population but also by the European. It is a significant fact, that Europeans, not only in the Madras Presidency but in all parts of India, prefer Hindus and Mohammedans to Christians as servants. Everywhere we heard the statement made by those who had lived for any time in India, that they would not have a native Christian in their houses. After having had several of them in our service we learned to appreciate the grounds on which this all-prevailing sentiment is based. We remember one lady missionary, who was in a state of great depression at the conduct of her Christianised domestics, but her position forbade her to employ unregenerate natives.

There is one peculiarity common to Indians of every race, religion, condition, and class—except perhaps the highest, which is too well-bred to show it—viz., curiosity. Without any apparent motive they put a string of questions nearly always the same to us on all occasions, the answers to which could not possibly be of any importance to them. These were, "Where do you come from? When did you leave there? What service to you belong to? What is your business here? How long do you stop? Where are you going?" In some cases, not satisfied with these, they asked us if we were bicycle agents. They could not understand otherwise, why we should take the trouble to travel on cycles.

These questions were answered as prudence dictated. After some experience we found it convenient to cut off too much impertinence by looking wise and mysteriously hinting we were on secret service making an examination of the district, which usually had the effect of putting an end to further questioning. But, as in Spain, where the customs have many points of resemblance to those of the East, we could not get the people to do much for us, till their curiosity had been satisfied.

At Jalarpet Junction there was no bungalow, so we were

obliged to pass the night in the waiting-room at the railway station, which was comfortable as such places go. At the larger railway stations the men's and women's waiting-rooms are provided with two or three cane couches each, and a dressing-room containing a washstand, pitcher, hand-basin, commode, and sometimes an iron bath-tub. If one is so fortunate as to be the sole occupant of the room, one can pass a fairly comfortable night; but usually one's rest is disturbed by the snores of other occupants, the screeching of locomotive whistles, the rumble of trains, the harsh and discordant shouting of natives on the platform, and the incoming of passengers. On several occasions parties of natives invaded the waiting-room and camped on the floor, making so much noise that sleep was impossible.

The waiting-rooms of the small stations possess only a table, straight-backed chairs, and wooden settees, and in these comfort is out of the question. One learns to doze on the wooden settees and even sitting upright on the chairs, but refreshing sleep cannot be obtained.

The next day we ran eighty-one miles to Salem Junction. This run was rather trying on account of thirst, for there was no town nor other place in the whole distance, where we could get soda-water or refill our water-flasks. The road was partly good and partly bad. It ascended for sixty miles over a high plateau, and then descended gently to Salem. Much of the way it was well shaded. We had to ford three rivers, the water in which was from ankle to knee-deep. The country became greener as we ascended, and the Shevaroy Hills appeared on the right clothed in a beautiful blue and picturesque in outline. On the horizon over them was a thin veil of cloud, which showed pinkish shades like sunset tints for several hours during the day. These hills serve as a summer resort to those who cannot go to Nilgiris. Their highest point is 6,347 feet.

Spending this night at the railway station at Salem we pushed on in the morning to Erode Junction forty miles to the south. Two miles before Erode we came to the Cauvery river, which here has a wide rocky bed, in which considerable water was flowing with an eddying current. There was no bridge, and when we reached the river no one was in sight, and no means of crossing was apparent.

After we had waited for some time, a native came up, and said there was a boatman a quarter of a mile above, whom he would call. In due time the boatman appeared with his boat, which was modelled after a lotus-leaf, or possibly, a frying-pan. It was circular, about six and a half feet in diameter, with a rim fifteen inches high turning up a right angle with the bottom. It was made of bamboo basketwork covered with buffalo hide.

As it danced about upon the water, it looked so frail, that we hesitated to trust ourselves to it, and suggested to the boatman, it would be advisable to take only one at a time over. He said the boat would hold all three, and we need have no fear. When the cycles and baggage had been placed in it, and we had stowed ourselves in the space which remained, the boat was completely filled. Only room enough was left for one leg of the boatman, by which he clung to the craft as only an Indian can cling, and wielded a spade-shaped paddle and a bamboo pole with great dexterity.

To our surprise the boat was exceedingly staunch and steady, and even when whirling round and round in the eddies in mid-stream did not tilt perceptibly. We at first felt ourselves in the position of the three wise men of Gotham who went to sea in a bowl, but we did not suffer the fate, which is supposed to have overtaken those adventurers, for our bowl proved strong, and we landed in safety on the other side.

For the third consecutive night we were obliged to put up at a railway station at Erode, where the waiting-rooms are well arranged. The couches were even provided with mosquito nettings, but alas! these were full of holes, and the host of mosquitos which took advantage of this defect made sleep a mockery.

The next day we rode sixty-two miles to Mettupalaiyam at the foot of the Nilgiri Hills. The road, which ascended moderately for about thirty miles, although without shade, was the smoothest we had seen since leaving Madras.

We passed two of the collections of figures of horses, horsemen, elephants, dogs and men, which are scattered about this part of the country. These figures, which are grotesque, of rude workmanship, and often of colossal size, are grouped together in semicircles under trees by the roadside, or in front of lonely country shrines, or arranged around walled enclosures with faces turned toward the centre of the enclosure. They are hollow, made of clay or chunam, and are painted in various colours.

The only explanation we were able to get as to their purpose came from an English official, who said the figures of animals were intended as mounts for the village gods, when they made their rounds in the region, and those of men to serve them as servants.

From their appearance, position, and arrangement, it might also be supposed, that they are intended as habitations for the spirits of the departed, when they revisit the scenes of their earthly activities, or as memorial or votive offerings, like the small animal figures of baked clay placed on and around tombs in Bengal. We did not see them farther north than the state of Mysore.

The approach to the Nilgiris on a cycle is like nearing an enchanted land on wings. As you bear down upon them they rise like an ethereal barrier blotting out the world beyond. They are well called the blue hills as the name implies. Whilst their vast wooded spurs are perfectly distinct in outline, the whole mass seems to soar above the plain in a film of azure blue. In the early morning a pink mist bathes them, at noon and evening a blue ether. At no hour do they like most hills appear real and commonplace. The Nilgiris are theatrical, resembling well-painted stage peaks yet possessing the one thing, that the at best but tawdry work of the artist cannot reproduce, the soul of nature.

At Mettupalaiyam we put up at Brown's bungalow, an establishment with four guest-rooms. The main building stands in a large enclosure bounded on three sides by sheds for the ponies employed in the tonga service to Ootacamund, which exhaled an odour none too agreeable to persons of delicate olfactory sense. The walls of the dining-room were well sprinkled with cheap prints, among which were numerous illuminated placards bearing such mottoes as "Dawson's Whiskies," "Dry Champagne, Geo. Goulet Rheims," "May Lee Cross cut," "The Lord will provide," "Faith, Hope and Charity," the last two evidently placed there by missionaries, doubtless as an antidote to the baleful effect of the others or with a view to create variety in the mural decorations, which might thus appeal to the taste of every one.

From Mettupalaiyam the road runs level for six miles to Kolar at the foot of the ghat leading to the Nilgiris. From Kolar to Coonoor sixteen miles it winds steeply upward, and thence on twelve miles with a somewhat easier gradient to Ootacamund. Although on this day the distance travelled was less than on any other of the six from Madras, the work was more fatiguing as we had to push our loaded cycles up the steep ascent twenty-two miles. The height climbed during the day must have been about 6,000 feet. The hills seen and passed were abrupt, of good shapes, and heavily wooded. Their bases were clothed with a jungle of bamboo, which was bare and brown having shed most of its foliage, then came dense forests of tropical trees largely deciduous, and higher these were replaced by evergreens.

The Nilgiri Hills consist of an isolated mountain massif adjoining the southern boundary of Mysore, extending fifty-one miles east and west, and twenty-one north and south, the sides of which rise everywhere sharply from the plain. The top is a rolling plateau of an average height of 6,500 feet above the sea, covered alternately with grass and forest. Its surface is intersected in all directions by narrow valleys. At several points it rises into peaks, the highest of which, Dodabetta, is said to be 8,728 feet.

The Nilgiris are a great blessing to South India affording a refuge from the heat in the warm season, which both the Madras Government and the people avail themselves of. The temperature is mild and equable being said to average 58° Fahr.

Ootacamund or Ooty, as the Anglo-Indian residents call it, the chief town on the plateau, lies at a height of 7,000 to 7,500 feet above the sea. With its delightful climate and attractive surroundings of wooded peaks, wild ravines, and grand forest, it is a by no means unpleasant place to live in. It is called by many the fairest hill-station in India, and it may indeed lay claim to certain attractions not possessed by the northern stations, prominent among which is the large amount of level area around it.

There are many miles of well-made roads extending in every direction over the hills and through the valleys, on which one may ride and cycle to his heart's content. There is plenty of room for polo, or golf, or any other game. It also offers attractions to the sportsman both in the surrounding district and in the mountains of the Kundas, on the wild slopes and crests of Murkurty and Avalanche peaks, as well as on the heavily wooded ones running down to the plains. Among the large game are the elephant, tiger, leopard, cheetah, bear, deer, wild boar, and muntjak, or mountain sheep. Tigers exist at all altitudes though more plentiful on the lower slopes.

A fine one was killed on Dodabetta a short time before our visit to it. There are also many varieties of birds and smaller animals. Darjeeling, Simla, and Murree, have their views of the "Snows" which may well be written with a capital. They also have their social life; but as one cannot live on views alone, so the interest in the social life of a hill-station, however agreeable, wanes after a time. At Ooty, if one becomes tired of gymkhanas and badminton, one can flee to the hills and forests without descending six or eight thousand feet to the plains or climbing to snowy heights. To escape Darjeeling one must descend to the Teesta, or the Terai, or attack a slope of Kanchenjanga.

The supreme grandeur of sunrise on Mounts Everest, Kabru, and Kanchenjanga, as seen from Sandakphu, cannot be seen in the Nilgiris, but sunrise moments may be enjoyed on the summit of Dodabetta, when the wide-spreading plains below are carpeted with fluffy mists, and the hills rise like sentinels of the morning in a garb of mystic blue toward the rose-tinted sky. Nor can one ever forget the evening hours, when the blood-red disk of the sun sinks in a dark mauve haze, which soon changes into the grey of twilight.

Besides three small aboriginal tribes the native inhabitants of the Nilgiris are the Badagas, a Hindu race said to have come from Mysore after the downfall of the kingdom of Vijayanagar about 350 years ago. They are tillers of the soil, hold their land under the Government, and pay a tribute in grain to the Todas.

The aboriginal tribe of the Todas, now reduced in number to less than seven hundred, is the most interesting of the native races. They regard themselves still as the real owners of the hills, and look with little favour on the more numerous and industrious people from the plains. They are tall, well built, with copper-coloured skin, elongated heads, and narrow foreheads. The men wear their hair in a frowzy shock, which, hanging over the temples and eyes gives them a wild appearance.

Some of the women are very good-looking. Their hair, which is long and black, is parted on the crown, combed back, and allowed to fall in long curls or waves. Their dress when clean makes an effective setting to the dark curls falling over it. It consists of coarse white cloth, which is draped gracefully over the shoulders like a toga leaving the right arm bare.

The Todas live in hamlets of four to six huts called *mands*. The huts are made of bamboo woven into a framework and covered with thatch, which is waterproof even during the monsoon. They are tent-shaped, about eighteen feet long, ten feet high, and nine wide. The ends are closed with stout planks. One end has a doorway, the sole opening to the hut, which is closed by a wooden door thirty-two inches high, eighteen wide, and four to six thick, so arranged as to slide forward and back. There is no chimney, and the smoke of the fire has to find its way out by the door if at all. The whole interior is black with soot.

On one side of the interior there is a raised clay platform covered with skins for sleeping purposes, and opposite a fireplace with a stand for cooking utensils, which are few and primitive. Among these is the usual pestle for pounding rice, whilst a hole in the ground beaten hard serves for a mortar. The huts are surrounded by walls of loose stones. A *mand* is usually occupied by one family, which also owns one or more others in different places, to which they move to graze their buffaloes.

The Todas are good-natured, lazy, and independent. They are wholly pastoral in their habits, depending for support on their herds of buffaloes, the tribute paid by the Badagas, and a small gratuity granted by Government in consideration of their claim to the land. Each householder has his own cattle, which are not interfered with by others. The buffaloes of different owners graze together in common under the supervision of the priest, who attends to the milking, and distributes each householder the milk due to him from his animals. The milk and butter are kept in one part of a separate hut entered by no one except the priest, the other part of which serves as a temple.

On the death of the head of a family the eldest son succeeds to the largest share of the buffaloes, and the youngest becomes owner of the house and has to support the women. Polyandry was formerly much practised but has fallen into disuse, and it is now the exception for a woman to have more than one husband. The marriage ceremony like most of those of the Todas is simple, consisting only of an exchange of buffaloes on the part of the husband and his father-in-law. The women cook, carry water, and, as a pastime, make a coarse sort of embroidery. Their position is low. When the men come home after an absence, the women greet them by falling on their knees and raising first one foot and then the other to their foreheads.

The language is a mixture of Dravidian dialects, and most strongly resembles Tamil, which some of the Todas speak. Now and then one of them is induced to attend the missionary schools at Ootacamund, but no converts are made. The religion has a pastoral tinge showing traces of ancestor and element worship.

There are higher and lower priests. The chief priest lives in a hut by himself apart from every one. No woman can approach his abode and no man speak with him without permission. He has great influence over the people, who believe God dwells in him and makes known His wishes through him as a medium. As to rites, happy mortals, they practise almost none. Some old men salaam to the rising sun or moon, others fast at the time of eclipses, but none except the priests do more than this.

Their only form of prayer is, "May all be well," or "May all be well with the buffaloes." The younger ones do not trouble themselves about even this form. The only really religious ceremony is said to be the sacrifice once a year of a male buffalo calf. Women are not permitted to be present at this.

It does not fall to the lot of most persons to have two funerals, but in this respect the Toda has the advantage of his fellow Indians. The first or green funeral takes place soon after death, when the corpse is placed in the open, and three handfuls of earth are thrown upon it. Two buffaloes of the deceased are then brought up to touch the corpse, after which they are immediately killed and placed beside it. The family and friends surround the three corpses and mourn, which ceremony is followed by the burning of the body. The ashes are left to be scattered by the winds.

The second or dry funeral takes place at the end of the year in commemoration of all who have died during it, at a funeral hut devoted to this purpose. The ceremony lasts two days and is evidently not a very sad affair. The first day is occupied with the assembling of the participators, buying, selling, and soothsaying, in fact with the semblance of a country fair. The crowning event is the arrival of selected buffaloes, which the next day are excited to a high pitch and then killed as an offering, which act closes the ceremony.

We heard a good deal in Ootacamund as in other parts of India of three bugaboos, of which the Europeans there appear to live in continual fear, "a touch of the sun," "fever," and "catching a chill," especially after a wetting even with the temperature at 85° and over. Without discussing these here we may say briefly that, in spite of constant exposure to heat, sun, cold, wet, and malarial emanations, in the course of many thousand miles of travel in all parts of India, we escaped all of these evils.

PART IV
Africa

16

ALEXINE TINNE
Gondokoro
1870

Alexine Tinne squeezed into the brief span of her life enough adventure to satisfy five ordinary mortals. She was born in The Hague in 1835, the heiress to a Dutch fortune, and at the age of nineteen she travelled to Egypt. She was so captivated by the idea of Africa that she decided to devote most of her active years to exploring the mysteries of the then almost unknown (to the West) continent.

In 1861, Alexine, accompanied by her mother, Harriet, and her Aunt Adriana, embarked from The Hague on the first stage of a voyage up the Nile in the hope of discovering the source of that river. (Captains Speke and Grant had already set out on such a search.) En route, they offered to take badly needed supplies to Speke and Grant, who were at Gondokoro, a small trading station in the Sudan, the farthest point up the Nile reachable by boat. The offer was turned down, and the three women pushed ahead in their little steamer. During the voyage, they survived bouts of dysentery and swarms of mosquitoes. Alexine used her spare time to start a notebook entitled "A Few General Directions for Travellers on the Nile." She recommended that one avoid drafts, wear flannels around the loins, and keep to a proper English diet—"not too much fruit and well-cooked vegetables."

Though they never reached Lake Victoria (the river passed into unmanageable rapids, as reconnaissance by foot revealed), their steamer was the first mechanical boat to get up the Nile as far as Gondokoro. The ladies spent a month among the Shilluk tribe (who, when asked about the source of the Nile, laughed and said it had none), packed up, and headed back to Khartoum. Their steamer later became The Prince Halim, *the first boat to provide passenger service on the upper Nile.*

On this journey Alexine had gathered ethnological specimens and had written letters home, but like the English church that was erected in The Hague in her memory, almost all these remains were destroyed during World War II. Harriet Tinne did keep a diary, but unfortunately the entries, probably intended for personal use, are so sketchy and incomplete that they do not provide a readable record. Hence, Alexine Tinne is represented in this volume by some verses she penned after returning from her epic voyage.

She died in 1868 when she was shot to death by a marauding Taureg while attempting to become the first woman to cross the Sahara. Her name is engraved on a little obelisk in southern Sudan, at the farthest point she reached on her Nile exploration, and her memory is preserved for posterity by none other than Dr. Livingstone, the famous explorer and missionary:

> *The work of Speke and Grant is deserving of highest commendation, inasmuch as they opened up an immense tract of previously unexplored country. . . . But none rises higher in my estimation than the Dutch lady, Miss Tinne, who after the severest domestic afflictions, nobly persevered in the teeth of every difficulty.*

The following poem appears in Penelope Gladstone's Travels of Alexine *(London: John Murray, 1970), the first and only serious study of this remarkable lady.*

Gondokoro

We've arrived! And whatever may happen
It never can alter the past.
We have been a long time in arriving,
But we're come to the Mountain at last.
And altho' there are yearly some merchants
Their ivory trade to pursue,
Few have braved all the dangers that we have
And got safely to Gondokoro.

We have passed through the Shilluks and Dinkas,
And done all the kindness we could.

Gondoroko

The Nuers, the Kitches, the Bari,
We have burnt their old tuguls for wood.
Passed elephants, buffaloes and lions,
Drunken captains and quarrelsome crew,
Crocodiles, hippopotami,
And got safely to Gondokoro.

We can boast we made friends with the Shilluks,
Rode on horseback with Mohammed Kher,
Bought our mutton for onions and turbans,
An ox for a lance or a spear.
We have ventured where very few ladies,
In fact I have heard but of two,
Who have suffered the hardships that we have
And got safely to Gondokoro.

For weeks we saw only green garches,
Where we'd nothing but pancakes to eat,
Been devoured by gnats in the marshes,
To whom we white men were a treat.
We have suffered from heat in the sunshine.
We have suffered from damp in the dew.
But at least here is earth where a biped
Walks safely at Gondokoro.

We've escaped many dangers of weather,
Wind, thunder and lightning, and rain.
We've escaped all the turnings and windings,
Without having dared to complain.
We've escaped being crashed in the steamer
In a cataract nobody knew,
And though rather the worse for the contact
We got safely to Gondokoro.

And here we've been feasted and shot for.
We've been to a torch ball at night,
Where the Negroes danced, drunk with merissa,
A beautiful curious sight.
We've sat under tamarhinds and citrons
Distributing presents not few,

For you must not be stingy in giving
To live safely at Gondokoro.

We've pitied the Austrian Mission,
Poor devils who die here like mice,
Though they planted a garden quite pretty
And built a brick house very nice.
At St. Croix six still are existing
Though the ague has turned them all blue,
Who declared it was useless attempting
To live safely at Gondokoro.

We've been to the Mountain Bellenia
O'er a plain with fine trees like a park,
With oxen and sheep and bad Negroes
Who would murder you after it's dark.
We took them five cows as a present.
It seems very odd but it's true,
Blue beads, copper bracelets and cattle
Give safety at Gondokoro.

We've been up as high as the Rejaf,
Which is quite at the back of beyond,
But there we could get on no further
For the steamer had stuck on the ground.
Now as we can't go further southward,
There is nothing more for us to do
Than to turn our boats round to the northward
And get safely from Gondokoro.

17

MARY KINGSLEY

Journey into the Jungle

FROM
Travels in West Africa (1897)

In the annals of West African exploration, few names rank above that of Mary Kingsley, one of those intrepid English ladies who feared neither the deepest jungle nor the highest mountain peak.

She was born in Islington in 1862. The love of travel and writing were ingrained from her childhood at Highgate. An omnivorous reader, she apparently created a world of her own amid books of travel, natural history, science, and literature. Both of her uncles were novelists, one the great Charles Kingsley. Her father, an eccentric physician, travelled widely in Asia, the South Seas, and America. In 1892, her parents died, leaving her a modest inheritance that enabled her to travel on her own. On a trip to the Canary Islands, she met the representatives of the West African trading firms who were to influence her views and to stimulate her to visit "the dark continent."

Charles Kingsley provided her with introductions to scientists, and she discovered that she could undertake valuable research by collecting West African fish. In 1893, she made her first trip to West Africa. She took notes on this journey, but decided against publishing them. Though she had travelled through the Congo Free State, she did not even hint at the terrible atrocities that the agents of King Leopold of Belgium were inflicting on the natives in a bloody regime of forced labor and monopoly, (that information would have to wait until the appearance of Joseph Conrad's Heart of Darkness *in 1899.)*

Though oblivious to the obvious, Mary Kingsley proved that a woman could travel alone in Africa on a small sum of money. Furthermore, her collection of fish so pleased the British Museum that she was awarded a collector's outfit for her next journey to the West African coast—which began in Liverpool in December of 1894 and ended there a year later.

Her second journey enabled her to collect many unknown specimens of fish and to study the social organization and religion of a cannibal tribe known as the Fan. Travels in West Africa, *her account of this adventure, was published in 1897. It was an immediate success and appeared in a popular abridged edition in 1900 and in a third edition in 1965, the rare sign of success for a travel book. Along with her* West African Studies *(1899), it marked the turning point in the history of West Africa, according to J. E. Flint, a historian at the University of Nigeria. Together, these books "helped to change in a profound way the attitude of European colonial administrators towards their African subjects, to create a scientific basis for the anthropological studies of Africans, and even to mould the ideas which educated Africans held about themselves in the early stages of the nationalist movement in West Africa."*

During that journey, she climbed the dangerous Mount Cameroon (the first woman to do so—native women did not ascend mountains). She died in 1900 in South Africa while serving as a nurse in the Boer War. Her last piece of writing was a sympathetic memoir prefixed to her father's Notes on Sport and Travel *(1900).*

Mary Kingsley's narrative style reminds us forcefully that her family bred novelists. No one can come away from Travels in West Africa *without feeling that it must be one of the most fascinating accounts of African exploration ever written. Its many beautiful passages evoke the nobility and the peril of the African forests, rivers, and mountains. Interwoven with these passages are scenes of great humor that gently satirize the blundering visitor rather than ridicule the behavior of the natives, as many such accounts so often did.*

My main aim in going to Congo Français was to get up above the tide line of the Ogowé River and there collect fishes; for my object on this voyage was to collect fish from a river north of the Congo. I had hoped this river would have been the Niger, for Sir George Goldie had placed at my disposal great facilities for carrying on work there in comfort; but for certain private reasons I was disinclined to go from the Royal Niger Protectorate into the Royal Niger Company's territory; and the Calabar, where Sir Claude MacDonald did everything he possibly could to assist me, I did not find a good river for me to collect fishes in. These two rivers failing me, from no fault of either of their own presiding genii, my only hope of doing anything now lay on the South West Coast river; the Ogowé. High-tide or low-tide, there is little difference in the water; the river, be it broad or narrow, deep or shallow, looks like a pathway of polished metal; for it is as heavy weighted with stinking mud as water e'er can be, ebb or flow, year out and year in. But the difference in the banks, though an unending alternation between two appearances, is weird.

At high-water you do not see the mangroves displaying their ankles in the way that shocked Captain Lugard. They look most respectable, their foliage rising densely in a wall irregularly striped here and there by the white line of an aërial root, coming straight down into the water from some upper branch as straight as a plummet, in the strange, knowing way an aërial root of a mangrove does, keeping the hard straight line until it gets some two feet above water-level, and then spreading out into blunt fingers with which to dip into the water and grasp the mud. Banks indeed at high water can hardly be said to exist, the water stretching away into the mangrove swamps for miles and miles, and you can then go, in a suitable small canoe, away among these swamps as far as you please.

This is a fascinating pursuit. For people who like that sort of thing it is just the sort of thing they like, as the art critic of a provincial town wisely observed anent an impressionist picture recently acquired for the municipal gallery. But it is a pleasure to be indulged in with caution; for one thing, you are certain to come across crocodiles. Now a crocodile drifting down in deep water, or lying asleep with its jaws open on a sand-bank, in the sun, is a picturesque adornment to the landscape when you are on the deck of a steamer, and you can write home about it and frighten your relations on your behalf; but when you are away among the swamps in a small dug-out canoe, and that crocodile and his relations are awake—a thing he makes a point of being at flood tide because of fish coming along—and when he has got his foot upon his native heath—that is to say, his tail within holding reach of his native mud—he is highly interesting, and you may not be able to write home about him—and you get frightened on your own behalf. For crocodiles can, and often do, in such

---

[1] A colonial administrator who served in the British East Africa Company.

places, grab at people in small canoes. I have known of several natives losing their lives in this way; some native villages are approachable from the main river by a short cut, as it were, through the mangrove swamps, and the inhabitants of such villages will now and then go across this way with small canoes instead of by the constant channel to the village, which is almost always winding. In addition to this unpleasantness you are liable—until you realise the danger from experience, or have native advice on the point—to get tide-trapped away in the swamps, the water falling round you when you are away in some deep pool or lagoon, and you find you cannot get back to the main river. For you cannot get out and drag your canoe across the stretches of mud that separate you from it, because the mud is of too unstable a nature and too deep, and sinking into it means staying in it, at any rate until some geologist of the remote future may come across you, in a fossilised state, when that mangrove swamp shall have become dry land. Of course if you really want a truly safe investment in Fame, and really care about Posterity, and Posterity's Science, you will jump over into the black batter-like, stinking slime, cheered by the thought of the terrific sensation you will produce 20,000 years hence, and the care you will be taken of then by your fellow-creatures, in a museum. But if you are a mere ordinary person of a retiring nature, like me, you stop in your lagoon until the tide rises again; most of your attention is directed to dealing with an "at home" to crocodiles and mangrove flies, and with the fearful stench of the slime round you. What little time you have over you will employ in wondering why you came to West Africa, and why, after having reached this point of absurdity, you need have gone and painted the lily and adorned the rose, by being such a colossal ass as to come fooling about in mangrove swamps. Twice this chatty little incident, as Lady MacDonald would call it, has happened to me, but never again if I can help it. On one occasion, the last, a mighty Silurian; as *The Daily Telegraph* would call him, chose to get his front paws over the stern of my canoe, and endeavoured to improve our acquaintance. I had to retire to the bows, to keep the balance right,[2] and fetch him a clip on the snout with a

---

[2]It is no use saying because I was frightened, for this miserably understates the case.

paddle, when he withdrew, and I paddled into the very middle of the lagoon, hoping the water there was too deep for him or any of his friends to repeat the performance. Presumably it was, for no one did it again. I should think that crocodile was eight feet long; but don't go and say I measured him, or that this is my outside measurement for crocodiles. I have measured them when they have been killed by other people, fifteen, eighteen, and twenty-one feet odd. This was only a pushing young creature who had not learnt manners.

I shall never forget one moonlight night I spent in a mangrove-swamp. I was not lost, but we had gone away into the swamp from the main river, so that the natives of a village with an evil reputation should not come across us when they were out fishing. We got well in, on to a long pool or lagoon; and dozed off and woke, and saw the same scene around us twenty times in the night, which thereby grew into an aeon, until I dreamily felt that I had somehow got into a world that was all like this, and always had been, and was always going to be so. Now and again the strong musky smell came that meant a crocodile close by, and one had to rouse up and see if all the crews' legs were on board, for Africans are reckless, and regardless of their legs during sleep. On one examination I found the leg of one of my most precious men ostentatiously sticking out over the side of the canoe. I woke him with a paddle, and said a few words regarding the inadvisability of wearing his leg like this in our situation; and he agreed with me, saying he had lost a valued uncle, who had been taken out of a canoe in this same swamp by a crocodile. His uncle's ghost had become, he said; a sort of devil which had been a trial to the family ever since; and he thought it must have pulled his leg out in the way I complained of, in order to get him to join him by means of another crocodile. I thanked him for the information and said it quite explained the affair, and I should do my best to prevent another member of the family from entering the state of devildom by aiming blows in the direction of any leg or arm I saw that uncle devil pulling out to place within reach of the crocodiles.

It is a strange, wild, lonely bit of the world we are now in, apparently a lake or broad—full of sandbanks, some bare and some in the course of developing into permanent islands by the growth on them of that floating coarse grass, any joint of which being torn off either by the current, a passing canoe, or hippos, floats down and grows wherever it settles. Like most things that float in these parts, it usually settles on a sandbank, and then grows in much the same way as our couch grass grows on land in England, so as to form a network, which catches for its adopted sandbank all sorts of floating *débris;* so the sandbank comes up in the world. The waters of the wet season when they rise drown off the grass; but when they fall, up it comes again from the root, and so gradually the sandbank becomes an island and persuades real trees and shrubs to come and grow on it, and its future is then secured.

We skirt alongside a great young island of this class; the sword grass some ten or fifteen feet high. It has not got any trees on it yet, but by next season or so it doubtless will have. The grass is stubbled down into paths by hippos, and just as I have realised who are the road-makers, they appear in person. One immense fellow, hearing us, stands up and shows himself about six feet from us in the grass, gazes calmly, and then yawns a yawn a yard wide and grunts his news to his companions, some of whom—there is evidently a large herd—get up and stroll towards us with all the flowing grace of Pantechnicon vans in motion. We put our helm paddles hard a starboard and leave that bank. These hippos always look to me as if they were the first or last creations in the animal world. At present I am undecided whether Nature tried "her 'prentice hand" on them in her earliest youth, or whether, having got thoroughly tired of making the delicately beautiful antelopes, corallines, butterflies, and orchids, she just said: "Goodness! I am quite worn out with this finicking work. Here, just put these other viscera into big bags—I can't bother any more."

Our hasty trip across to the bank of the island on the other side being accomplished, we, in search of seclusion and in the hope that out of sight would mean out of mind to hippos, shot down a narrow channel between semi-island sandbanks, and those sandbanks, if you please, are covered with specimens—as fine a set of specimens as you could wish for—of the West African crocodile. These interesting animals are also having their siestas, lying sprawling in all directions on the sand, with their mouths wide open. One immense old lady has a family of lively young crocodiles running over her, evidently playing like a lot of kittens. The heavy musky smell they give off is most repulsive, but we do not rise up and make a row about this, because we feel hopelessly in the wrong in intruding into these family scenes, uninvited, and so apologetically pole ourselves along rapidly, not even singing. The pace the canoe goes down that channel would be a wonder to Henley Regatta. When out of ear-shot I ask Pagan whether there are many gorillas, elephants, or bushcows round here. "Plenty too much," says he; and it occurs to me that the corn-fields are growing golden green away in England; and soon there rises up in my mental vision a picture that fascinated my youth in the *Fliegende Blätter,* representing "Friedrich Gerstaeker auf der Reise." That gallant man is depicted tramping on a serpent, new to M. Boulenger, while he attempts to club, with the butt end of his gun, a most lively savage who, accompanied by a bison, is attacking him in front. A terrific and obviously enthusiastic crocodile is grabbing the tail of the explorer's coat, and the explorer says "Hurrah! das gibt wieder einen prächtigen Artikel für *Die Allgemeine Zeitung.*" ["Hurrah! This will give us an article for the newspapers."] I do not know where in the world Gerstaeker was at the time, but I should fancy hereabouts. My vigorous and lively conscience also reminds me that the last words a most distinguished and valued scientific friend had said to me before I left home was, "Always take measurements, Miss Kingsley, and always take them from the adult male." I know I have neglected opportunities of carrying this commission out on both those banks, but I do not feel like going back. Besides, the men would not like it, and I have mislaid my yard measure. I will not bore you with my diary in detail regarding our land journey; because the water-washed little volume attributive to this period is mainly full of reports of law cases, for reasons hereinafter to be stated; and at night, when passing through this bit of country, I was usually too tired to do anything more than make an entry such as: "5 S., 4 R. A., N.E Ebony. T. I—50, &c.,&c."—entries that require amplification to explain their significance, and I will proceed to explain.

Our first day's march was a very long one. Path in the ordinary acceptance of the term there was none. Hour after hour, mile after mile, we passed on, in the under-gloom of the great forest. The pace made by the Fans, who are infinitely the most rapid Africans I have ever come across, severely tired the Ajumba, who are canoe men, and who had been as fresh as paint, after their exceedingly long day's paddling from Arevooma to M'fetta. Ngouta, the Igalwa interpreter, felt pumped, and said as much, very early in the day. I regretted very much having brought him; for, from a mixture of nervous exhaustion arising from our M'fetta experiences, and a touch of chill, he had almost entirely lost his voice, and I feared would fall sick. The Fans were evidently quite at home in the forest, and strode on over fallen trees and rocks with an easy, graceful stride. What saved us weaklings was the Fans' appetites; every two hours they sat down, and had a snack of a pound or so of meat and aguma apiece, followed by a pipe of tobacco. We used to come up with them at these halts. Ngouta and the Ajumba used to sit down; and rest with them, and I also, for a few minutes, for a rest and chat, and then I would go on alone, thus getting a good start. I got a good start, in the other meaning of the word, on the afternoon of the first day when descending into a ravine.

I saw in the bottom, wading and rolling in the mud, a herd of five elephants. I am certain that owing to some misapprehension among the Fates I was given a series of magnificent sporting chances, intended as a special treat for some favourite Nimrod of those three ladies, and I know exactly how I ought to have behaved. I should have felt my favourite rifle fly to my shoulder, and then, carefully sighting for the finest specimen, have fired. The noble beast should have stumbled forward, recovered itself, and shedding its life blood behind it have crashed away into the forest. I should then have tracked it, and either with one well-directed shot have given it its quietus, or have got charged by it, the elephant passing completely over my prostrate body; either termination is good form, but I never have these things happen, and never will. (In the present case I remembered, hastily, that your one chance when charged by several elephants is to dodge them round trees, working down wind all the time, until they lose smell and sight of you, then to lie quiet for a time, and go home.) It was evident from the utter unconcern of these monsters that I was down wind now, so I had only to attend to dodging, and I promptly dodged round a tree, thinking perhaps a dodge in time saves nine—and I lay down. Seeing they still displayed no emotion on my account, and fascinated by the novelty of the scene, I crept forward from one tree to another, until I was close enough to have hit the nearest one with a stone, and spats of mud, which they sent flying with their stamping and wallowing came flap, flap among the bushes covering me.

One big fellow had a nice pair of 40 lb. or so tusks on him, singularly straight, and another had one big curved tusk and one broken one. If I were an elephant I think I would wear the tusks straight; they must be more effective weapons thus, but there seems no fixed fashion among elephants here in this matter. Some of them lay right down like pigs in the deeper part of the swamp, some drew up trunkfuls of water and syringed themselves and each other, and every one of them indulged in a good rub against a tree. Presently when they had had enough of it they all strolled off up wind, a way elephants have;[3] but why I do not know, because they know the difference, always carrying their trunk differently when they are going up wind to what they do when they are going down—arrested mental development,[4] I suppose. They strolled through the bush in Indian file, now and then breaking off a branch, but leaving singularly little dead water for their tonnage and breadth of beam. One laid his trunk affectionately on the back of the one in front of him, which I believe to be the elephant equivalent to walking arm-in-arm. When they had gone I rose up, turned round to find the men, and trod on Kiva's back then and there, full and fair, and fell sideways down the steep hillside until I fetched up among some roots.

It seems Kiva had come on, after his meal, before the others, and seeing the elephants, and being a born hunter, had crawled like me down to look at them. He had not expected to find me there, he said. I do not believe he gave a thought of any sort to me in the presence of these fascinating creatures, and so he got himself trodden on. I suggested to him we should pile the baggage, and go and have an elephant hunt. He shook his head reluctantly, saying "Kor, kor," like a depressed rook and explained we were not strong enough; there were only three Fans—the Ajumba, and Ngouta did not count—and moreover that we had not brought sufficient ammunition owing to the baggage having to be carried, and the ammunition that we had

---

[3]Foolish, because natives always attack them in the rear.
[4]The usual explanation for anything you do not understand in a native of Africa's conduct.

must be saved for other game than elephant, for we might meet war before we met the Rembwé River.

We had by now joined the rest of the party, and were all soon squattering about on our own account in the elephant bath. It was shocking bad going—like a ploughed field exaggerated by a terrific nightmare. It pretty nearly pulled all the legs off me, and to this hour I cannot tell you if it is best to put your foot into a footmark—a young pond, I mean—about the size of the bottom of a Madeira work arm-chair, or whether you should poise yourself on the rim of the same, and stride forward to its other bank boldly and hopefully. The footmarks and the places where the elephants had been rolling were by now filled with water, and the mud underneath was in places hard and slippery. In spite of my determination to preserve an awesome and unmoved calm while among these dangerous savages, I had to give way and laugh explosively; to see the portly, powerful Pagan suddenly convert himself into a quadruped, while Gray Shirt poised himself on one heel and waved his other leg in the air to advertise to the assembled nations that he was about to sit down, was irresistible. No one made such palaver about taking a seat as Gray Shirt; I did it repeatedly without any fuss to speak of. That lordly elephant-hunter, the Great Wiki, would, I fancy, have strode over safely and with dignity, but the man who was in front of him spun round on his own axis and flung his arms round the Fan, and they went to earth together; the heavy load on Wiki's back drove them into the mud like a pile-driver. However we got through in time, and after I had got up the other side of the ravine I saw the Fan let the Ajumba go on, and were busy searching themselves for something.

I followed the Ajumba, and before I joined them felt a fearful pricking irritation. Investigation of the affected part showed a tick of terrific size with its head embedded in the flesh; pursuing this interesting subject, I found three more, and had awfully hard work to get them off and painful too for they give one not only a feeling of irritation at their holding-on place, but a streak of rheumatic-feeling pain up from it. On completing operations I went on and came upon the Ajumba in a state more approved of by Praxiteles than by the general public nowadays. They had found out about elephant ticks, so I went on and got an excellent start for the next stage.

By this time, shortly after noon on the first day, we had struck into a mountainous and rocky country, and also struck (more, more, more) a track—a track you had to keep your eye on or you lost it in a minute, but still a guide as to direction.

The forest trees here were mainly ebony and great hard wood trees,[5] with no palms save my old enemy the climbing palm, *calamus*, as usual, going on its long excursions, up one tree and down another, bursting into a plume of fronds, and in the middle of each plume one long spike sticking straight up, which was an unopened frond, whenever it got a gleam of sunshine; running along the ground over anything it meets, rock or fallen timber, all alike, its long, dark-coloured, rope-like stem simply furred with thorns. Immense must be the length of some of these climbing palms. One tree I noticed that day that had hanging from its summit, a good one hundred and fifty feet above us, a long straight rope-like palm stem. Interested, I went to it, and tried to track it to root, and found it was only a loop that came down from another tree. I had no time to trace it further; for they go up a tree and travel along the surrounding tree-tops, take an occasional dip, and then up again.

The character of the whole forest was very interesting. Sometimes for hours we passed among thousands upon thousands of gray-white columns of uniform height (about 100—150 feet); at the top of these the boughs branched out and interlaced among each other, forming a canopy or ceiling, which dimmed the light even of the equatorial sun to such an extent that no undergrowth could thrive in the gloom. The statement of the struggle for existence was published here in plain figures, but it was not, as in our climate, a struggle against climate mainly, but an internecine war from over population. Now and again we passed among vast stems of buttressed trees, sometimes enormous in girth; and from their far-away summits hung great bush-ropes, some as straight as plumb lines, others coiled round, and intertwined among each other, until one could fancy one was looking on some mighty battle between armies of gigantic serpents, that had been arrested at its height by some magic spell. All these bush-ropes were as bare of foliage as a ship's wire rigging, but a good many had thorns. I was very curious as to

---

[5]*Diospyros* and *Copaifua mopane*.

how they got up straight, and investigation showed me that many of them were carried up with a growing tree. The only true climbers were the *calamus* and the rubber vine *(Landolphia)*, both of which employ hook tackle.

Some stretches of this forest were made up of thin, spindly stemmed trees of great height, and among these stretches I always noticed the ruins of some forest giant, whose death by lightning or by his superior height having given the demoniac tornado wind an extra grip on him, had allowed sunlight to penetrate the lower regions of the forest; and then evidently the seedlings and saplings, who had for years been living a half-starved life for light, shot up. They seemed to know that their one chance lay in getting with the greatest rapidity to the level of the top of the forest. No time to grow fat in the stem. No time to send out side branches, or any of those vanities. Up, up to the level, and he among them who reached it first won in this game of life or death; for when he gets there he spreads out his crown of upper branches, and shuts off the life-giving sunshine from his competitors, who pale off and die, or remain dragging on an attenuated existence waiting for another chance, and waiting sometimes for centuries. There must be tens of thousands of seeds which perish before they get their chance; but the way the seeds of the hard wood African trees are packed, as it were, in cases specially made durable, is very wonderful. Indeed the ways of Providence here are wonderful in their strange dual intention to preserve and to destroy; but on the whole, as Peer Gynt truly observes, *"Ein guter Wirth—nein das ist er nicht."*

We saw this influence of light on a large scale as soon as we reached the open hills and mountains of the Sierra del Cristal, and had to pass over those fearful avalanche-like timber falls on their steep sides. The worst of these lay between Efoua and Egaja, where we struck a part of the range that was exposed to the south-east. These falls had evidently arisen from the tornados, which from time to time have hurled down the gigantic trees whose hold on the superficial soil over the sheets of hard bed rock was insufficient, in spite of all the anchors they had out in the shape of roots and buttresses, and all the rigging in the shape of bush ropes. Down they had come, crushing and dragging down with them those near them or bound to them by the great tough climbers.

Getting over these falls was perilous, not to say scratchy work. One or another member of our party always went through; and precious uncomfortable going it was I found, when I tried it in one above Egaja; ten or twelve feet of crashing creaking timber, and then flump on to a lot of rotten, wet *débris,* with more snakes and centipedes among it than you had any immediate use for, even though you were a collector; but there you had to stay, while Wiki, who was a most critical connoisseur, selected from the surrounding forest a bush-rope that he regarded as the correct remedy for the case, and then up you were hauled, through the sticks you had turned the wrong way on your down journey.

The Duke had a bad fall, going twenty feet or so before he found the rubbish heap; while Fika, who went through with a heavy load on his back, took us, on one occasion, half an hour to recover; and when we had just got him to the top, and able to cling on to the upper sticks, Wiki, who had been superintending operations, slipped backwards, and went through on his own account. The bush-rope we had been hauling on was too worn with the load to use again, and we just hauled Wiki out with the first one we could drag down and cut; and Wiki, when he came up, said we were reckless, and knew nothing of bush ropes, which shows how ungrateful an African can be. It makes the perspiration run down my nose whenever I think of it. The sun was out that day; we were neatly situated on the Equator, and the air was semisolid, with the stinking exhalations from the swamps with which the mountain chain is fringed and intersected; and we were hot enough without these things, because of the violent exertion of getting these twelve to thirteen-stone gentlemen up among us again, and the fine varied exercise of getting over the fall on our own account.

When we got into the cool forest beyond it was delightful; particularly if it happened to be one of those lovely stretches of forest, gloomy down below, but giving hints that far away above us was a world of bloom and scent and beauty which we saw as much of as earth-worms in a flower-bed. Here and there the ground was strewn with great cast blossoms, thick, wax-like, glorious cups of orange and crimson and pure white, each one of which was in itself a handful, and which told us that some of the trees around us were showing a glory of colour to heaven alone.

Sprinkled among them were bunches of pure stephanotis-like flowers, which said that the gaunt bush-ropes were rubber vines that had burst into flower when they had seen the sun. These flowers we came across in nearly every type of forest all the way, for rubber abounds here.

I will weary you no longer now with the different kinds of forest and only tell you I have let you off several. The natives have separate names for seven different kinds, and these might, I think, be easily run up to nine.

A certain sort of friendship soon arose between the Fans and me. We each recognised that we belonged to that same section of the human race with whom it is better to drink than to fight. We knew we would each have killed the other, if sufficient inducement were offered, and so we took a certain amount of care that the inducement should not arise. Gray Shirt and Pagan also, their trade friends, the Fans treated with an independent sort of courtesy; but Silence, Singlet, the Passenger, and above all Ngouta, they openly did not care a row of pins for, and I have small doubt that had it not been for us other three they would have killed and eaten these very amiable gentlemen with as much compunction as an English sportsman would kill as many rabbits. They on their part hated the Fan, and never lost an opportunity of telling me "these Fan be bad man too much." I must not forget to mention the other member of our party, a Fan gentleman with the manners of a duke and the habits of a dustbin. He came with us, quite uninvited by me, and never asked for any pay; I think he only wanted to see the fun, and drop in for a fight if there was one going on, and to pick up the pieces generally. He was evidently a man of some importance from the way the others treated him; and moreover he had a splendid gun, with a gorilla skin sheath for its lock, and ornamented all over its stock with brass nails. His costume consisted of a small piece of dirty rag round his loins; and whenever we were going through dense undergrowth, or wading a swamp, he wore that filament tucked up scandalously short. Whenever we were sitting down in the forest having one of our nondescript meals, he always sat next to me and appropriated the tin. Then he would fill his pipe, and turning to me with the easy grace of aristocracy, would say what may be translated as "My dear Princess, could you favour me with a lucifer?"

I used to say, "My dear Duke, charmed, I'm sure," and give him one ready lit.

I dared not trust him with the box whole, having a personal conviction that he would have kept it. I asked him what he would do suppose I was not there with a box of lucifers; and he produced a bush-cow's horn with a neat wood lid tied on with tie tie, and from out of it he produced a flint and steel and demonstrated. Unfortunately all his grace's minor possessions, owing to the scantiness of his attire, were in one and the same pine-apple-fibre bag which he wore slung across his shoulder; and these possessions, though not great, were as dangerous to the body as a million sterling is said to be to the soul, for they consisted largely of gunpowder and snuff, and their separate receptacles leaked and their contents commingled, so that demonstration on fire-making methods among the Fan ended in an awful bank and blow-up in a small way, and the Professor and his pupil sneezed like fury for ten minutes, and a cruel world laughed till it nearly died, for twenty. Still that bag with all its failings was a wonder for its containing power.

The first day in the forest we came across a snake[6]—a beauty with a new red-brown and yellow-patterned velvety skin, about three feet six inches long and as thick as a man's thigh. Ngouta met it, hanging from a bough, and shot backwards like a lobster, Ngouta having among his many weaknesses a rooted horror of snakes. This snake the Ogowé natives all hold in great aversion. For the bite of other sorts of snakes they profess to have remedies, but for this they have none. If, however, a native is stung by one he usually conceals the fact that it was this particular kind, and tries to get any chance the native doctor's medicine may give. The Duke stepped forward and with one blow flattened its head against the tree with his gun butt, and then folded the snake up and got as much of it as possible into the bag, while the rest hung dangling out. Ngouta, not being able to keep ahead of the Duke, his Grace's pace being stiff, went to the extreme rear of the party, so that other people might be killed first if the snake returned to life, as he surmised it would. He fell into other dangers from this caution, but I cannot chronicle Ngouta's afflictions in full without running this book into an old-fash-

---

[6]*Vipera nasicornis;* M'pongwe, *Ompenle.*

ioned folio size. We had the snake for supper, that is to say the Fan and I; the others would not touch it, although a good snake, properly cooked, is one of the best meats one gets out here, far and away better than the African fowl.

The Fan also did their best to educate me in every way: they told me their names for things, while I told them mine, throwing in besides as "a dash for top" a few colloquial phrases such as: "Dear me, now," "Who'd have thought it," "Stuff, my dear sir," and so on; and when I left them they had run each together as it were into one word, and a nice savage sound they had with them too, especially "dearmenow," so I must warn any philologist who visits the Fans, to beware of regarding any word beyond two syllables in length as being of native origin. I found several European words already slightly altered in use among them, such as "Amuck"—a mug, "Alas"—a glass, a tumbler. I do not know whether their "Ami"—a person addressed, or spoken of—is French or not. It may come from "Anwĕ"—M'pongwe for "Ye," "You." They use it as a rule in addressing a person after the phrase they always open up conversation with, "Azuna"—Listen, or I am speaking.

They also showed me many things: how to light a fire from the pith of a certain tree, which was useful to me in after life, but they rather overdid this branch of instruction one way and another; for example, Wiki had, as above indicated, a mania for bush-ropes and a marvellous eye and knowledge of them; he would pick out from among the thousands surrounding us now one of such peculiar suppleness that you could wind it round anything, like a strip of cloth, and as strong withal as a hawser; or again another which has a certain stiffness, combined with a slight elastic spring, excellent for hauling, with the ease and accuracy of a lady who picks out the particular twisted strand of embroidery silk from a multi-coloured tangled ball. He would go into the bush after them while other people were resting, and particularly after the sort which, when split is bright yellow, and very supple and excellent to tie round loads.

On one occasion, between Egaja and Esoon, he came back from one of these quests and wanted me to come and see something, very quietly: I went, and we crept down into a rocky ravine, on the other side of which lay one of the outermost Egaja plantations. When we got to the edge of the cleared ground, we lay down, and wormed our way, with elaborate caution, among a patch of Koko; Wiki first, I following in his trail.

After about fifty yards of this, Wiki sank flat, and I saw before me some thirty yards off, busily employed in pulling down plantains, and other depredations, five gorillas: one old male, one young male, and three females. One of these had clinging to her a young fellow, with beautiful wavy black hair with just a kink in it. The big male was crouching on his haunches, with his long arms hanging down on either side, with the backs of his hands on the ground, the palms upwards. The elder lady was tearing to pieces and eating a pine-apple, while the others were at the plantains destroying more than they ate.

They kept up a sort of a whinnying, chattering noise, quite different from the sound I have heard gorillas give when enraged, or from the one you can hear them giving when they are what the natives call "dancing" at night. I noticed that their reach of arm was immense, and that when they went from one tree to another, they squattered across the open ground in a most inelegant style, dragging their long arms with the knuckles downwards. I should think the big male and female were over six feet each. The others would be from four to five. I put out my hand and laid it on Wiki's gun to prevent him from firing, and he, thinking I was going to fire, gripped my wrist.

I watched the gorillas with great interest for a few seconds, until I heard Wiki make a peculiar small sound, and looking at him saw his face was working in an awful way as he clutched his throat with his hand violently.

Heavens! think I, this gentleman's going to have a fit; it's lost we are entirely this time. He rolled his head to and fro, and then buried his face into a heap of dried rubbish at the foot of a plantain stem, clasped his hands over it, and gave an explosive sneeze. The gorillas let go all, raised themselves up for a second, gave a quaint sound between a bark and a howl, and then the ladies and the young gentleman started home. The old male rose to his full height (it struck me at the time this was a matter of ten feet at least, but for scientific purposes allowance must be made for a lady's emotions) and looked straight towards us, or rather towards where that sound came from. Wiki went off into a paroxysm of falsetto sneezes the like of which I have never heard; nor evidently had the gorilla, who doubtless thinking, as one of his black co-relatives would have thought, that the phenomenon favoured Duppy, [a ghost] went off after his family with a celerity that was amazing the moment he touched the forest, and disappeared as they had, swinging himself along through it from bough to bough, in a way that convinced me that, given the necessity of getting about in tropical forests, man has made a mistake in getting his arms shortened. I have seen many wild animals in their native wilds, but never have I seen anything to equal gorillas going through bush; it is a graceful, powerful, superbly perfect hand-trapeze performance.[7]

After this sporting adventure, we returned, as I usually return from a sporting adventure, without measurements or the body.

When I was in Gaboon in September, 1895, there was great Ukuku excitement in a district just across the other side of the estuary, mainly at a village that enjoyed the spacious and resounding name of Rumpochembo, from a celebrated chief, and all these phenomena were rife there. Again, when I was in a village up the Calabar there were fourteen goats and five slaves killed in eight days by leopards, the genuine things, I am sure, in this case; but here, as down South, there was a strong objection to proceed against the leopard, and no action was being taken save making the goat-houses stronger. In Okyon, when a leopard is killed, its body is treated with great respect and brought into the killer's village. Messages are then sent to the neighbouring villages, and they send representatives to the village and the gall-bladder is most carefully removed from the leopard and burnt *coram publico,* each person whipping their hands down their arms to disavow any guilt in the affair. This burning of the gall, however, is not ju-ju, it is done merely to destroy it, and to demonstrate to all men that it is destroyed, because it is believed to be a deadly poison, and if any is found in a man's possession the punishment is death, unless he is a great chief—a few of these are allowed to keep leopards' gall in their

---

[7] I have no hesitation in saying that the gorilla is the most horrible wild animal I have seen. I have seen at close quarters specimens of the most important big game of Central Africa, and, with the exception of snakes, I have run away from all of them; but although elephants, leopards, and pythons give you a feeling of alarm, they do not give that feeling of horrible disgust that an old gorilla gives on account of its hideousness of appearance.

possession. John Bailey tells me that if a great chief commits a great crime and is adjudged by a conclave of his fellow chiefs to die, it is not considered right he should die in a common way, and he is given leopards' gall. A precisely similar idea regarding the poisonous quality of crocodiles' gall holds good down South.

The ju-ju parts of the leopard are the whiskers. You cannot get a skin from a native with them on, and gay, reckless young hunters wear them stuck in their hair and swagger tremendously while the elders shake their heads and keep a keen eye on their subsequent conduct.

I must say the African leopard is an audacious animal, although it is ungrateful of me to say a word against him, after the way he has let me off personally, and I will speak of his extreme beauty as compensation for my ingratitude. I really think, taken as a whole, he is the most lovely animal I have ever seen; only seeing him, in the one way you can gain a full idea of his beauty, namely in his native forest, is not an unmixed joy to a person, like myself, of a nervous disposition. I may remark that my nervousness regarding the big game of Africa is of a rather peculiar kind. I can confidently say I am not afraid of any wild animal—until I see it—and then—well I will yield to nobody in terror; fortunately as I say my terror is a special variety; fortunately because no one can manage their own terror. You can suppress alarm, excitement, fear, fright, and all those small-fry emotions, but the real terror is as dependent on the inner make of you as the colour of your eyes, or the shape of your nose; and when terror ascends its throne in my mind I become preternaturally artful, and intelligent to an extent utterly foreign to my true nature, and save, in the case of close quarters with bad big animals, a feeling of rage against some unknown person that such things as leopards, elephants, crocodiles, &c., should be allowed out loose in that disgracefully dangerous way, I do not think much about it at the time. Whenever I have come across an awful animal in the forest and I know it has seen me I take Jerome's advice, and instead of relying on the power of the human eye rely upon that of the human leg, and effect a masterly retreat in the face of the enemy. If I know it has not seen me I sink in my tracks and keep an eye on it, hoping that it will go away soon. Thus I once came upon a leopard. I had got caught in a tornado in a dense forest. The massive, mighty trees were waving like a wheat-field in an autumn gale in England, and I dare say a field mouse in a wheat-field in a gale would have heard much the same uproar. The tornado shrieked like ten thousand vengeful demons. The great trees creaked and groaned and strained against it and their bush-rope cables groaned and smacked like whips, and ever and anon a thundering crash with snaps like pistol shots told that they and their mighty tree had strained and struggled in vain. The fierce rain came in a roar, tearing to shreds the leaves and blossoms and deluging everything. I was making bad weather of it, and climbing up over a lot of rocks out of a gully bottom where I had been half drowned in a stream, and on getting my head to the level of a block of rock I observed right in front of my eyes, broadside on, maybe a yard off, certainly not more, a big leopard. He was crouching on the ground, with his magnificent head thrown back and his eyes shut. His fore-paws were spread out in front of him and he lashed the ground with his tail, and I grieve to say, in face of that awful danger—I don't mean me, but the tornado—that depraved creature swore, softly, but repeatedly and profoundly. I did not get all these facts up in one glance, for no sooner did I see him than I ducked under the rocks, and remembered thankfully that leopards are said to have no power of smell. But I heard his observation on the weather, and the flip-flap of his tail on the ground. Every now and then I cautiously took a look at him with one eye round a rock-edge, and he remained in the same position. My feelings tell me he remained there twelve months, but my calmer judgment puts the time down at twenty minutes; and at last, on taking another cautious peep, I saw he was gone. At the time I wished I knew exactly where, but I do not care about that detail now, for I saw no more of him. He had moved off in one of those weird lulls which you get in a tornado, when for a few seconds the wild herd of hurrying winds seem to have lost themselves, and wander round crying and wailing like lost souls, until their common rage seizes them again and they rush back to their work of destruction. It was an immense pleasure to have seen the great creature like that. He was so evidently enraged and baffled by the uproar and dazzled by the floods of lightning that swept down into the deepest recesses of the forest, showing at one second every detail of twig, leaf, branch, and stone round you, and then leaving you in a sort of swirling dark until the next flash came; this, and the great conglomerate roar of the wind, rain and thunder, was enough to bewilder any living thing.

I have never hurt a leopard intentionally; I am habitually kind to animals, and besides I do not think it is ladylike to go shooting things with a gun. Twice, however, I have been in collision with them. On one occasion a big leopard had attacked a dog, who, with her family, was occupying a broken-down hut next to mine. The dog was a half-bred boarhound, and a savage brute on her own account. I, being roused by the uproar, rushed out into the feeble moonlight, thinking she was having one of her habitual turns-up with other dogs, and I saw a whirling mass of animal matter within a yard of me. I fired two mushroom-shaped native stools in rapid succession into the brown of it, and the meeting broke up into a leopard and a dog. The leopard crouched, I think to spring on me. I can see its great, beautiful, lambent eyes still, and I seized an earthen water-cooler and flung it straight at them. It was a noble shot; it burst on the leopard's head like a shell and the leopard went for bush one time. Twenty minutes after people began to drop in cautiously and inquire if anything was the matter, and I civilly asked them to go and ask the leopard in the bush, but they firmly refused. We found the dog had got her shoulder slit open as if by a blow from a cutlass, and the leopard had evidently seized the dog by the scruff of her neck, but owing to the loose folds of skin no bones were broken and she got round all right after much ointment from me, which she paid me for with several bites. Do not mistake this for a sporting adventure. I no more thought it was a leopard than that it was a lotus when I joined the fight. My other leopard was also after a dog. Leopards always come after dogs, because once upon a time the leopard and the dog were great friends, and the leopard went out one day and left her whelps in charge of the dog, and the dog went out flirting, and a snake came and killed the whelps, so there is ill-feeling to this day between the two. For the benefit of sporting readers whose interest may have been excited by the mention of big game, I may remark that the largest leopard skin I ever measured myself was, tail included, 9 feet 7 inches. It was a dried skin, and every man who saw it said, "It was the largest skin he had ever seen, except one that he had seen somewhere else."

Bibliography

Bird, Isabella. *Unbeaten Tracks in Japan: An Account of Travels on Horseback in the Interior.* New York: G. P. Putnam's Sons, 1880.

Blunt, Lady Ann. *A Pilgrimage to Nejd* (Second Edition). London: John Murray, 1881.

Bremer, Frederika. *Travels in the Holy Land,* II. Translated by Mary Howitt. London: Hurst and Blackett, 1862.

Field, Kate. *Ten Days in Spain.* Boston: James R. Osgood, 1875.

Fuller, Margaret. *Memoirs,* II. Boston: Phillips, Sampson and Co., 1852.

Hart, Mrs. Ernest. *Picturesque Burma.* London: Dent, 1897.

Kingsley, Mary. *Travels in West Africa.* London: Macmillan and Co., 1897.

Marsden, Kate. *On Sledge and Horseback to Outcast Siberian Lepers.* London: Record Press, 1892.

Martineau, Harriet. *Eastern Life: Present and Past.* London: E. Moxon, 1848.

Montagu, Lady Mary Wortley. *The Selected Letters, 1716-1718,* edited by Robert Halsband. London: Longmans, Green, 1970.

Pfeiffer, Ida. *A Lady's Voyage Round the World.* New York: Harper and Bros., 1852.

Piozzi, Hester Lynch. *Observations Made in the Course of a Journey Through France, Italy, and Germany.* Reproduction of the 1789 edition. Ann Arbor: University of Michigan Press.

Stanhope, Lady Hester. *The Memoirs.* London: Colburn, 1845.

Tinne, Alexine. "Gondokoro" in Penelope Gladstone, *Travels of Alexine.* London: John Murray, 1970.

Tweedie, Mrs. Alec. *Through Finland in Carts.* London: Adam and Charles Black, 1897.

Wollstonecraft, Mary. *Letters Written During a Short Residence in Sweden, Norway, and Denmark.* The 1796 edition, published by Joseph Johnson, London, edited by Carol Poston. Lincoln: University of Nebraska Press, 1976.

Workman, Fanny Bullock. *Through Town and Jungle.* London: Unwin, 1904.

Other Accounts of Interest

EDITOR'S NOTE

Were it not for the limitations of space, I would have represented many other women travellers between the covers of this book. However, readers who found as much pleasure in the narratives included here as I did, may pursue their interest in the subject by way of the following list of recommended readings.

As the headings suggest, both the famous and the near-anonymous searched out almost every interesting corner of the world, some of them lighting in one place for a period, others girdling the globe in their consuming desire to see and experience it all. Some of these accounts are based on diaries and letters, others are shaped into skillful narratives with all the elements of a fascinating novel.

Like their male counterparts, a few of these women travellers were not always happy with what they encountered in "strange" surroundings, nor content with their circumstances, and occasionally (as we have seen in one or two selections in this book) they could speak in ugly accents as well as with the tongues of men and angels. But the offense is rarely gross, and most of these accounts fairly burst with curiosity and compassion toward the inhabitants of the new worlds that these writers have discovered for themselves. That sense of excitement, discovery, and sympathy is conveyed to the reader who is willing to appreciate the fact that these women were not totally exempt from the prejudices of their class and their society.

At least two of these writers (Montez and Tristan) await the hand of the practiced translator and several of the books (Jameson, Hore, and Lott) would profit from reprinting. Other titles by writers represented in this volume appear in the headnotes.

In Europe

D'Aulnoy, Madame. *Travels into Spain.* London: Samuel Crouch, 1692 (reprinted by Robert McBride, 1936).

Elliot, Frances. *Diary of an Idle Woman in Spain.* Leipzig: Bernard Tauchnitz, 1884.

Eyre, Mary. *Over the Pyrenees into Spain.* London: Richard Bentley, 1865.

Hajek, Rosa. "My Life as a Revolutionary," *Ararat* (Spring 1974).

Jackson, Helen Hunt. *Bits of Travel.* Boston: J. R. Osgood, 1872.

Kirkland, Caroline Matilda. *Holidays Abroad or Europe from the West.* New York: Baker and Scribner, 1849.

Radcliffe, Ann. *A Journey Made in the Summer of 1794 Through Holland . . . Germany . . . the Lakes.* Dublin: W. Porter, 1795.

Sand, George. *My Life 1854–1855.* New York: Harper & Row, 1979.

Sedgwick, Catharine. *Letters from Abroad to Kindred at Home.* New York: Harper & Bros., 1841.

Shelley, Mary Wollstonecraft (Godwin). *History of a Six Weeks Tour Through a Part of France, Switzerland, Germany, and Holland.* London: T. Hookman and C. & J. Ollier, 1817.

Stowe, Harriet Beecher. *Sunny Memories of Foreign Lands.* Boston: Phillips, Samson and Co., 1854.

Yates, Mrs. Ashton. *A Winter in Italy.* London: Colborn, 1845.

In the Americas

Child, Lydia Maria. *Letters from New York.* Boston: C. S. Frances and Co., 1843.

Gripenberg, Alexandra. *A Half Year in the New World, 1888.* Newark: University of Delaware Press, 1954.

Hale, Susan. *Mexico.* Boston: D. Lothrop and Co., 1889.

Hall, Margaret Hunter. *The Aristocratic Journey, 1827–1828.* New York: G. P. Putnam's Sons, 1931.

Howe, Julia Ward. *A Trip to Cuba, 1860*. New York: Praeger, 1969.
Jameson, Anna Brownell. *Sketches in Canada and Rambles Among the Red Men*. London: Longman, Brown, Green, and Longmans, 1852.
Kemble, Frances Ann. *Journal . . . 1838–1839*. London: John Murray, 1841.
Magoffin, Susan. *Down the Santa Fe Trail, New Mexico, 1846–1847*. New Haven: Yale University Press, 1926.
Modjeska, Helen. *Memoirs and Impressions of Helen Modjeska*. New York: Macmillan and Co., 1910.
Riedesel, Baroness Frederika Charlotte Louise von. *Letters and Journals Relating to the War of the American Revolution*. Chapel Hill: University of North Carolina Press, 1905.
Tristan y Moscozo, Flora. *Pérégrinations d'une Paria, 1833–1834*. Paris: A. Bertrand, 1838.
Trollope, Frances Milton. *Domestic Manners of the Americans*. London and New York: Whittaker, Treacher & Co., 1832.
Webb, Beatrice. *American Diary, 1898*. Madison: University of Wisconsin Press, 1963.
Wright, Frances. *Views of Society and Manners in America, 1819*. Cambridge: The Belknap Press, 1963.

In the Middle East

Anonymous. *Letters of a German Countess Written During Her Travels in Turkey, Egypt, the Holy Land, Syria, Nubia, etc.*, translated by H. Evans Lloyd. London: Coburn, 1845.
Asmar, Maria Theresa. *Memoirs of a Babylonian Princess*. London: Coburn, 1845.
Hale, Susan (with Edward Everett Hale). *A Family Flight Over Egypt and Syria*. Boston: D. Lothrop and Co., 1882.
Lagerlof, Selma. *Harvest*. Garden City, N.Y.: Doubleday, Doran, 1935.
Lott, Emmeline. *Harem Life in Egypt and Constantinople*. London: Richard Bentley, 1865.

In the Far East

Eden, Emily. *Up the Country*. London: Richard Bentley, 1866.
Elwood, Mrs. Colonel. *Narrative of a Journey Overland from England*. London: Colburn, 1830.

Fay, Mrs. *Letters from India, 1779–1815*. London: Hogarth Press, 1925.
Inglis, Lady Julia. *The Siege of Lucknow*. London: Osgood, McIlvaine and Co., 1892.
Leonowans, Anna. *The English Governess at the Siamese Court*. Boston: Field, Osgood and Co., 1870.
Metcalfe, Emily. "A Reminiscence of India," from *The Golden Calm: An English Lady's Life in Moghul India*, edited by M. M. Kaye. New York: Viking Press, 1981.

IN AFRICA

Hore, Annie. *To Lake Tanganyika in a Bath Chair*. London: S. Low, Marston, Searl and Rivington, 1886.

IN OTHER PLACES

Bly, Nelly (Elizabeth Cochrane). *Nelly Bly's Book: Around the World in Seventy-Two Days*. New York: Pictorial Weeklies Co., 1890.
Brassey, Mrs. Anne. *Around the World in the Yacht "Sunbeam."* New York: Henry Holt & Co., 1889.
Judd, Laura Fish. *Honolulu: Sketches of Life from 1826 to 1861*. New York: Anson Randolph, 1880.
Montez, Lola. *Memoiren der Lola Montez*. Berlin: Graffin von Landsfeld, 1851.
Parks, Fanny. *Wanderings of a Pilgrim in Search of the Picturesque*. Oxford: Oxford University Press, 1850.
Schaw, Janet. *Journal of a Lady of Quality, Being the Narrative of a Journey from Scotland to the West Indies, North Carolina, and Portugal, in the Years 1774 to 1776*. New Haven: Yale University Press, 1934.
Thurston, Lucy Goodale. *The Life and Times of Lucy Thurston*. Ann Arbor: S. C. Andrewes, 1882.